CANDIDATE

FOR

FCE

**FIONA
JOSEPH**

+

**PETER
TRAVIS**

PRENTICE HALL
PHOENIX ELT

New York   London   Toronto   Sydney   Tokyo   Singapore

Contents

Vocabulary development	Use of English	Language Awareness
	Error correction	Present tenses Adverbs of frequency
Words connected with literature	Understanding a cloze	Question tags Past simple and continuous
	Exam focus: (Part 1) multiple choice cloze Sentence transformation	Comparatives and superlatives Defining and non-defining relative clauses
Food and drink Entertainment	**Exam focus: (Part 3) 'key' word transformations** Error correction	Modal verbs of obligation Past perfect simple and continuous
Science and technology	Error correction	Future (1) Present perfect simple and continuous
Negative prefixes Similar words and opposites	**Exam focus: (Part 2) open cloze**	Conditionals (1) Articles

	Reading	Writing	Speaking	Listening	
7 **The Natural World** *page* 76	Magazine article about weather and health: •prediction •scanning **Exam focus: (Part 3)** **gapped text**	A letter of complaint A short story competition entry	Giving and exchanging personal information	A talk on energy conservation: •prediction •specific information Two learners practise for Paper 5: •global understanding	
8 **Pastimes and Passions** *page* 88	**Exam focus: (Part 1)** **multiple matching** Newspaper article on pop obsessions: •confirming your own ideas	An account of a hobby A letter of invitation	**Exam focus: (Part 2)** **comparing two** **photographs**	An artist's tips on successful drawing: •global understanding •comprehension and inference How to salsa: •following instructions News reports on obsessed fans: •global understanding •finding the details	
9 **The Things People Do** *page* 100	Sociability quiz: •skimming •comprehension The stories of Eric Cantona and Diane Modahl: •scanning and information sharing	A short story **Exam focus: (Part 2)** **a description of a** **sporting hero**	Discussion and negotiating **Exam focus: (Part 3)** **sharing opinions**	A radio phone-in about problem flatmates •specific information •inference An experiment into personal ethics: •global understanding •specific information A documentary on: Diego Maradona: •prediction •specific information and note taking	
10 **Transport** *page* 112	Two young people's stories: •comparing texts Extract from *Gridlock*: •prediction •comprehension and inference	A letter giving directions A letter to a newspaper editor		Interview about daily journeys to work/school: •specific information **Exam focus: (Part 3)** **multiple matching**	
11 **Dangerous Creatures** *page* 124	A 'true confession' magazine article •skimming **Exam focus: (Part 2)** **multiple choice**	An opinion article on animal issues	Sharing opinions	Interview with a zoologist •global understanding •specific information A radio talk on vivisection: •global understanding •note taking	
12 **Skills and Abilities** *page* 136	A questionnaire on first aid: •specific information **Exam focus: (Part 4)** **multiple matching**	A magazine article A letter of advice	Asking questions **Exam focus: (Parts 3** **and 4) exchanging** **information,** **exchanging and** **justifying opinions**	Two life-saving stories: •global understanding •specific information Five learners talk about taking the FCE exam: •understanding feelings and opinions	

Vocabulary development	Use of English	Language Awareness
Weather words	'Key' word transformations **Exam focus: (Part 1) multiple choice cloze** **Exam focus: (Part 5) word formation**	Passives Future (2)
Words with a similar meaning Music	Error correction	Reported speech Conditionals (2)
Colloquial language Right and wrong	Multiple choice cloze and open cloze	Verb forms (1) Possibility and certainty
Phrasal verbs On the road Word groups	**Exam focus: (Part 4) error correction**	Review of tenses Verb forms (2)
Words with a similar meaning Word formation	Multiple choice cloze **Exam focus: (Part 5) word formation**	Time conjunctions Expressing quantity
Parts of the body and injuries Dependent prepositions and word formation Negative prefixes	Open cloze	Ability Grammar check

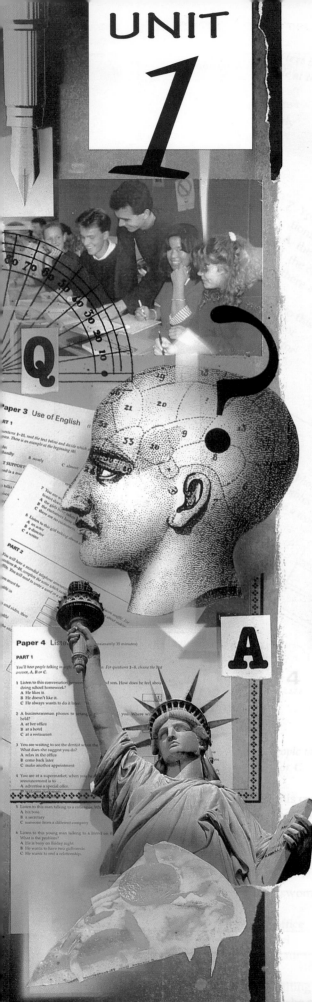

UNIT 1

Starting Points

PART ONE
Getting to know each other

Lead-in

1 Ask your partner questions to get information similar to that shown below. Write each of your partner's answers on a separate piece of paper.

Example:
A: 'If I had the chance I'd really like to go to New York.'
Q: 'Which city would you most like to visit?'   New York

'A sister called Chloe. I haven't got a brother.'
'May 11th.'
'Tom Cruise. I think he's great.'
'Listening to music and reading.'
'No doubt about it. Pizza. I love it!'
'People who smoke in restaurants. It drives me mad!'

2 Now put all the pieces of paper together, mix them up and share them out equally amongst all the students in the class. Look at the things that are written on the pieces of paper you now have. Can you find the people who said each one?

Listening technique: specific information

Listen to the following interview with a student from Greece. Fill in the first column of the Student Profile questionnaire below.

STUDENT PROFILE	student	partner
Name	Dimitris	
Age		
Marital status		
Length of time spent studying English		
Languages spoken		
Reason for studying English		
Things you most like about yourself		
Things you least like about yourself		
How you think other people see you		
Ambition		

Reading technique: correcting mistakes

1 Now read the following profile of the same student, which was written in a hurry by a classmate. There are some *factual* mistakes. How many can you find?

2 You will also have noticed that there were several grammar mistakes. Work with a partner and try to find and correct them.

> Dimitris has 17 years old and lives in Zographou near the centre of Athens. He's single and lives with his parents, his brother and two sisters. He's a student at high school and has spent three years study English. He speaks also little German and French. He's studying English for (to) pass FCE but he's not sure if he'll need in the future because he doesn't know yet what job he wants to do.
>
> Dimitris describes himself as be rather lazy and likes to spend most of time talking rather than working. However, he also thinks he's good friend and is happy always to listen people if they will have any problems. He spends usually his spare time to go out with friends and have a good time. He really likes playing and watching football and his ambition is play football for Panathinaikos, although he doesn't think this will happen.

3 Now use the second section of the questionnaire to find out similar information about your partner.

Writing skill: a personal profile

Now write a couple of paragraphs about the person you interviewed. Follow the model of Dimitris' profile and then give it to a third student to check for accuracy.

See **Language awareness: present tenses and adverbs of frequency**

PART TWO
You the language learner

Lead-in

Look at the photographs below, which show different ways of studying. Working with a partner, compare and contrast these different methods in relation to yourself. For example, do you (or would you) prefer to:

- be part of a small class rather than a large one?
- have private lessons with your own tutor?
- work by yourself in class or with your friends?
- use a computer rather than a book?
- work without a teacher sometimes?
- do lots of the things you are good at (for example speaking)?
- spend more time on the things you find difficult (for example, writing)?

Reading technique: global understanding

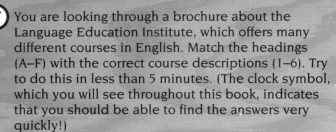

You are looking through a brochure about the Language Education Institute, which offers many different courses in English. Match the headings (A–F) with the correct course descriptions (1–6). Try to do this in less than 5 minutes. (The clock symbol, which you will see throughout this book, indicates that you should be able to find the answers very quickly!)

A Holiday English
B Academic English
C Self-study English
D English for Examinations
E Business English
F Conversational English

Language Education Institute
Summer courses

1
An ideal course for students who like to learn at their own pace and without a teacher. Improve your listening and grammar using the latest in computer and multimedia software. You choose when to study and for how long. Warning! Not suitable for the unmotivated.

2
Forget your grammar books and learn English for real communication. You will practise your speaking skills through discussions and role plays. You will learn to understand a variety of English accents by watching authentic videos. You will also find out about the cultural habits of the British. Ideal for those coming to live in the United Kingdom for a long period.

3
Learn the art of telephoning, letter writing, meetings and negotiations in English. This is the perfect course for top executives, as well as students of commerce. All our English teachers have had experience in industry, so we can teach you essential work vocabulary. We specialise in small groups and one-to-one teaching.

Speaking skill: sharing opinions

1 Look at the adverts again. Which course would most appeal to you, if you had the choice? Why?

Example:
The thought of doing lots of discussion work really appeals to me – I'd choose the Conversational English course.

Which course would be the least useful or interesting for you? Compare your opinions with the rest of your group.

Example:
Well, I'm not very good at organising my own language learning, so the self-study course would be a waste of time and money for me.

2 What were the most and least popular courses in your class?

Use of English: error correction

1 The English teachers at the Language Education Institute were asked what were the typical language errors made by their students. They produced the following list. Working in small groups, see if you can identify the mistake and then correct it.

Example:
This classroom is not enough warm.
This classroom is not warm enough.

1 It was so hot weather that we all got sunburnt on our last trip.
2 My teacher at home said me that I was no good at grammar.
3 Can you give me some informations about other language courses?
4 What means 'cabbage'?
5 I'm not used to speak in English all the time – it makes me nervous.
6 To smoke isn't really very good for you.
7 I've known my boyfriend since seven years.
8 He go to class every day by bus.
9 She works like an English teacher.
10 I must make my essay tonight for homework.
11 Can you explain me why my grade is so low?
12 Shall we go in Scotland for the vacation?
13 What kind of music do you like to listen?
14 My teacher he is very good.

2 Which of these mistakes do *you* sometimes make? There are opportunities to improve your grammatical accuracy in the Language Awareness sections at the end of each unit.

4
Thousands of people learn English just for fun. Our classes will give you the chance to meet people from all around the world who have a common interest – the English language! You will learn useful expressions to help you get by in shops, banks, restaurants, and other everyday situations. If you're taking a trip to England, why not try this course as part of your vacation?

5
Are you planning to study at an English-speaking university? If so, you may need help understanding lectures, reading textbooks and writing essays or dissertations. This course will help you to understand and write formal English.

6
Do you want a recognised qualification in English? We offer classes at beginner, intermediate and advanced levels to help you prepare. You will study with a coursebook and do regular progress tests along the way. You must be prepared to attend all classes if you wish to be entered for the certificate.

EXAM FOCUS
(Writing, Part 1)
a transactional
letter

You **must** answer this question. You are interested in going to Britain to study for four weeks in the summer. You have seen the advertisement below, but you need more information before you decide. Your task is to write to the Director of Studies.

Read carefully the advertisement and the notes which you have made below. Then write your letter to the language school, covering the points in your notes and adding any other relevant points.

Write a letter of between 120 and 180 words in an appropriate style. Do not write any addresses.

trips included in price?

Come and study English at the Language Education Institute. We offer a wide range of courses from Holiday English to Academic English, in beautiful surroundings. Our teaching rooms are modern and well-equipped, and there is a leisure centre nearby.

what facilities?

- course length?
- cost?
- number of hours tuition?
- accommodation provided?
- date of next course?

S T R A T E G I E S

1 If you don't know the name of the person you are writing to, how should you begin and end your letter?

Dear Sir   Dear Sir or Madam   Dear Sirs
With love   Yours sincerely   Yours faithfully

2 Write a first draft of your letter, including all the points mentioned in the task. You can use some of the following phrases:

I saw your advertisement for ... in ...
First of all, I would like to know ...
In addition, could you tell me ...
Furthermore, I was wondering if ..., and whether ...
I look forward to hearing from you/your reply.

3 Now ask your partner to read your letter and comment on the following points:

- Have you missed out any of the points you should have covered?
- Have you made any spelling or grammatical mistakes?
- Is your handwriting easy to read?
- Have you kept within the word limit?

▶ **Look at the 'Exam skills' section on the Review page.**

PART THREE
A candidate for FCE

Lead-in

How much do you know about the FCE examination? Try this quiz with a partner to find out!

1 How many people take FCE each year?
   a) 100,000   b) 150,000   c) 200,000

2 Which country has around 100,000 candidates?
   a) Greece   b) Brazil   c) Argentina

3 Why is it called the 'new FCE'?

4 CAE and CPE are higher exams. True or False?

5 More males than females enter for the FCE. True or False?

6 There are five papers in all. Which one lasts the longest?
   a) Reading   b) Writing   c) Use of English
   d) Listening   e) Speaking

7 Which is the shortest?

Reading technique: scanning and inference

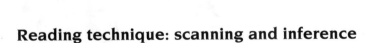

1 Now read the information below to check your answers. A useful reading technique is to highlight or underline the part of the text where you find the answer.

The aim of the FCE exam is to test your general proficiency in English through tests of reading, writing, grammar/vocabulary, listening and speaking. It is taken by over 200,000 candidates every year. Approximately half of the entries are from Greece, and it is a popular exam throughout Europe, Argentina and Brazil. In 1996 the exam was changed; so it is sometimes referred to as the 'new' or 'revised' FCE. If you pass the FCE, you may want to go on to take the CAE or CPE exams. The majority of candidates are in their teens or early twenties and around two thirds of candidates are female.

PAPER 1: READING
(Time allowed: 1 hour 15 minutes)

You have to read and answer 35 questions in total on four long texts (or three long and two or more short texts). The texts are usually from authentic sources. There are questions where you have to match information (Parts 1 & 4), answer multiple-choice questions (Part 2) and fill in a text which has gaps (Part 3). You have to be able to understand main points, pick out specific information, put jumbled texts back together, as well as reading between the lines.

PAPER 2: WRITING
(Time allowed: 1 hour 30 minutes)

You have to do two writing tasks: Part 1 is a transactional letter and is compulsory; Part 2 gives you a choice out of four tasks, which may include an article, a report, a non-transactional letter, a discursive composition, a descriptive or narrative composition/ short story plus a question on a set text you may have read. The length of both writing tasks is 120–180 words. You have to be able to write accurately and appropriately according to the type of text.

PAPER 4: LISTENING
(Time allowed: approximately 40 minutes)

Part 1 of this paper consists of multiple-choice questions based on a series of short unrelated extracts. In Part 2 you have to listen to a continuous text and complete notes or fill in blanks. Part 3 is a series of extracts that are on the same theme or topic, involving matching information. In the final part you listen to a continuous text and choose between two or three possible answers, for example true/false or multiple choice.

PAPER 3: USE OF ENGLISH
(Time allowed: 1 hour 15 minutes)

There are five parts in this paper, which aims to test your grammar and vocabulary. Part 1 is a multiple-choice cloze and Part 2 an open cloze. In Part 3 you have to rewrite a sentence using a given 'key' word. Part 4 consists of a short text with errors which you have to correct. Part 5 tests your ability to form new words from a 'stem' word.

PAPER 5: SPEAKING
(Time allowed: approximately 14 minutes)

This paper is usually done with a partner and two examiners (one will ask you questions and the other will assess your performance). You will have to give personal information about yourself (Part 1), talk about a photograph in relation to yourself (Part 2), complete a problem-solving task with your partner (Part 3) and take part in a general discussion of the theme in Part 3 (Part 4).

2 All of the papers in FCE are divided into Parts. Look back at the details of each paper and see if you can identify which Part each of these instructions come from.

Example:
Writing Paper
You *must* answer this question.   Part 1

a Reading Paper
For questions 8–15, choose the answer (A, B, C or D) which you think fits best according to the text.

b Writing Paper
Write an answer to one of the questions 2–5 in this Part.

c Use of English Paper
For questions 31–40, complete the second sentence so that it has a similar meaning to the first sentence, using the word given.

d Listening Paper
You will hear people talking in eight different situations. For questions 1–8, choose the best answer, A, B or C.

3 When you have finished, find one example of each of these Parts in this book, by looking for the 'Exam Focus' box.

Example:
Page 10

EXAM FOCUS
(Writing, Part 1)
a transactional letter

e Speaking skill: sharing ideas

1 Look at the following list of suggestions for preparing for the FCE exam. Rate each on a scale of 1–3 (1 = not much use, 2 = might be useful, 3 = very useful). Note the **e** symbol which shows that an activity is particularly useful for the exam.

a doing past FCE papers or practice tests in class
b communicating with an English-speaking pen-pal (e.g. by phone, letter, e-mail)
c reading English newspapers, magazines and novels
d using a coursebook in class
e checking each other's essays for grammar mistakes
f keeping a record of useful vocabulary
g listening to English programmes on the radio
h working in pairs or groups in class

2 When you have finished, share your answers with your partner and explain your ratings to each other.

Listening technique: global understanding

You are going to hear a teacher giving his opinion about the above suggestions. As you listen for the first time, put the suggestions in the correct order (e.g. 1 = e, etc.).

1
2
3
4
5
6
7
8

Listening technique: specific information and inference

1 Listen to the tape again. Make notes in the table above on the advice the teacher gives about each point.

2 Compare your notes with a partner and then against the tapescript, if necessary.

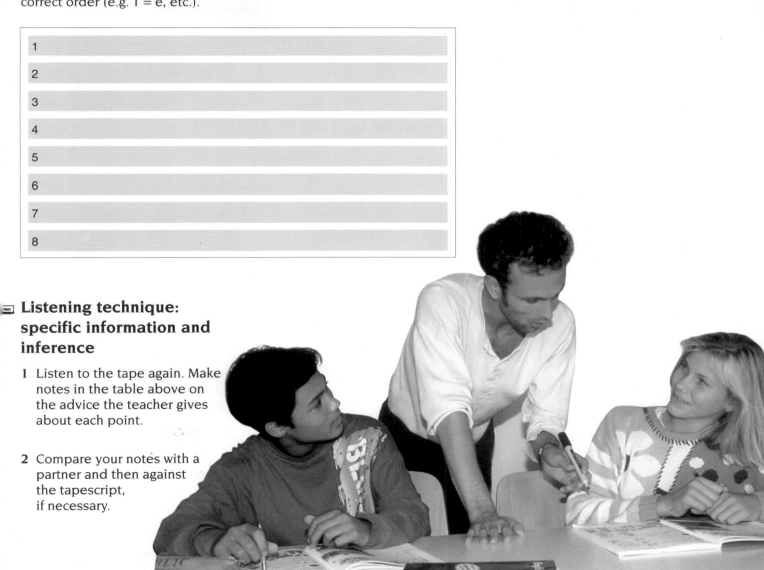

LANGUAGE AWARENESS
present tenses and adverbs of frequency

1 Find somebody in the class who:

a can tell you at what temperature water boils.
b can tell you the name of a good book they're reading at the moment.
c can tell you what colour socks they're wearing without looking.
d comes to school/college by bike.
e can tell you the date your English course finishes.
f can tell you if the days are getting longer or shorter.
g is seeing a friend this evening.

2 Match each of the sentences above with one of the uses below. Which tense is used in each case?

an action/situation happening 'now'
a permanent situation, for example a fact
a timetable/calendar event
a temporary action/situation
a future arrangement
a changing/developing situation
a habitual action/situation

3 ▱ Complete the following dialogue, supplying the correct form of the verb in brackets. Then listen to the tape to check your answers.

A: Hello, sir. I (a) .... (do) some market research. I wonder if you would mind answering a few questions?
B: Well, I (b) .... (try) to do some shopping actually .
A: What toothpaste (c) .... (you use), sir?
B: Well, we usually (d) .... (use) Cowgate, but at the moment we (e) .... (use) McGreens.
A: I see. Have you thought about trying Crust, sir? It (f) .... (clean) whiter than white.
B: No. My wife (g) .... (not like) Crust. She says it (h) .... (burn) her mouth.
A: How often (i) .... (you wash) your hair, sir?
B: About twice a week. My wife (j).............................. (wash) hers every day. It (k) .... (cost) us a fortune in shampoo!

A: And who (l) .... (choose) the brand?
B: My wife. She usually (m) .... (get) it in the supermarket. In fact, that's where I (n) .... (go) now.
A: Really, sir. And what brand (o).............................. (she buy)?
B: I (p) .... (not know), to be quite honest. Have you got many more questions? It (q) .... (get) rather late. The shops (r) .... (close) in a few minutes.
A: Only a few more, sir. What perfume (s).............................. (your wife wear)?
B: No idea. I never (t) .... (buy) her any. Listen. I'm very sorry, but she (u).............................. (wait) for me at home. She (v) .... (not feel) very well and the doctor (w) .... (come) round this evening to have a look at her. Oh look! The man (x).............................. (close) the shop. I must go. Bye!

4 Some of the following sentences contain mistakes in word order. Which ones and why? And which job do I do?

a I go usually to work and then leave quickly with something I didn't arrive with.
b Always I work harder at big religious festivals like Christmas.
c I don't get given often tips.
d I occasionally have been bitten by a dog.
e I can often make people very happy.
f I rarely am unpopular on people's birthdays.
g A pair of shoes lasts me never more than a few months.
h I wear always a uniform.
i I always am disappointed when lifts are out of order.
j I have sometimes to get people out of bed.

5 Which verbs do adverbs of frequency precede and which verbs do they follow? See the Grammar Reference on page 165 to check your ideas.

6 Now think of a job and write similar clues. Try them out on the class.

Keeping a record of your learning

1 It can be a good idea to record regularly what you have done in class. There is a review sheet for this purpose at the end of every unit. Use this page to do the following:

a make a note of useful vocabulary
b try out the suggestion for organising your vocabulary learning
c record your performance in Exam Focus activities
d assess your strong and weak areas
e record general points about classroom activities

2 Look at this example and read the notes.

Use this section to record vocabulary from the unit – choose the words that <u>you</u> want to remember.

Your review of Unit 1

(Vocabulary)

Your selection:

single = not married e.g. My teacher is single.
computer software
ambition = dream e.g. His ambition is to get a good job.
(un)ambiti(ous) (adj.)
(un)motivated (adj.) – to motivate (v.) – motivation (n.)

In each unit we give you a different suggestion to help you:
a) record vocabulary so that you remember it more effectively, or
b) extend your vocabulary.

(Suggestion:)

Write the words you want to remember on a piece of card and, on the back, put a translation, a picture, a definition or a sentence in English. Carry your cards around with you and review them before every English class.

Answer the questions to check that you remember the format of the exam task.

(Exam skills)

(Complete the summaries by underlining the appropriate answer:)

Your teacher or colleagues can give you feedback.

Writing, Part 1, a transactional letter
• Part 1 contains a) one task b) a choice of writing tasks.
• You a) must b) don't have to answer this part.

(How well did I do?)

This is a nice question. My friend checked my work for me. My grammar is quite good, but (I need to improve my spelling.) Also, I missed out some of the information from the question.

What do you need to do to improve?

Use this section to record what you have done.

(General)

My reading skills are good, but the listening is too difficult for me. I would like to speak more in class, but I am too shy.

UNIT 2

Communication

PART ONE
Towards a global language

Lead-in

1 It has been claimed that the following English words have become more or less universal. How many are now used in your country on an everyday basis, maybe with a slightly different spelling? Can you add any more to the list?

airport	passport	hotel	telephone	bar	no problem
cigarette	sport	golf	tennis	stop	sex appeal
weekend	Internet	soda	know-how	jeans	

2 In groups, consider the following questions:

● How many pop songs in the charts in your country are sung in English?
● How many British or American TV soap operas are on TV at present?
● How many British or American writers are well known in your country?
● How many shops in your town have an English name?
● How many items of clothing are your classmates wearing with English words on them?

Reading technique: specific information

1 Work in pairs. Student A look at the text on page 148. Student B read the text below. Make notes on the points that are dealt with in your article:

- English used in advertising
- Everyday English
- English words with non-English spelling
- English words with different uses

In Hong Kong you can find a place called 'The Plastic Bacon Factory'. In Sarajevo you can find graffiti saying 'Heavy Metal is law!' and 'Hooligan Kings of the North!' I bring this up here to make the somewhat obvious observation that English has become the most global of languages. Products are seen to be more exciting if they carry English messages even when, as often happens, the messages don't make a lot of sense.

I have before me a Japanese eraser which says: 'Mr Friendly Quality Eraser. Mr Friendly Arrived!! He always stay near you, and steals in your mind to lead you a good situation.' On the bottom of the eraser is a further message: 'We are ecologically minded. This package will self-destruct in Mother Earth.' It is a product that was made in Japan only for Japanese consumers, yet there is not a word of Japanese on it.

Coke cans in Japan come with the slogan I FEEL COKE & SOUND SPECIAL. A shopping bag carried a picture of dancing elephants above the legend: ELEPHANT FAMILY ARE HAPPY WITH US. THEIR HUMMING MAKES US FEEL HAPPY.

English words are everywhere. Germans speak of *die Teenagers* and *das Walkout* and German politicians snarl '*No comment*' at German journalists. Italian women coat their faces with *col-cream*, Romanians ride the *trolleybus*, and Spaniards, when they feel chilly, put on a *sueter*. Almost everyone in the world speaks on the *telephone* or the *telefoon* or even, in China, the *te le fung*. And almost everywhere you can find *hamburgers*, *night-clubs* and *television*.

Some nations have left the words largely intact but given the spelling a novel twist. Thus the Ukrainian *herkot* might seem foreign to you until you realize that a herkot is what a Ukrainian goes to his barber for.

(Bill Bryson: *Mother Tongue*)

2 Now share your information with Student A.

3 Has English entered your language in any of these ways? Do you think your country imports too much language and culture from Britain and America?

Use of English: understanding a cloze

1 Work with somebody who read the same text as you. Can you think of examples of the following:

modal verb   auxiliary verb   pronoun   preposition
relative pronoun   conjunction   article

2 Look at the first paragraph of your article and find examples of these language items. When you've found as many examples as you can, write out the paragraph missing out one example of each type (replace them with a line: _____). Make sure you leave a few words between each line.

3 Swap your exercise with a pair who are working on the other text. Now try to complete the cloze exercise you have been given.

EXAM FOCUS
(Listening, Part 1)
unrelated extracts

🔊 **You will hear people using English in eight different situations. For questions 1–8, choose the best answer, A, B or C.**

1 You hear the following advertisement on the radio. It is for
   A a newspaper.
   B a holiday.
   C a review of movies and plays.

2 You hear a man talking on the phone. He is trying to make an appointment with
   A a doctor.
   B a dentist.
   C an optician.

3 A woman is being interviewed on the radio about a summer school. It has courses in
   A music.
   B languages.
   C drama.

4 A radio presenter is talking about Hollywood. He is explaining about
   A families from Hollywood.
   B a competition.
   C a movie.

5 A man is talking on the phone about a car. Is he phoning to
   A sell it?
   B have it fixed?
   C report it stolen?

6 Somebody has been stealing wild birds from Trafalgar Square and selling them to restaurants. Listen to the conversation. The man talking thinks the story is
   A terrible news.
   B a good idea.
   C untrue.

7 Listen to this woman talking about a recent trip abroad. She went away
   A for a holiday.
   B on business.
   C for her health.

8 You overhear a woman talking about the possibility of life on other planets. She thinks
   A Mars has seas and deserts.
   B Mars has no life on it.
   C Mars could have life on it.

S T R A T E G I E S

1 You need to be aware of words and phrases acting as distractors. For example, just because you hear the word 'cinema' doesn't mean that the extract is about films. Listen to Question 1 and make a note of any words or phrases that refer to:
   a newspapers.
   b holidays.
   c movie or theatre reviews.

2 Which of the words or phrases do you think are there to distract you? What evidence have you got for this?

3 Now try the other extracts.

▶ **Go to the Review page to record your performance.**

See **Language awareness: question tags**

PART TWO
A *good read*

Lead-in

1 Would you describe yourself as a keen reader? How do your reading habits compare with your colleagues'? Is there anybody in your group who does the following?

in their own language:
- finishes one book then starts another almost immediately
- only reads books for studying not for pleasure
- likes a particular type of book or has a favourite author
- prefers reading magazines or newspapers to books
- prefers watching the TV to reading

in English:
- ever reads British or American magazines or newspapers
- has ever read a simplified English novel or 'reader'
- prefers to read authentic English rather than simplified novels
- has learnt lots of vocabulary through reading English for pleasure
- actually prefers reading books in English rather than in their own language
- has absolutely no interest in reading English books

2 You may be aware that you have the opportunity to study an English novel as part of the FCE examination. Would you or your colleagues be interested? What would be the advantages or disadvantages of doing this?

Listening technique: global understanding

You will hear four students talking about their experiences of studying a reader. As you listen for the first time decide if the student enjoyed reading the book. Make a list of the words or expressions that helped you and share your ideas with a partner.

Listening technique: specific information

Listen again and list the advantages and disadvantages that are mentioned by each speaker. How many correspond to the ones you talked about? Which of the opinions do you most identify with?

Vocabulary development: words connected with literature

1 The students in the previous listening activity were sometimes
   unable to remember a particular word in English. However, this did
   not stop them talking; they simply used other words or expressions
   to explain what they meant. Write your own definitions of the words
   below and then check against the definitions given in the tapescript
   on pages 175–6.

   Example:
   author – *the person who wrote the book*

author	characters
title	theme
plot	biography
thriller	dialogue

2 Work in teams. Listen to the following clues about some more
   words that relate to literature. The words appear below but the first
   letter only has been supplied. How many do your team know?

   a   e _ _ _ _ _

   b   s _ _ _ _ _ _   f _ _ _ _ _ _

   c   c _ _ _ _ _ _ _

   d   h _ _ _ _ _

   e   s _ _ _ _

   f   s _ _ _ _   s _ _ _ _

   g   s _ _ _ _ _ _ _ _

   h   h _ _ _

   i   n _ _ _ _ _ _ _

   j   p _ _ _ _ _ _ _

3 To help you remember them, can you organise the
   words in activities 1 and 2 into three (or more)
   different categories? How would the following words
   fit into these categories?

whodunnit	best-seller	illustration
portrayal	fiction	tragedy
narrator	setting	novel

4 Choose a favourite book or a film you have seen recently.
   Do not tell anyone else the title. Describe your choice to the
   members of your group. Can they guess what it is? The
   following points might help you:

   What kind of a book or a film is it?
   Where is it set?
   What, generally, is the theme of
   the book or film?
   Who are the main characters?
   What is the basic plot?
   What did you particularly like
   about it?

⊃ Writing skill: describing events in a book

1 You have been given the following composition to write.

Describe an important event in a book that you have read, stating why you think it is significant and the effect that it had on you.

Look at the list of points below and put them into a logical order.

- the significance of the event
- background to the event
- introduction
- the effect it had on you
- description of the event

2 Now look at this sample composition, and see if your plan matches the one used here.

There are many important events in Aldous Huxley's 'Brave New World' but, for me, the most significant one is the death of Linda.

Linda and her son, John, are brought from the Reservation (and the old world) to London, where family life, loyalty and love are despised. The society in this 'brave new world' does not approve of Linda because she looks old and is ugly, so she is given the drug 'soma' in large quantities in the hope that she will die soon. Not long after they arrive in London, John receives a phone call to say that his mother is in hospital, dying. He rushes to her bedside, and sits there watching her, remembering how she used to be when she was younger. However, the moment is spoiled when a group of children surround her bed to look at and make fun of her. Linda dies shortly.

This event shows the contrast between the old and new world, particularly as the nurse cannot understand why John is unhappy at the death of his mother. I felt sympathy for John for being in a world where there is no one to share his pain.

3 Study the composition again and look at the use of the present simple and the past simple. With a partner, try to explain why each one has been used.

4 Now write a composition of your own. When you have finished, exchange compositions with your partner and give each other marks out of 20 for the following areas:

- content (did the description make you interested in reading the book for yourself?) – 5 marks
- correct use of language (especially tenses) – 5 marks
- organisation (did it follow the plan?) – 5 marks
- presentation (was the handwriting easy to read?) – 5 marks

5 Compare your compositions with the one on page 161, which was also written by an FCE student. Are yours as good, or better?

See Language awareness: past simple and past continuous

PART THREE
TV: entertainment or information?

Lead-in

1 Do you watch a lot of television? What type of programme do you
watch the most? Rank your top 5 (1 = your favourite).

- ☐ international news and current affairs
- ☐ local news and events
- ☐ sports
- ☐ films and dramas
- ☐ soaps and serials
- ☐ light entertainment (comedies, chat shows, quiz shows, etc.)
- ☐ documentaries
- ☐ nature programmes
- ☐ music and the arts
- ☐ leisure and hobbies
- ☐ children's programmes
- ☐ home shopping
- ☐ foreign channels

2 Look at your list. Do you like programmes that are mainly for
entertainment or for information?

3 Compare your viewing habits with others in the class. Does the class
have similar or different tastes?

Reading technique: prediction

1 A group of young people were asked to write a report about the role
of television. Look at the title of the first report and, with a partner,
see if you can predict what the report is about.

> Entertainment for all the family? That's a joke.

 2 Quickly skim read the text to see if your prediction was right.

> It's Saturday night, it's 8 o'clock, and my best friend
> has just called to cancel our date this evening. In
> desperation I turn to the TV guide to see what's on telly
> tonight. I wish I hadn't bothered. It's a choice between
> the movie 'A Few Good Men' (a great film, but like all
> my friends I've already seen it at the cinema and on
> video), the opera 'Carmen' (not really my style, more my
> mum's) and a stupid game show where the host has a
> string of very irritating catchphrases. When are the
> middle-aged programme controllers going to wake up
> and realise that people of my age group (15–20) want
> something more?
>
> Stephanie May, 16, Wales

Reading technique: global understanding

You are going to read four more of the reports. Decide whether each report is about TV's role as:

- entertainment
- information
- entertainment *and* information
- neither of these

1

Some people argue that soaps are a load of rubbish, that they're badly made and don't deal with real issues. Well, the final point is certainly true of some American imports. Remember when everybody was mad about 'Dallas'? It was all about money, big cars, swimming pools and beautiful women. No attention was ever paid to any realistic problems in this world, the problems of ordinary people. But isn't that why we enjoyed them so much as an escape from reality once a week?

Cristina Suarez, 20, Spain

2

Watching television is the dominant leisure activity for most people in Britain. Almost every home has a television set, and on average around one third of the total free time of British people is spent watching television. I did some of my own research amongst my friends at school and discovered that the majority (80%) have a television of their own in their bedrooms! Am I the only person who finds these statistics disturbing and rather sad? In the competition you asked us whether the role of TV was to entertain or to inform. I would argue that we should turn our TV sets off and get out into the real world.

Marie O'Connor, 16, England

3

At its best, television is a wonderful form of entertainment that can stimulate a life-long interest in the arts. We can see top class artists at the touch of a button and in the comfort of our own home. A piano recital by Rubenstein, an orchestra conducted by Stokowski: both of these would be beyond the pocket of most of us. As a student of music, I certainly can't afford to go to concerts on a regular basis.

Television is also the major source of news and information for most people. Documentary programmes about foreign countries, and educational programmes about medicine, science or natural history, are brought into the homes of ordinary people who, without television, would know very little about these things.

Rosliana Bt Ahmad Rosli, 17, Malaysia

4

Despite the developments in computer technology and the Internet, television still remains the main medium to reach out to people and educate them about social issues. Many chat shows deal with the real problems facing people today – poverty and homelessness, mental illness, AIDS, to name but a few. What is also interesting is that, increasingly, the scriptwriters of many soaps are no longer afraid to deal with these issues too. Domestic violence, drug-dealing, alcoholism may not be pleasant or light-hearted viewing, but it seems that even soaps – traditionally very escapist entertainment – can now play a vital role in educating young people.

Anastasia Vloutsis, 18, Greece

Reading technique: summary skills

Read each of the four reports again and match them to one of the following titles (A–E). There is one title that you don't need.

A Don't just sit there – get a life!
B Excellent quality, excellent value
C Of course they're awful, but that's why we love them!
D Just a load of repeats
E The changing role of soaps

Speaking skill: sharing opinions and decision making

1 Working in groups of four, imagine that you are part of an advisory panel to a television channel which has decided to launch a new soap opera aimed at people in your age group.

2 Give the channel advice on the following:

How often should it be shown?
On what days of the week?
At what time?
Should it seek to entertain only or to inform as well?

3 The following themes or topics are often dealt with in soaps. Decide which three would be of *most* interest to young people in your country:

- rich people and their lifestyles
- love and relationships
- marriage and divorce
- family issues (e.g. parents and teenagers, a teenage pregnancy)
- addictions (e.g. drugs, alcohol, food, gambling)
- illness or disability
- social problems (e.g. homelessness, racism, debt)
- problems at school/work (e.g. bullying)

Are there any of the above topics that should be avoided?

4 Look at the pictures of the four main actors who have been chosen to act in this soap. Make up some information about them and their lifestyles, their relationship to each other, and decide an outline of the story for the first episode. Try to end with a cliff-hanger.

5 Share your group's ideas with the rest of the class and decide which group has the most promising plans.

EXAM FOCUS
**(Writing, Part 2)
a discursive essay**

An international magazine is investigating the following question:

> Information or entertainment? Television isn't much good at providing either any more.

Write a short article (120–180 words) which gives your reaction to this statement, based on television in your country.

S T R A T E G I E S

1 In a question like this, you need to decide if you agree completely, agree in part or disagree with the statement. Why not work in a group with people who have the same opinion as you?

2 Your article will have five main parts:

- introduction
- your opinion
- reasons
- the effect of future developments
- conclusions

3 Work together to make notes under the 'reasons' and 'future developments' headings, and write a first draft of your article in class.

▶ **Go to the Review page to record your performance.**

LANGUAGE AWARENESS
question tags

1 🔲 Decide which of the following question tags are correct and then listen to check your ideas.

a We'd better be leaving, hadn't we?
b Are you from Greece, aren't you?
c Nobody called while I was out, did nobody?
d Let's go to the cinema, shall we?
e We hardly ever go out, don't we?
f I'm next, am't I?
g You don't speak English, do you?
h You haven't got the time, have you?
i We should be all right, shouldn't we?
j We met at the sales conference, didn't we?
k We have to turn left here, haven't we?

2 Of those that you got wrong, which of these general rules did you forget or were you not aware of?

- Affirmative statements generally have negative tags and vice versa.
- The auxiliary verb ('do', 'be', 'have') or modal verb ('must', 'should', etc.) in the main clause is repeated in the tag. (Remember that 'have' can sometimes be used as an ordinary verb.)
- An ordinary verb in the main clause means 'do' is used in the question tag.
- Negative words, like 'nobody', 'nothing', 'never', 'hardly', take a positive question tag.
- 'I am' takes 'aren't I?' in the question tag.
- 'Somebody', 'someone', 'nobody' and 'no one' take 'they' in the tag.
- 'Let's' is followed by 'shall we?' in the tag.
- Question tags do not follow questions.

3 🔲 Intonation is extremely important when using question tags as it is this that carries the meaning. Rising intonation (↗) indicates the speaker is asking a genuine question or making a request, falling intonation (↘) is used if the speaker is sure. Decide if the speaker is probably sure (S) or not sure (NS) of the statements about you below and then listen to check your answers.

a You're probably studying for FCE, aren't you? (S)
b You've been studying English for at least a year, haven't you? (S)
c You can't speak any other languages, can you? (NS)
d You think question tags are easy, don't you? (NS)

4 Work in pairs and complete the following statements about your partner, supplying the correct question tag. You will need to decide which is most suitable, a positive or a negative main clause. Then ask him or her the questions, using the correct intonation. Don't forget, question tags are an aid to conversation, so if an interesting point is raised or there's disagreement, talk about it.

a You have/haven't been to America ...
b You (don't) smoke ...
c You were/weren't at the last lesson ...
d You are/aren't doing FCE ...
e I'm better/worse at question tags than you are ...
f You hardly ever/always do your homework ...
g We had to/didn't have to do homework from the last lesson ...
h Nothing/something interesting happened in the news yesterday ...
i This time next year, you will/won't be studying English ...
j Let's talk about something else ...

5 🔲 Listen and answer the following questions. Then check your ideas with your partner, using a question tag and the appropriate intonation.

6 In pairs, think of as many things as you can about your teacher that

a) you're sure are true, or
b) you're not sure.

Ask your teacher each question, with an appropriate question tag and the appropriate intonation.

Examples:

You're not married, are you? ↗

Your birthday's in May, isn't it? ↘

LANGUAGE AWARENESS
past simple and past continuous

1 ▭ One of the authors of this book once had a rather embarrassing experience. Look at the following words and try to guess what happened. Then listen to see how close you were.

parents' house/rat/socks/scratching/hangover/
visitors/embarrassed

2 Turn to the tapescript on pages 176–7. Can you match the sections in italics with a use of the past simple or continuous below? Write each one in the chart.

Use	Example
a sequence of events	
past (permanent) habit	
past (temporary) habit	
an action that interrupts or happens in the middle of another	
an action that is interrupted by another	
two or more actions happening at the same time (sometimes used to set the scene)	

3 Look at the following extracts. Which is an anecdote, a novel extract, a news bulletin? Complete the extracts with either the past simple or the past continuous form of the verb provided.

A The explosion (a) .... (take) place just as commuters (b) .... (make) their way to the station. The emergency services (c) .... (rush) to the scene which witnesses (d) .... (describe) as being like a scene from hell. Tim Hancock, a builder who (e) .... (work) in the area at the time of the explosion, (f) .... (give) us the following account.

'I (g) .... (have) my tea break and (h) .... (play) cards with my mates when we (i) .... (hear) this enormous "bang". We (j) .... (run) outside, (k) .... (see) what had happened and just (l) .... (try) to help.'

B It (a) .... (be) about 7.15 when Sam (b) .... (leave) home. He (c) .... (get) into the car and (d) .... (turn) left into Main Street. The stranger (e) .... (stand) menacingly at the end of the road but (f) .... (pay) no attention as Sam (g) .... (drive) up beside him and (h) .... (lower) the window.

C Yeah, well anyway it (a) .... (happen) while me and the wife (b) .... (work) in the garden. I (c) .... (plant) some roses and Mavis (d) .... (talk) to the woman next door, who (e) .... (complain) about the weather. Anyway, I (f) .... (dig) this hole when all of a sudden I (g) .... (see) this bright light in the sky. It (h) .... (come) out of nowhere, (i) .... (fly) quickly over our heads, (j) .... (stop) for a few seconds and then (k) .... (disappear).

4 Think about your journey to school or college today. Try to remember the scene when you left your house, what you did when you left and what was happening at any particular moment. Complete the following text supplying your own description of what happened using past simple and past continuous.

When I left home ... (set the scene) ...
I ... (sequence of events) ...
While I was ... (what were other people doing?)
Then I ...
While I was ... (what happened?)

5 Now continue the description until the moment the lesson started. Then swap your text with a partner and comment on each other's use of tenses.

Your review of Unit 2

Vocabulary

Your selection:

Suggestion: Compare your vocabulary selection with a partner. Ask him/her to test you on some of your chosen words, by giving you a clue. (This will help *both* of you to remember the word)

Example:
'This word has six letters, the fourth letter is 'h', it's the name given to the person who writes a book.'
'Is it "author"'?
'Correct!'

Exam skills

Complete the summaries by underlining the appropriate answer:

Listening, Part 1, extracts
• You will hear people using English in eight a) similar b) different situations.
• You have to choose from a) two b) three c) four answers.

Your score _____ /8
How well did I do?

Writing, Part 2, a discursive essay
• This question is a test of your ability to a) write a description b) argue a point.

How well did I do?

General

Problems and Solutions

PART ONE
A problem shared

Lead-in

In your country, at what ages must you or are you allowed to do the things below? Write the ages in the first column. Then compare your answers with other members of the group.

	your country	England	other countries
start school		5	Sweden 7
leave school		16	Spain 14, Greek 14.5
get a part-time job			
drive a car			
ride a small motorbike			
buy cigarettes			
marry (with your parents' consent)		16	Greece 17 any / Italy 17, Home 15
vote in a general election			
drink alcohol in a bar			
be held responsible for a crime		10	Scotland 8, Greece 7, Poland/Germany 14

Listening technique: global understanding

You are going to hear an extract from a radio programme that answers questions sent in by its teenage listeners. The programme begins by looking at the different ages of consent across Europe. As you listen for the first time, decide which points are discussed and in which order. (For example, start school = 1, etc.)

Listening technique: specific information

1 Listen again and write in the ages of consent for England and for one of the other countries mentioned.
2 There is a big difference between countries on some issues. Whose laws do you most agree with?

Speaking skill: problem solving

1 Do you agree with the rights young people have in your country, or would you change any of the ages of consent?

2 The letters below were sent in to the same radio programme. What advice would you give to each person? Make brief notes with a partner and save these notes for later.

I've been planning to get a small motor bike for my 16th birthday next month. I know my parents have never wanted me to have one as they think they're too dangerous. However, they promised me last year that if I saved up half the money they would put up the rest. I've been working part-time and have nearly saved up the amount I need. Now they're telling me that they're not going to give me the money. They didn't expect me to save up enough and now they're breaking their promise. Somebody recently died in a motor bike accident near our house and they're using that as an excuse. I really think they're acting unfairly.

Steve

Me and my boyfriend have been going out together for almost a year now and we're very much in love. He's 17 and I'm 16. The problem is my parents don't like him and refuse to let me see him. They think I should be concentrating on my school work and not spending all my time going out with him or talking to him on the phone. We still see each other secretly and the more my parents try to keep us apart, the more I seem to want to be with him. We've talked about running away together and getting married, but I'd hate to make a decision like that without the blessing of my parents, who I also love very much. How can I make them see how much he means to me?

Carol

I've been having a lot of problems at school lately. I'm nearly 16 and had planned to stay on for two more years to get the qualifications I need to go to university. However, lately I've been feeling very irritated with all the petty rules that our school has. We're not treated like adults! I hate having to wear a school uniform, we have to call all the teachers 'Sir' or 'Miss', while they only refer to us by our surnames, and they're always ordering us about. A lot of my friends have left school and are now looking for work. I desperately want to be independent and make my own decisions and I'm beginning to think leaving school and going to work would be the best way to achieve this. What should I do?

Kelly

3 As a teenager who do/did you listen to most/least for advice? Why? Share your ideas in a group.

- a teacher
- a parent
- a grandparent
- a friend of the same age
- an older brother or sister
- an agony aunt in a teenage magazine

📼 Listening technique: specific information

1 Now, listen to the second part of the radio programme, in which a teacher, an agony aunt and a student counsellor give their advice on the three problems. Make notes of what each of them says in the table below.

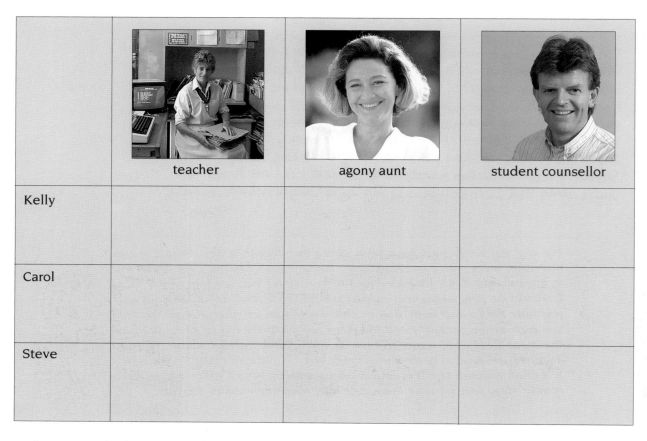

	teacher	agony aunt	student counsellor
Kelly			
Carol			
Steve			

2 If you were the letter writers whose advice would you take?

Writing skill: a reply to a problem page

1 Choose one of the problems that you discussed in the Speaking activity and, using the notes you have made, write your own reply to the letter of around 150 words. You can use some of the following phrases for giving advice:

Have you tried ...?
What about ...?
In my experience ...
The best solution would be ...
If that doesn't work, you could always ...

2 When you've finished, ask your partner to assess your work out of 20 on the following points:

● advice (was it useful?) – 10 marks
● grammatical accuracy – 10 marks

PART TWO
Brain-teasers

Lead-in

Work in small groups. Which group can give the best answers to the following questions?

Why is it that women live longer than men?
Why do moths fly towards light?
Why is it that we clap to show our appreciation?
Why does your voice sound different when you hear yourself recorded?
Why do some countries put a line across the stem on a number seven?
Why does the earth revolve to the east but the weather come from the west?
Why is it that one person yawning often makes another person yawn?

Listening technique: global understanding

You are going to hear two lateral thinking problems. The first time you listen match each problem to the appropriate picture. One picture is not used.

a   b   c

Listening technique: specific information

1 Here is a chance to practise your listening and grammatical skills. Listen to the recording two or three times, making a note of all the key words in each problem. After each listening, share your ideas in groups.

2 Now rewrite each problem, paying attention to grammatical accuracy.

3 Compare your versions with other groups before checking the facts against the tapescript on page 178.

Speaking skill: asking questions

Can you solve the problems? Work in pairs. Each of you will be given the answer to one of the problems. The other person should ask 'yes/no' questions to solve the problem. You are only allowed twenty questions. Try to make sure your questions are grammatically correct.

***See* Language awareness: comparatives and superlatives**

EXAM FOCUS
(Use of English, Part 1)
multiple-choice
cloze

For questions 1–15, read the text below and decide which word A, B, C or D best fits each space. There is an example at the beginning (0).

Example:

(0)   A area   B ground   Ⓒ land   D space

There were three farming families: Smith, Brown and Jones. Mr and Mrs Smith had a triangle of (0) land which they wanted to divide in such a (1) ...... that each of their offspring would have a piece of land (2) ...... the same size and shape.

Down the road, the Browns had four children. The parents wanted to divide their land – an L-shaped plot which (3) ...... like a square with one of its quarters (4) ...... out – into four equal pieces for their offspring. Again, (5) ...... piece of land had to be the same shape.

In the (6) ...... village, (7) ......, Mr and Mrs Jones had a piece of farmland in a (8) ...... square. They had five children. (9) ...... with the Smiths and the Browns, they were eager to make (10) ...... that each child should have a single piece of land (11) ...... in size and shape: the square had to be divided into five.

The three families (12) ...... in the local surveyor, Theo D. Lite, to ask his (13) .... Mr Lite looked at the Smiths' triangle of land and quickly (14) ...... a sketch of how to divide the land into three. At the Browns' house, he thought a little longer; then he (15) ...... up with a plan which would give each of the four children an L-shaped piece of land. Finally, he turned his attention to the Jones' problem and, after a little thought, came up with a solution.

#	A	B	C	D
1	A way	B method	C system	D style
2	A utterly	B totally	C completely	D exactly
3	A seemed	B appeared	C looked	D showed
4	A removed	B subtracted	C taken	D moved
5	A each	B both	C some	D all
6	A near	B close	C neighbouring	D next-door
7	A meanwhile	B then	C while	D during
8	A exceptional	B perfect	C correct	D flawless
9	A Like	B Similar	C Same	D As
10	A certainly	B ensure	C sure	D definite
11	A identical	B same	C corresponding	D like
12	A asked	B called	C phoned	D rang
13	A suggestion	B advice	C thought	D idea
14	A wrote	B painted	C lined	D drew
15	A came	B went	C thought	D decided

S T R A T E G I E S

1 Read the whole text through first to get a general understanding.

2 Are there any words near the gaps that are used in combination with another word? For example: phrasal verbs, dependent prepositions, words which collocate (go) with other words?

3 Compare your answers with a partner before checking them with your teacher.

4 Have you found the solution yet?

▶ **Go to the Review page to record your performance.**

PART THREE
A problem in the workplace

Lead-in

1 What kind of an employee/student are you? Give yourself a grade of good, average or weak in the following areas.

	good	average	weak
punctuality			
attendance			
relationship with other colleagues/students			
attitude to your boss/teacher			
commitment to job/studying			
ability to finish work under pressure			
quality of written reports/essays			
computer skills			
general impression			

2 Tell your partner your good and weak points.

Example:
Well, I'm usually quite punctual, but I don't always attend class as often as I should.

3 What do you think is the most important aspect of being a good employee/student? Choose from the above list or think of your own ideas. If you were a boss or teacher, how would you deal with somebody who scored 'weak' in the above areas? Share your ideas with a small group.

EXAM FOCUS
(Reading, Part 4)
multiple matching

You are going to read an extract from a book which tells you how to identify different types of employee. For questions 1–13, choose from the list of employee types A–H. Some of the types may be chosen more than once. When more than one answer is required, these may be given in any order. There is an example at the beginning (0).

Which employee type(s):

arrives at work the earliest?	0	**A**	
is often absent on Monday morning?	1		
can take too long to finish reports?	2	3	
hands in reports of poor quality?	4		
is unhappy with the amount of work he/she is given?	5	6	7
will moan about the journey to work?	8		
is often late for work?	9	10	
will phone his/her friends and family during work time?	11		
is friendly towards colleagues but less so to the manager?	12		
suffers the least from stress?	13		

Identifying Employee Types

A The Manager

Donna arrives at work at 8:30 am, her usual time. The office is not scheduled to open until 9 am, but she likes the quiet time to get organised and plan for the day ahead. As department manager, she's also setting an example to her staff, which had some punctuality problems when she took over the department about six months ago. Punctuality has improved slightly, but several other problems are now emerging.

B The Complainer

Jeff hurries in at just about 9, out of breath and obviously agitated. He immediately starts complaining about his difficulties with public transport, crowds, the weather or the traffic. He looks at his in-tray and loudly states that he seems to have more assignments than the other staff members. Throughout the day, he continues to complain that he is the only one working diligently.

C The Sickly

Marie regularly calls in five minutes after nine to report that she cannot make it into work due to horrible colds, assorted viruses, migraine, headaches or back pain. These maladies seem to occur right before or after a holiday or weekend.

D The Not-My-Jobber

Vicky is usually on time and always very cheerful. She sorts through her in-tray, and promptly delivers to Donna all those assignments that are 'clearly not her job'. Whenever Donna points out that most of the tasks do come within her range of responsibilities, she pleasantly replies that although she disagrees, she'll do them because she wants to keep her job.

E The Perfectionist

Gina arrives precisely five minutes before 9 every day. She gets down to work at exactly nine o'clock and doesn't stop until exactly noon when she promptly leaves for lunch, regardless of her workload or deadlines. Her reports are so scrupulously prepared that it takes her an incredible amount of time to produce even the simplest document.

F The Procrastinator

Frank arrives anywhere from five to thirty-five minutes late every day. He stopped making excuses long ago because lateness is not an issue for him – it's a custom. He is so pleasant and charming that when he does arrive, everyone is happy to see him and no-one mentions the time. Few people are able to stay angry with him, although he gives everyone ample reason. He regularly misses appointments and delays every task to the last minute. Frank never feels pressure because his personality remains calm and confident.

(J. Miskell & V. Miskell: *Motivation at Work*)

G The Half-hearted Employee

Sal arrives for work anywhere from fifteen minutes early to fifteen minutes late. Whenever he's questioned about overdue reports, he never seems sure which report is being requested, but he always answers vaguely that it is almost finished. Sal always hands in his reports, but they usually need extensive revision. He spends a lot of time making personal calls.

H The Angry Underminer

Leon arrives at 9 am and greets the staff in a friendly manner. When he passes Donna's office he simply says, 'Good morning', as if it takes some great effort. Leon will do anything that is asked of him but is sure to mention to the others that he has yet another new task that he has no choice but to accept. He usually talks about Donna in a negative way. It is no secret that Leon was interviewed for the manager's job six months ago and became bitter when Donna got the job instead.

S T R A T E G I E S

1 First of all, look at the paragraph headings. With a partner, try to predict what each employee type is like.

   Example:
   The Perfectionist. 'I think this is somebody who likes to do everything perfectly ... maybe s/he spends a long time doing particular jobs.'

2 Now quickly read each paragraph to see if your predictions were correct.

3 Look at the numbered points in turn and follow the Exam Focus instructions. Try to underline evidence in each section and then check your answers in a small group.

▶ **Go to the Review page to record your performance.**

Speaking skill: discussion and reaching agreement

1 In small groups, imagine that you are Donna, the department manager, and you have been told by your boss that you have to get rid of two members of your team. One employee is to be sacked, and the other is to be made redundant and given a year's salary.

2 Read the text above again, as well as the confidential notes on each employee on the right. Try to reach agreement in your group about which employees should leave the department.

3 Report your decision to the rest of the class, giving reasons for your choices.

4 Now think about the following points:

- How much did you contribute to the discussion?
- Did you use (or hear) any interesting phrases?
- Did you make any mistakes?

MEMO

Jeff	not popular with colleagues, can't cope with the stress of working in a big city?
Marie	47 days off sick last year, looks after elderly father (also in poor health).
Vicky	wants very limited role in company, won't accept new responsibilities, doesn't seem to want promotion. Gets on well with others.
Gina	afraid of making mistakes, works rather slowly, a bit of a 'clock-watcher'.
Frank	good for staff morale, but very unreliable! Often plays computer games during office time.
Sal	rather quiet, doesn't talk to colleagues much, no commitment to the job.
Leon	spends a lot of time in other departments, prefers making jokes instead of useful suggestions in department meetings, uncooperative.

CONFIDENTIAL

Use of English: sentence transformation

The following sentences are part of an advertisement for a new member of staff. However, you have decided that they need to be redrafted. Rewrite each sentence so that it is grammatically correct and still means exactly the same thing. The underlined words need to be changed.

See **Language awareness: defining and non-defining relative clauses**

Example:

If your application is successful you will be responsible for organising a team of five.
The successful ... (general noun to personal noun)

The successful applicant will be responsible for organising a team of five.

1 We prefer that applicants are over the age of 25.
   It ... (active to passive)
2 It is desirable that you have practical experience.
   Candidates ... (modal verb)
3 It is essential that you can demonstrate good communication skills, particularly in writing.
   You ... (modal verb)
4 You should be able to work under pressure.
   You should have ... (adjective to noun)
5 You must show that you can work as part of a team.
   It ... (active to passive)
6 You must be familiar with the latest information technology.
   You must be used ... (different preposition)
7 It would be an advantage to hold a current driving licence.
   It would be ... (noun to adjective)
8 If you want to apply you should submit a CV and covering letter.
   Those interested ... (infinitive to gerund – but be careful!)
9 We will hold interviews three weeks after the closing date.
   Interviews ... (active to passive)

LANGUAGE AWARENESS
comparatives and superlatives

1 Some of the following statements contain grammatical mistakes. How many can you correct?

a Your teacher is tallest person in the class.
b This coursebook is not as interesting than your last coursebook.
c Your shoes were more expensive than your trousers.
d It's more warm today than it was yesterday.
e More English you study, more English you can speak.
f You live more far from school/college than the person sitting on your left.
g You're a little younger than the person sitting on your right.
h This grammar point is difficulter than the last one.

2 Decide if the statements are true or false. Change any of those that are false.

Example:
Paula is the tallest in the class.

3 Write the comparative and superlative forms of the following words, then complete the sentences below.

	comparative	superlative
old		
tall		
hot		
thin		
happy		
cosy		
responsible		
intelligent		

Most one-syllable words add ...
One-syllable words ending in a vowel + a consonant ...
Words ending in 'y' ...
Words with three or more syllables ...

4 How do the following words differ?

	comparative	superlative
pretty		
good		
bad(ly)		
far		
many		
well		

5 Use the words in box B to compare some of the things in box A.

A

| Britain/Greece/Spain |
| Mercedes/BMW/Fiat |
| A lawyer/A secretary/A doctor |
| A film/A play/A book |

B

| a lot/far/a bit/a little |
| slightly/rather/even |
| much/any/no |

Example:
A Greek summer is a lot hotter than a British one.

6 Write six sentences about somebody in the class, comparing this person with other people. You must use comparatives, superlatives and 'as...as' structures (e.g. 'She's not quite as tall as Carlos.'). See if your partner can guess who you're describing and maybe correct any mistakes that you have made!

7 Read the following text and then create similar texts using the sentences below.

The better he became at his job, the higher up the company he went. The higher up the company he went, the more responsibility he had. The more responsibility he had, the harder he worked. The harder he worked, the more tired he became. The more tired he became, the less he enjoyed his job.

The more I study English ...
The older I get ...
The more I think about life ...
The more money I have ...

8 Look back at activity 1. Are there any sentences that still need correcting?

LANGUAGE AWARENESS
defining and non-defining relative clauses

1 How good is your work vocabulary? How many of the following do you know?

a A _ _ _ _ _ _ _ _ _ _ is a machine *which people use to write letters.*
b A _ _ _ _ _ _ _ _ _ _ _ is a machine *that copies paper.*
c The person *that organises the boss' routine* is called a _ _ _ _ _ _ _ _ _ .
d The person *who you see working at reception* is called a _ _ _ _ _ _ _ _ _ _ _ _ .
e A _ _ _ _ _ _ _ _ _ , *which outlines your terms and conditions,* is signed by both you and the employer.
f In Britain _ _ _ _ _ _ _ _ _ _ is taken at the age of 65, *which isn't soon enough for some people.*
g Your _ _ _ _ _ _ _ , *which is often paid at the end of each month,* is usually taxed.
h A _ _ _ _ _ , *which is sent to people in the office,* is like a short note.

2 In which of the sentences above can 'who' or 'which' be replaced by 'that'?
Which of the clauses in italics contain 'essential' and which contain 'extra' information?

3 The relative pronoun can be omitted in two of the sentences. Which ones and why?

4 Sentences a, b, c and d are examples of defining relative clauses, sentences e, f, g and h non-defining. Using the sentences as guides, fill in the table below.

	defining	non-defining
essential information		
extra information		
commas		
use of 'that'		
omission of pronoun	*(when it's the object)*	

5 Try this vocabulary exercise. This time you must supply the correct relative pronoun and commas, if required, as well as the word being described.

a This is the word _____ describes a person without a job.
b This is the period of time _____ you work beyond your contracted hours.
c This person _____ job it is to keep an eye on the building is often an ex-policeman.
d This is an organisation _____ defends workers' rights.
e This room _____ company directors have their meetings is often beautifully furnished.
f This person _____ is often employed after leaving school is taught how to do a particular job.

6 Now test another group. Work in pairs and write six similar questions. You should use one of the following in each of your questions:

which/that
when
whose
who
where

You score two points for a grammatically correct question, two for a correct answer.

7 Fill in the gaps in the following report, supplying defining or non-defining relative pronouns and commas where required. Put brackets around the pronouns that can be missed out. You will need to choose from the following pronouns: who, that, which, where, when, whose.

Jeff _____ has worked with the company for two years has earned a reputation as being rather a complainer. The regular problems _____ he has with public transport often lead to him arriving late and colleagues _____ have worked with him often complain about his attitude. Hardly a day goes by _____ he isn't claiming to be the only person _____ is working hard. This behaviour _____ often creates a bad atmosphere is leading to a breakdown in staff morale. However, his work _____ is always of a very high standard cannot be faulted and it would be a pity to lose a man _____ contribution to the company has been immeasurable. He has also developed a large number of business contacts _____ are of great benefit to us all. Unfortunately, he is working in an environment _____ co-operation and the ability to get on with colleagues is vital.

Your review of Unit 3

Vocabulary

Your selection:

Suggestion: Look at the words you have recorded from this unit. Why did you record them? Tell your partner.

Example:

'I've chosen a lot of words from Part 3 to do with work and the workplace, like "memo", "job applicant", "redundant". I might find them useful in the future.'

Cross out any words you are not likely to use in the near future.

Exam skills

Complete the summaries by underlining the appropriate answer:

Use of English, Part 1, multiple-choice cloze
- This question is a test mainly of a) grammatical structures b) vocabulary.
- You a) have a choice of four answers b) fill in the gap yourself.

Score _____/15
How well did I do?

Reading, Part 4, multiple matching
- With this type of multiple matching the questions come a) before b) after the text(s).
- You are being tested on your ability to read for a) the main ideas b) specific information.

Score _____/13
How well did I do?

General

UNIT 4

English Matters

PART ONE
A *taste* of Britain

Lead-in

How would you cope with British food and eating habits? Try the quiz below.

a How many different ways could you be served a potato?
b If you were invited for 'tea' what might it mean?
c What time would you probably eat your evening meal?
d What would it mean if your host decided to get a 'take-away'?
e If you were asked 'How do you take your tea?' what would you say?
f If you were offered 'dessert' what would you have just finished eating?
g What would you be given if you asked for a traditional English Sunday roast?

Vocabulary development: food and drink collocation

1 Complete the table below with the opposite of the word supplied.

> spicy/hot mature fresh dry light well-done sweet soft
> tough sparkling strong hard-boiled natural stale

	crusty	*bread*	sweet		*wine*
soft		*egg*		weak	*tea*
fresh		*bread*	mild		*curry*
	sour	*milk*	mild		*cheese*
still		*water*		stodgy	*pudding*
	tender	*steak*	rare		*steak*
	fruit	*yoghurt*	savoury		*snack*

2 Which items of food can you think of that are:

mashed scrambled poached steamed boiled
barbecued baked grilled fried

3 Ask your partner about some of their food preferences.
For example, do they like soft or hard-boiled eggs?

◫ Listening technique: global understanding

Look at the map of Britain below and the pictures of some traditional food. Do you recognise any of them? You are going to hear a radio programme explaining what these foods are and where you can go to try them. As you listen for the first time decide which type of food is being described in each case.

Haggis:
Scottish speciality made from lamb's liver and heart. Served with (1) .... Try it at: Charles McSween and Son, (2) .... Bruntsfield Place, Edinburgh.

Welsh Lamb Pie:
Made with lamb and vegetables and cooked for (9) .... Covered in a light crusty pastry. Some delicious examples can be found at Blas ar Gymru (The Taste of Wales) (10) .... Crwys Road, Cardiff.

Yorkshire Pudding:
Served as part of a traditional Sunday roast dinner. Made from milk, flour, eggs and (3) .... Sometimes made with (4) .... for added taste. A wide range can be found at The Spurriergate Centre, York.

Cornish Pasties:
First eaten over (7) .... years ago by the Cornish tin miners. Basic ingredients of (8) .... held together in a pastry parcel. Pop in and try one at the Cornwall Patisserie, Lower Lemon Street, Truro.

Cream Teas:
Best Cream Teas to be found in the West Country, particularly Devon, home of Britain's (5) .... industry. A dry, crumbly cake topped with (6) .... and served with a pot of tea. Try one at the Old Forge at Totnes.

◫ Listening technique: specific information

◫ Listen again and fill in the gaps 1–10.

Speaking skill: sharing information

Are there any regional specialities in your country that are internationally famous, or should be? Work alone or with somebody else from your country and decide what you would include in your country's top five foods. Consider the points opposite :

- Where is this food produced? (you could draw a map)
- When is it usually eaten?
- What is it made of?
- What is special about it?

PART TWO
Host families

Lead-in

1 Imagine you are coming to stay with a host family
in Britain while you study English. What are the
main advantages of living with an English family?
Can you think of any drawbacks? Write a brief list
with your partner.

2 Which of the following aspects would cause
problems for you? Put a tick in the first column,
where appropriate, and then discuss your
answers with a partner, giving reasons for your
views.

	You	Middle East	France	Italy	Turkey	Belgium	Japan	Thailand	General
Not being sure of the house rules or if you are being polite enough									
Sharing a house with others of the same mother tongue									
Your host having pets									
Not having a daily conversation with your host									
Using a bath instead of a shower									
Your host having teenage children of the opposite sex									
English food									

Reading technique: scanning

The text you are going to read gives an account of some of the
problems faced by foreign students who stay with host families in
Britain. Scan the text as quickly as you can (5 minutes) in order to
discover which nationalities have which problems. Tick the relevant
boxes in the chart above. Use the final box for problems that are not
specific to any nationality.

There's no place like home

1 As hundreds of thousands of overseas students do battle with the English language in schools across the UK this summer, many will be struggling with a culture for which they are totally unprepared. Misunderstandings can occur which, if not sorted out, can ruin a student's trip.

2 Much of this is the result of false perceptions and expectations of British families and the way they live. For example, a Middle East student in his forties wrote before his arrival in England to request an orthopaedic mattress, a family willing to discuss the day's news, no pork in his diet and no alcohol. Then, after his second day in England, his host rang the college welfare officer to say he wouldn't eat the food she'd cooked for him. The college solved the problem by the student taking evening meals at the college, where he could try out the food by eating a little at a time, and only taking breakfast with his host. 'They later got on like a house on fire,' said his welfare officer. 'He just hadn't got on with the food.'

3 A number of leading EFL organisations have commissioned research among foreign students to discover what they felt were the most important factors in their stay.

They found that, although UK EFL courses were heavily praised, what concerned students was the quality of host families and welfare during their stay.

4 In one report, French agents described cases of two students of the same mother tongue living with the same family, lack of attention to guests by host families (with few opportunities for English conversation), and problems to do with food. According to the research: 'The Italians have a phobia about British packed lunches (which they consider to be soggy sliced bread and chocolate biscuits) but are happy to eat them if they contain wholesome things.'

5 In a British Council report, a majority (71 per cent) cited as 'very important' the time a host family spent with them in English conversation. Other important features included the family's welcome, a place to study in peace and not having another student with the same mother tongue in the same family.

6 Matching students to families is often difficult. 20–30 per cent of students don't like pets, yet trying to find a family without pets is very difficult. Turks do not allow dogs into their homes, and one Belgian girl told her hosts it was abhorrent

to allow them into bedrooms. Then there is the problem of baths. 'Some cultures think it disgusting to lie in one's own dirty water,' says one accommodation officer. 'Without a shower there is no way they can wash their hair. Some students want three showers a day.'

7 Host families need to be warned about wide cultural differences to avoid misunderstandings. An advice leaflet on hosting Japanese families points out that they will wait for permission or an invitation to do most day-to-day things in a host's home. Some countries insist on certain hosting rules. The Thai embassy, for example, stipulates that Thai girls are not allowed to be placed in a family which has boys over the age of 12 under the same roof.

8 Students should also be clearer about the true nature of an English family. 'Another part of the problem is that people abroad think of an English family as a white, married couple with two kids. But that is not a typical English family. There is a wide ethnic spread, single parent families and so on. We're interested in a warm, welcoming atmosphere where students get a lot of English and interest and care. That's the important thing - and for that you need standards.'

(Guardian)

Reading technique: summary skills

1 Match the paragraph (1–8) with the correct paragraph summary (a–j). There are two which you do not need.

a Aspects that foreign students most dislike
b A question of hygiene
c What host families need to know
d What English families are really like
e Culture shock! (Not just a language problem)

f How to keep your host family happy
g The most important things for foreign students
h Reaching a compromise
i Researching the problems
j Wanting to go home

2 Try to justify your answers to the teacher.

3 Have you ever experienced problems like these? Share your experiences with the class.

See **Language awareness: modal verbs of obligation**

EXAM FOCUS
(Use of English, Part 3) 'key' word transformations

For questions 1–10, complete the second sentence so that it has a similar meaning to the first sentence. Use the word given and other words to complete the sentence. You must use between two and five words. Do not change the word given. There is an example at the beginning (0).

Example:

0 I don't mind your dog sleeping on my bed.
matter

It ...*doesn't matter*.... if your dog sleeps on my bed.

1 Don't bother to wash my clothes. I prefer to do it myself.
need
There .... wash my clothes. I prefer to do it myself.

2 I wish we had a system of government as good as your British one.
only
.... system of government was as good as your British one.

3 Gold is much cheaper in my country than in Britain so please accept this bracelet.
expensive
In my country gold .... in Britain so please accept this bracelet.

4 Your food is the best I've ever eaten.
never
I've .... good food.

5 I'd prefer to have a bath once a week.
rather
I .... once a week.

6 You really must start charging your guests more money.
essential
It .... charging your guests more money.

7 I haven't had such a good time for years.
since
It's been years .... a good time.

8 I can't believe you are 59 – you look much younger.
far
You .... than 59.

9 Would you like to go out for a meal this evening?
feel
Do .... out for a meal this evening?

10 The laws of my country do not permit me to change back this currency, so I would like you to have it.
allowed
According to the laws of my country, I .... change back this currency, so I would like you to have it.

STRATEGIES

1 In English (as in your own language) there are a number of ways you can express the same idea.

I don't feel like working today.
I'm not in the mood to work today.

As well as a vocabulary difference ('don't feel like'/ 'am not in the mood') there is also a grammatical change ('working'/ 'to work').

2 Read the humorous sentences 1–10 above (which will make your host very happy!). Work with a partner and complete as many as you can, before checking your answers with your teacher.

3 When you have finished, remember to check that you have not used more than five words in the space. (In the exam, you will not get a mark if you exceed the word limit, even if your answer is absolutely correct.) Contractions, e.g. 'I'm', are counted as two words.

▶ **Go to the Review page to record your performance.**

◻ Listening technique: specific information and inference

1 You are going to hear a conversation between Dimi and her friend about Dimi's stay with her host family. As you listen, complete the questionnaire below for the Accommodation Office who arranged the stay. When you've finished compare your answers with your partner.

Overseas student questionnaire

Host family accommodation

1 Please state the name and address of the family you stayed with:

....

2 Overall, did you enjoy your stay with them?

Yes, very much ☐   It was OK ☑   No, not much ☐

3 Did you feel welcome in their home (i.e. were they friendly towards you)?

Yes ☐   Some of the time ☐   No ☐

4 How was your room? Please comment.

Very good ☐   OK ☐   Too small ☐   Poor ☐

....

5 Did you enjoy the food they gave you?

Yes ☐   It was OK ☐   Not much ☑

....

6 Did your hosts invite you out if they were going somewhere?

Often ☐   Sometimes ☐   Never ☐

7 Did you and your host take the time to talk to each other?

Yes ☐   Some time ☐   She was too busy ☑   I was too busy ☑

8 Did your host help you to find which bus stop and bus to use?

Yes ☐   No ☐

9 Is there anything in particular that you did not like about your host/accommodation?

....

10 Is there anything in particular that you did like?

....

ⓔ Writing skill: a semi-formal letter to a host family

1 You are going to work or study in England and it has been arranged that you will stay with Mrs Smith. Read the notes which you have made and then write a polite letter to Mrs Smith, introducing yourself and addressing the following points.

- Allergic to potatoes/possible to cook own food?
- Able to practise English conversation every day?
- Possible to have use of her car? (long journey by public transport, willing to pay for petrol/ maintenance)
- Can her dog sleep outside bedroom?

2 Begin your letter in the following way:

> Dear Mrs Smith,
> I am delighted to have the opportunity of coming to stay with you and your family ...

3 When you have finished, exchange letters with your partner and check the following:

- register (is it polite enough?) – 5 marks
- content (are all the points covered?) – 5 marks
- grammar and vocabulary – 5 marks
- organisation (are the ideas in a logical order?) – 5 marks

4 Now read the sample letter on page 162 and compare it with your own.

PART THREE
Out and about in England

Lead-in

1 Which of the following can you do in your home town/city? How
  often do you do them? Are there any other things you would
  add to the list? Share your views with a partner.

	often	sometimes	rarely	never
Going to a pub/bar				
Seeing a film				
Going to see a play or concert				
Going to a restaurant				
Playing bingo				
Going to the gym/sports centre				
Late-night shopping				
Going to a café				
Going dancing in a club				

2 How do you think overseas visitors feel about social activities in
  your area?

3 How might the climate, the character of the people, or the working
  hours affect the kind of popular social activities in different
  countries?

Reading technique: global understanding

Read the following article written by an overseas
student who has been studying in England for
several months. How many of the above
points are mentioned?

LIVING IT UP IN ENGLAND

How's the social life in England like? It's OK! Even if my first impression wasn't
very good. I still remember my first day clearly in Britain; all shops were shut
down. I thought, 'How I am going to live here?'

But as time went by, I knew about the British lifestyle. You could find that
most leisure places are inside because the weather is often very cold or wet.
Most British like going to the pub with friends. The big pubs are very wonderful
and although I don't drink alcoholic, the pubs are welcome and friendly. And you
can meet some very nice boys!

And English persons also like doing indoor activities like bowling or pool and
Bingo. You can join local people on shopping excursions also but every shops
close at 5.30. So this makes it difficult to shop if people working. But the
bowling and pool is very good. And maybe you would win a lot of money play
Bingo. It's also worth to go for short walks in the beautiful parks but just if
the weather is good!

Yes, according to my advice, come to England, you have a great time!

Use of English: error correction

1 In pairs, discuss this student's strengths and weaknesses.
Has the student:

- organised the article well?
- made it interesting?
- used appropriate vocabulary?
- used grammar correctly?

2 Can you find and correct at least 20 grammar and vocabulary mistakes?

Vocabulary development 1: adverb and adjective collocation

1 What was the mistake in the following sentence?

'The big pubs are very wonderful ...'

2 Match an adjective from column A
with a similar but more extreme
adjective from column B:

A	B
bad	fascinating
tasty	fantastic
poor	thrilling
pretty	awful
exciting	gorgeous
good	delicious
interesting	wonderful
nice	terrible

3 Which of the adjectives can be preceded by 'very' and which by 'absolutely'? Can you work out why?

4 Work in pairs and give your opinion of leisure facilities in your local area.

Example:
'What's the area like for shopping?'   'Absolutely fantastic!'

Vocabulary development 2: entertainment

1 In which category or categories would you put the words below:

screen	audience	customer	aisle	spectator	instructor	waiter
stage	programme	court	ticket	bill	pitch	dressing room	conductor
actor	menu	changing room	interval	bar		

sports club	restaurant	theatre/concert hall	cinema

2 Can you think of at least five more words to add to each of the categories?

3 Test your partner by giving definitions of some of the words.
Your partner must guess which words you are describing.

Writing: an article for a travel magazine

1 Imagine you have been asked to write an article called 'Living it up in ...' for a travel magazine. You can write about your own country <u>or</u> another country you have visited.

2 Look at the Lead-in activity on page 46 again, and make a list of all the leisure activities you are going to put in your article. Think about the following:

- indoor or outdoor?
- young people or all generations?
- daytime or evening?
- cheap or expensive?

3 Write the article (120–180 words) paying particular attention to the language points you examined in the previous Use of English activity on page 47. You could also use some of the 'entertainment' vocabulary you have just practised.

See **Language awareness: past perfect simple and continuous**

EXAM FOCUS
(Speaking, Part 2) comparing two photographs

Choose two of the photographs below and be prepared to talk about them with a partner.

a

b

c

d

STRATEGIES

1 🖭 Look at the four photographs on page 148. You will hear two students practising for Part 2 of the Speaking paper. Listen to what they are asked to do and then decide which pictures they are talking about.

2 Now look at the photographs above. Work in groups of three. One of you should act as the examiner, giving the instructions which the teacher will supply. When you've finished, comment on how well the interview went before changing roles and trying again with a new examiner.

▶ **Go to the Review page to record your performance.**

LANGUAGE
AWARENESS
modal verbs
of obligation

1 ▭ Listen to the following dialogues, the first between a landlady and a student, the second between two students. What are the rules about the following:

breakfast?
dinner?
tidying the bedroom ?
bedtime?
getting home late?
using the bathroom?
washing clothes?

2 ▭ Turn to the tapescript on pages 179–80 and listen again, underlining all the modals of obligation.

3 Which of the modal verbs that appeared in the dialogues express the following:

strong obligation/necessity?
weaker obligation/necessity?
no obligation/necessity?

4 Study the tapescript again. Why does Mrs Sproggit use 'must' but Carlos use 'have to' when talking about getting home late? How would the same statements be expressed with future reference? What's the difference in meaning between 'mustn't' and 'don't have to'? Refer to the Grammar Reference section to confirm your ideas.

5 Complete the sentences below with an appropriate form of 'must (not)' or '(not) have to'.

a I didn't have any cash, so I .... pay by cheque.
b You .... come to visit as soon as you have time.
c You .... do it if you don't want to.
d We .... arrive early tonight if we want a good seat.
e Keys .... be left at reception. (notice)
f We .... leave the keys at reception. (guest)
g I .... forget to pay the electricity bill.
h We .... go to work tomorrow if there's a train strike.

6 Read the following statements. Who did something that was unnecessary? Who didn't do something because it wasn't necessary?

It was sunny so Terry *didn't need to* take an umbrella.
It was sunny so John *needn't have* taken an umbrella.

Find further examples like this in the tapescript.

7 Rewrite the following statements using the verb in brackets. Be careful not to change the meaning of the sentences.

Example:
They reserved a seat on the train but it was empty. (need)
They needn't have reserved a seat on the train.

a Yesterday was great. I had a day off school because the teacher was sick. (have to)
b If this tooth doesn't get better, it's a trip to the dentist for him. (have to)
c Don't worry about giving me a lift. I've called a taxi. (need)
d It's our anniversary next week. I hope I don't forget to buy some flowers. (must)
e John passed his exam without doing any revision. (need)
f I was told to stay in bed until my temperature went down. (have to)
g You won't pass the exam unless you do a bit more work. (ought to)
h He took his umbrella out, but it didn't rain. (need)
i I expected you to phone if you were going to be late. (should)

8 Form two groups: Group A are landlords or landladies, Group B students looking for accommodation. Refer again to the categories in activity 1 and decide what you require in each case.

Example:

Landlord:	You have to ...
	You needn't ...
Tenant:	Do we have to ...?
	Do I need to ...?

When you're ready, interview people from the other group. Can you find a perfect host/guest?

LANGUAGE AWARENESS
past perfect simple and continuous

1 Miguel, an EFL student studying in England, has disappeared. Read the police inspector's report opposite.

2 Read the report again and underline all the examples of the past perfect simple and continuous. All of them are used to show 'past in the past', but which of them:

a make the order of events clear?

b refer to an action/state at an indefinite time?

c refer to an action/state at a definite time?

d refer to an unfinished/ interrupted activity?

e emphasise 'duration' or a repeated action?

3 Now read the second half of the report opposite, completing the sentences with the correct form of the verb in brackets. You will have to use past or past perfect tenses.

4 What's happened to Miguel? For some more clues, look at the pictures below. Work in pairs and list all the things he'd done and all the things he'd been doing before he left his landlady's house.

Example:
He'd been studying cookery.

I received a phone call on the evening of September 11. It seemed that Miguel had gone missing and hadn't been seen at college since his last English class. I went straight to the college and interviewed all the people who knew him. Apparently on the days leading up to his disappearance he'd been complaining rather a lot about life in England. One of his colleagues had heard him say that one more meal of potatoes and he wouldn't be responsible for his actions.

When I had spoken to all his classmates I was taken to see his host family. The woman of the house showed me his room and gave me an account of his last known movements. She confirmed that he had been behaving rather strangely but she was unable to offer any reason for this. I carried out a thorough search of his room. I found his diary opened at September 11. He'd clearly been writing in it when he'd been disturbed - the entry was unfinished and he had cut short the final sentence. There had to be a logical explanation somewhere.

His landlady was able to tell me that she (a) .... (see) him running down the road on the evening of the 11th. Just before this she (b) .... (go) into his room and (c)............................. (offer) him a plate of chips. She (d) .... (confirm) my earlier suspicions when she (e) .... (tell) me that he (f) .... (write) in his diary when she (g)............................. (enter) the room. While looking around the room earlier I (h)............................. (notice) the name and address of a local Spanish restaurant which Miguel, I presume, (i) .... (write) on a scrap of paper. I (j)............................. (leave) her house and (k) .... (go) straight to the restaurant. I (l)............................. (arrive) a few moments later and (m)............................. (take) a table in the corner. When I (n)............................. (order) my coffee I (o)............................. (sit) back in my chair and relaxed. While I (p)............................. (wait) for the coffee to arrive I (q) .... (examine) the evidence. According to those who knew him, Miguel (r)............................. (act) strangely. He (s)............................. (develop) an almost irrational dislike of potatoes, so much so that the sight of a plate of chips (t)............................. (make) him run from his landlady's house in panic. On the way to the restaurant I (u) .... (think) of that big sack of potatoes I (v) .... (see) in the landlady's kitchen. 'Who could blame him?' I thought. 'It was enough to send anyone crazy!' There was no doubt in my mind where I would find Miguel.

Simple SPANISH Cooking

COOK

Required for busy Spanish restaurant

Phone Carlos on:
0171 323 7070

chips patatas fritas
prawns gambas
carrots zanahorias
dessert postre

✓ apply for a job
✓ cancel the cheque to college
• tell landlady I'm leaving

Your review of Unit 4

Vocabulary

Your selection:

Suggestion: Copy the mind map below on to a large sheet of paper and extend it with as much vocabulary as you can think of.

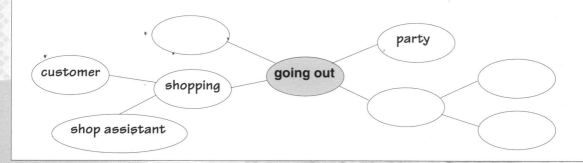

Exam skills

Complete the summaries by underlining the appropriate answer:

Use of English, Part 3, 'key' word transformations
• This question is a test of a) grammar b) vocabulary or c) both.
• You a) may or b) may not change the form of the word given.

Your score _____ /10
How well did I do?

Speaking, Part 2, comparing two photographs
• In the first part of this section you talk mainly to a) your partner or b) the examiner.
• You have to a) describe what is in your picture or b) talk about the picture in relation to yourself.

How well did I do?

General

UNIT 5

Science and Technology

PART ONE
It doesn't add up!

Lead-in

1 How many of the following sums can you do:

- in your head?
- with pen and paper?
- only with a calculator?

6×12 $45 \div 9$ $1 - 0.92$ $4{,}783 + 5{,}003$

$\frac{1}{2} + \frac{1}{3}$ 16^2 $\sqrt{81}$ $3^2 + 4^2$

2 Which of the above sums would you expect an 11 year old to be able to do without a calculator?

❸ Use of English: error correction

1 The following sentences have been taken from a newspaper article about the use of calculators in primary schools (5–11 years) in Britain. In each sentence there is an unnecessary word. Cross the word out to make the sentence grammatically correct.

Example:
It is recommended that calculators should be banned in primary schools after national tests showed young pupils are making basic mistakes in the mathematics.
Answer: ... basic mistakes in ~~the~~ mathematics.

1 Children had the same problems doing so simple sums at the age of 14 as they did at 11.
2 This it seems to indicate that they had not understood the fundamentals of maths while still at primary school.
3 In tests this year, many 14 year olds could not answer to questions such as 1 minus 0.92. Others failed to divide the 45 by 5 correctly. (2 mistakes)
4 Many did not understand the questions because of they had not learned the mathematical language needed to answer correctly.
5 Teachers will to be told to review the use of calculators.
6 In the long-term Britain could follow to other countries in banning them from primary schools.
7 Calculators who are banned in many primary schools on the continent.
8 Therefore, children must to learn their times tables.
9 The Education Minister argued such that children must not be allowed to rely on calculators to do simple sums.
10 'If pupils will continue to overuse calculators, it will be very damaging indeed,' she said.

2 When you have finished, compare your answers with a partner. Try to explain why the sentence is wrong.

3 Do children use calculators for maths in your country?

🔊 Listening technique: prediction and global understanding

1 You are going to hear an extract from an interview with the headteacher of a primary school. She talks about the advantages and disadvantages of her pupils using computers in their story-writing lessons. Before you listen, what points do you think she is going to mention? Make a list.

2 Now listen to the extract. Does she mention any of your ideas?

EXAM FOCUS
(Listening, Part 4)
true or false

⌨ **Listen to the extract again. For questions 1–7 decide whether the statements are True or False, in the headteacher's opinion.**

Most children are not allowed to use their parents' computer at home.	T	F	1
Children's handwriting has improved as a result of using computers.	T	F	2
Using a computer does not make children better authors.	T	F	3
Some children are afraid of using computers.	T	F	4
Computer skills are important for all jobs.	T	F	5
Being able to check your spelling on a computer is a good thing.	T	F	6
All children should be able to use their own computer at school.	T	F	7

S T R A T E G I E S

1 First of all, always read through the statements before you begin to listen, as this will help you to understand the order of the information.

2 Listen and try to answer as many questions as possible. You can use the second listening as a chance to confirm your answers. In the exam, remember to transfer your answers to the answer sheet.

3 Compare your answers in a small group.

▶ **Go to the Review page to record your performance.**

Speaking skill: a panel discussion

1 Look at the following recent newspaper headlines about the effect of technology on educational standards. You are going to take part in a public debate about the issue.

Computers are turning our children into dunces

Calculator kids can't add up!

Teachers fear computers replacing books in the classroom

2 Work in groups of four. Turn to page 149 and choose one of the role cards each.

3 Take some time to prepare what you are going to say before you begin your discussion. Use the information from the unit and your own ideas as well as the points on your role card.

4 When your group is ready, let your chairperson start the discussion.

See **Language awareness: future (1)**

PART TWO
Useful inventions?

Lead-in

1 How or for what reason might the following objects be used to solve everyday problems? Be imaginative!

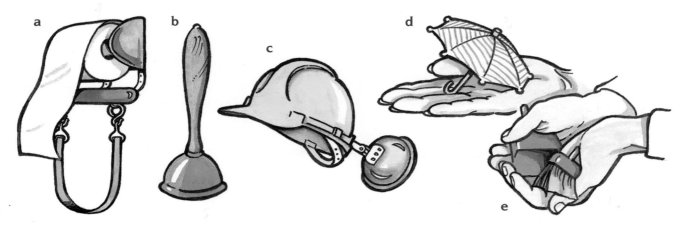

a   b   c   d   e

2 Which of the following people might each of these objects help:

somebody who always falls asleep on the train?
somebody who has a terrible cold or has hay fever?
somebody who wears expensive shoes?
somebody who never gets a seat on a crowded train?
somebody who is fanatical about keeping their house clean?

3 Now turn to page 150 to see the uses an inventor made of them!

Listening technique: global understanding.

You will hear five adverts, one for each of the objects. As you listen for the first time match the adverts with the objects by numbering them 1–5.

Listening technique: specific information

1 Listen to the five adverts again. Match the questions (A–F) with an advert (1–5). Use each letter once only. There is one letter you do not need to use.

Which object:

A helps to avoid embarrassing situations?   Advert 1 ☐
B is advertised as a possible gift?   Advert 2 ☐
C will make others jealous?   Advert 3 ☐
D is expected to sell quickly?   Advert 4 ☐
E is ideal for the people living next door?   Advert 5 ☐
F comes with a money back guarantee?

2 Think of three or four household objects. What imaginative uses could you put them to?

e Vocabulary development: science and technology

1 Complete the table with the correct form of the word.

verb	person	general noun	adjective
analyse	*analyst*	*analysis*	*analytical*
—		biology	
—			chemical
		discovery	
	engineer		
—			experimental
	inventor		
	mechanic		
—			physical
research			
—		science	
—			technical

2 Match the following stress patterns with each of the words in the box.

Example:

□□ □ *c*   □□ □ *c*   □ □□ □ *f*   □□ □□□ □ *h*
analyse   analyst   analysis   analytical

a   □ □   f   □ □ □□
b   □ □   g   □□ □ □
c   □□□   h   □□ □ □□
d   □ □ □   i   □□□ □ □
e   □□□

Speaking skill: description and persuasion

1 Here are some more amazing inventions. Which is your favourite?
   Refer back to the tapescripts of the adverts on pages 180–81. Look at
   the following features:

   ● identifying with the customer's problem
   ● addressing the listener directly with questions
   ● outlining the benefits of the gadget

2 In groups, invent similar adverts for each of the inventions shown
   here. Try to 'sell' your invention to another group.

Writing skill: linking ideas

1 The jumbled sentences below come from a text that outlines the life of a famous inventor. Put the sentences in order.

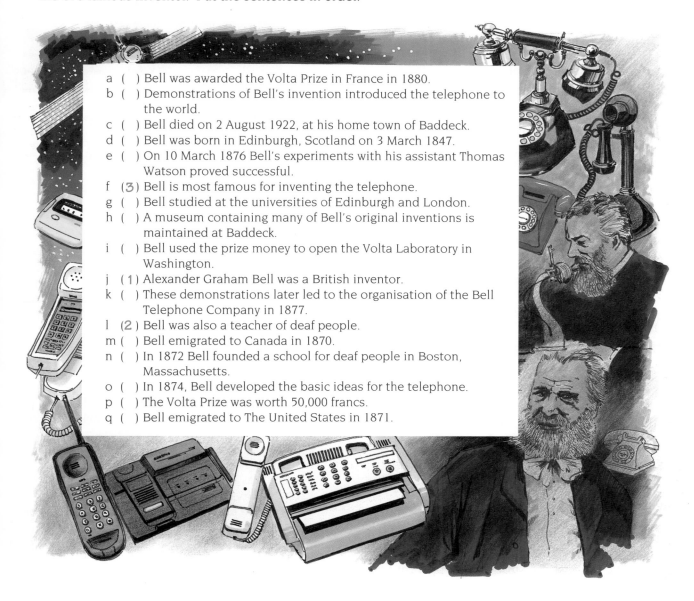

a ( ) Bell was awarded the Volta Prize in France in 1880.
b ( ) Demonstrations of Bell's invention introduced the telephone to the world.
c ( ) Bell died on 2 August 1922, at his home town of Baddeck.
d ( ) Bell was born in Edinburgh, Scotland on 3 March 1847.
e ( ) On 10 March 1876 Bell's experiments with his assistant Thomas Watson proved successful.
f (3) Bell is most famous for inventing the telephone.
g ( ) Bell studied at the universities of Edinburgh and London.
h ( ) A museum containing many of Bell's original inventions is maintained at Baddeck.
i ( ) Bell used the prize money to open the Volta Laboratory in Washington.
j (1) Alexander Graham Bell was a British inventor.
k ( ) These demonstrations later led to the organisation of the Bell Telephone Company in 1877.
l (2) Bell was also a teacher of deaf people.
m ( ) Bell emigrated to Canada in 1870.
n ( ) In 1872 Bell founded a school for deaf people in Boston, Massachusetts.
o ( ) In 1874, Bell developed the basic ideas for the telephone.
p ( ) The Volta Prize was worth 50,000 francs.
q ( ) Bell emigrated to The United States in 1871.

2 You will notice that many of the sentences are rather short and a little repetitive. Work in groups and rewrite the text combining and/or linking some of the sentences. You will need to concentrate on:

a substituting nouns for pronouns
b using defining and non-defining clauses (see the Language awareness section on page 38)
c using suitable linking words
d missing words out that aren't necessary
e paragraphs

3 Half of your group should examine 'a' and 'b' while the others consider 'c' and 'd'. Then share your ideas on these points and on paragraphing before writing the text.

PART THREE
Is Big Brother watching you?

Lead-in

1 How common is the use of surveillance cameras in your country?

2 What crimes do you think cameras in the following places are trying to prevent? (Fill in the first column.) Decide which of the uses are acceptable to you (put a tick, cross or question mark in the third column). Share your ideas with a small group.

Use of cameras	Type of crime they are trying to prevent		A good thing?	
	Your view	*Police view*	*Your view*	*Police view*
6 in car parks				
4 at football stadiums				✓
7 in schools and colleges				
2 on the motorway				
8 in lifts				
1 in shopping centres				
3 on the front of your house				✓
5 in hospitals				

🔊 Listening technique: global understanding

Listen to a talk on this subject by a police officer and decide in which order the points are mentioned.

Example:
in shopping centres = 1

🔊 Listening technique: specific information and speaker's attitude

Listen a second time and make a note of the types of crimes the cameras are supposed to prevent and whether the police officer thinks this is a good or bad thing.

Reading technique: prediction

1 You are going to read two texts about surveillance, which have been mixed up. Work in small groups, on either text A or text B.

2 Here are the title and first paragraph of your text (opposite). Discuss some ideas for what your text is going to be about.

Text A
Is your boss spying on you?
As Val Forster lifted her suitcase on to the conveyer belt at the airport, she was able to forget the pain in her arthritic knee for just a moment. 'A sunshine holiday in Portugal is just what I need,' thought the 52-year-old grandmother. She had worked as a secretary in a hospital for 16 years, but her illness meant that, in June this year, she was forced to go on sick leave. Her doctor told her that a break in the sun would help her.

(Bella)

Text B
Caught in the act!
A controversial new video has just been released and is set to cause a storm; it is called 'Caught in the Act!' As the title might suggest, the video features footage from closed circuit television (CCTV) cameras that have been installed all over Britain. Victoria Coren meets the man behind the video, Barry Goulding.

(Guardian)

Reading technique: skimming

1 Try to find the five remaining paragraphs which belong to your text from the following list A–J. The following tips may help you to read more effectively.

If you are working on text A, look for:
- references to Val Forster
- words to do with work.

If you are working on text B, look for:
- references to Barry Goulding
- words to do with crime
- words to do with video/filming.

2 Compare your paragraph choices with someone from the other group. You should have different answers!

A 'Surveillance is necessary because it's clearly understood that businesses have to be able to police their own affairs,' says David Benn, Director of an equipment distributor in London. 'And you can't always do that effectively if your work-force knows about it. We now supply equipment to most public companies in the UK,' he adds.

B Simon Davies, who runs a group concerned about privacy, says: 'Even official estimates say that there is now one surveillance camera for every 300 people in the UK. I'd say it was more like one for every 150 and many of these miniature cameras are in the workplace.'

C CCTV surveillance has increased beyond recognition and is set to continue doing so. It can be and is a threat to individual freedom. It can also provide the promise of greater security and protection from crime in inner cities. Somewhere there is a balance to be struck.

D I asked Goulding first how easy it was to obtain the footage. 'From surveillance cameras installed by the police on motorways, from security firms, from local authority cameras in city centres. It's easy; we are living in a surveillance society.' Questioned as to whether the police and other providers had actually received payment for the footage, he became remarkably coy. 'We got most of it from slipping fifty pounds to fat boys in various places,' says James Hunt, his helpful assistant.

E Surprisingly, there are signs that monitoring of work-forces is already becoming accepted. 'Listening in' on phone calls is now relatively common and bosses now have the technology to access files on your computer without you knowing. 'The technology will get smaller and smaller and be available more cheaply,' says Simon Davies. 'Then it will be everywhere.'

F Clearly the thought of being spied upon causes concern. Studies have shown that monitored workers are nervous, less efficient, cold to customers and it can make stress levels very high indeed. However, under British law at present, there is no right to privacy, so employers can do what they like.

G He set up the film-making company Eduvision ('*edu*cational tele*vision*') two years ago in order to make 'films with a point'. The point of making this film, he claims, was to spark a national debate about the increasing use of surveillance cameras. But is this film performing any kind of public service, or is it just an excuse to charge £11.99 a time?

H But, as she went through customs, she didn't see the private detective hiding in a telephone booth on the other side of the airport. Nor did she see the zoom lens camera capturing all her actions on film. When she got back home she received a letter from the hospital management, saying 'How can you be sick if you can do this?' She was totally shocked. However, surveillance in Britain is more widespread than you think.

I Watching this video, you will see all sorts of crimes and misdemeanours that the cameras have caught, from robberies and street crimes, to drug-taking and even a couple kissing in a lift. Remember though, that this is not fiction, but real life, with real people just like you and me.

J The stars of this film remain anonymous but, despite this, we are told that CCTV produces evidence which can be used to convict criminals of their crimes. The filmmaker is quick to point out that the faces are not clear and 'really, it's no more than you would see in a newspaper photograph.' Even so, it is disturbing that anyone could become the 'victim' of one of these videos.

e Reading technique: text organisation

1 Each text has a similar organisation. Read the following plan, and put your chosen paragraphs in the correct order.

Organisation	Text A	Text B
1 Title and Introduction 2 Examples of people filmed in secret 3 Living in a surveillance society 4 Justifying the use of cameras 5 The rights of the individual 6 Conclusion: surveillance will continue to grow		

2 Share your information with someone from the other group. What do you think about this kind of surveillance?

See **Language awareness: present perfect simple and continuous**

EXAM FOCUS
(Writing, Part 2)
a report for a magazine

You are looking through your school or work magazine when you see the following announcement. Write a report of 120–180 words in an appropriate style.

Vandalism of property and theft of people's belongings are two of the biggest problems facing us at the moment. In addition, three computers were stolen only last week … It has been proposed that we introduce two surveillance cameras, one at the entrance to the building and one in the men's locker room (where the majority of thefts have occurred). We are interested in your views – please write a short report about what YOU think of this plan.

S T R A T E G I E S

1 Working with a partner, list the advantages and disadvantages of the proposal. Decide what your view is. If you support the proposal, state why. If you are against the proposal, can you think of any alternative solutions?

2 Use some of the following phrases to give a balanced view.

While some people argue that … , my view is …
Despite … , I am still concerned that …
On the one hand … , but on the other …

However, make sure the reader is clear about your viewpoint.

3 Exchange your report with your partner for feedback.

▶ **Go to the Review page to record your performance.**

LANGUAGE AWARENESS
future (1)

1 How many mistakes in the underlined future forms can you find in the following letter?

Dear Anna

How are you? Just a quick note about the summer vacation. My college term <u>will finish</u> in July and the new one <u>will start</u> in October, so I've got two months holiday!

<u>I'm spending</u> July with a friend in Scotland – he's arranged a walking holiday through the mountains! And I've decided that in the last few weeks of the holiday I <u>prepare</u> for the new term. So that leaves me with a whole month with nothing to do! I'm sure the weather <u>is being</u> lovely around that time so <u>shall</u> I come up to stay with you? Write back and tell me what you think.

Anyway, I think <u>I'm going to finish</u> now. <u>I'll be</u> busy tomorrow – I've got an essay to hand in to my teacher and I haven't done any work for it yet.

Write back soon

Lots of love

Carl

2 Read the Grammar Reference on pages 168–9 and then fill in the 'form' section in the table below. Then read the letter again and find examples of the functions listed in the table. Do you need to make any further corrections? Write the correct sentence in the table.

Function	Form	Example
intention		
arrangement		
firm prediction		
simple prediction		
timetable/ calendar event		
spontaneous decision		
suggestion	shall	... *so shall I come up to stay with you?*

3 🔊 Read the following dialogue between Anna and Cathy. Choose the best future form and then listen to the dialogue to check your answers.

Anna: Have you heard? Carl wants to come and visit me during the summer.

Cathy: That (a) .... (be) nice. You know how much he likes you!

Anna: That's exactly why I don't want him to come! I've heard from one of his friends that he (b) .... (ask) me for a date!

Cathy: Wonderful news, I think I (c) .... (cry)! I'm only joking. So when (d) .... (he come)?

Anna: Don't say it like that. You make it sound as if it's all arranged! He (e) .... (go) on another walking holiday in Scotland with a friend. He (f) .... (get) back from there at the end of July. He wants to come after that.

Cathy: Well, I (g) .... (see) Joanne then. We've already made plans to visit the coast.

Anna: But you can't leave me on my own with Carl! I (h) .... (go) mad if I have to spend a week alone with him.

Cathy: (i) .... (I phone) Joanne and ask if you can come along as well?

Anna: Great idea! I (j) .... (write) back now and tell him it's not possible.

Cathy: Poor Carl. He was saying on the phone how much he was looking forward to seeing you. He (k) .... (be) really disappointed.

Anna: Not half as disappointed as I (l) .... (be) if Joanne says I can't come!

4 Did any of your answers differ from the recorded dialogue? If so, can you justify your choice of structure?

5 Imagine you are Anna. Write a short reply to Carl putting him off from coming. Include the following:

an outline of your school/college timetable
your intentions for the summer
the arrangements you've made
a prediction or two about your intentions and arrangements
suggest seeing each other next year
finish with an excuse

6 Swap letters with another student and check each other's use of future structures.

LANGUAGE AWARENESS
present perfect simple and continuous

1 🎧 Listen to the following sentences. How many words are there in each? Remember to include contractions as two words.

   a   I ...
   b   We ...
   c   ... you
   d   He ...
   e   I ...
   f   The ...

2 Grammar books often explain that the present perfect connects the past with the present. How do each of the sentences relate the past to the present?

Example:
I've worked for the company for 25 years.
(I still work there)

3 Which sentences refer to the meanings below?

   a past action that is important now
   a period of time up until now

4 Change the sentences into the past tense. How do the meanings change?

5 🎧 Listen to the following radio report and then answer the questions below.

   a What has the college been doing?
   b What has it done to upset Mark?
   c What has the Student Union tried to do on several occasions?
   d What has the college been suffering from recently?
   e How long has Karen been studying at the college?
   f What, according to the Principal, has the college always done?

6 Underline examples of the present perfect simple and continuous in the questions. Which tense is used to focus on:

   a the result of a completed action
   b the action (maybe complete, maybe not)
   c how long
   d how much/many/often
   e a permanent action or state
   f a temporary action or state

7 Some English students were asked to give an example of each of these uses. Decide which student uses the tense correctly (C) and which incorrectly (I)? Correct those that you think are wrong.

   a I've been cutting my finger! It really hurts!
   b We have learnt phrasal verbs today.
   c I've been eating potatoes all month!
   d The English! My host family have been drinking 20 cups of tea today.
   e I think the English have always been suffering from terrible weather.
   f Our teacher has given us a lot of homework lately.

8 Supply the correct form of the verb in the following texts. You will need to use the past simple, present perfect or present perfect continuous.

   a I .... (work) for IT Engineering since 1985. I .... (start) in the Sales Department and then .... (move) into Personnel in 1989. I .... (always enjoy) working with people, and during the past few months I .... (attend) a course in Counselling.

   b Chris:
     I .... (order) the taxi and I .... (reserve) two seats on the train. Oh yes, and I .... (phone) your mum last night to tell her to feed the cat. I .... (pack) since I .... (get back) from work so I .... (not have) the chance to do any shopping yet. Can you do it when you get back?

   c Ben: You look exhausted! What .... you .... (do)?
     Jan: I .... (decorate). We .... (move) last week and the new house is a mess!
     Ben: .... you .... (finish) yet?
     Jan: No. I .... (do) all the painting but I still .... (not do) the wallpapering.

9 Your teacher will give you a questionnaire examining your experience as a language student. Work in pairs and interview each other using the structures you have looked at in this session.

Your review of Unit 5

Vocabulary

Your selection:

Suggestion: When you write new words, do you remember to record the correct pronunciation as well as the meaning? Choose six words from the list above that you are likely to use when speaking and use a good dictionary to record how the word is pronounced and where the stress falls.

Example: inventor /ɪnˈventə/

Exam skills

Complete the summaries by underlining the appropriate answer:

Listening, Part 4, true or false
- In this question you listen to a) a continuous text b) some extracts.
- You have the chance to listen a) once only b) twice.

Score _____ /7
How well did I do?

Writing, Part 2, a report for a magazine
- In this question you have to a) give your opinion b) tell a story about a particular topic.
- You a) should b) shouldn't use sub-headings or bullet points.
- The minimum number of words you should write is a) 100 b) 110 c) 120.

How well did I do?

General

In Search of Happiness

PART ONE
Finding your perfect soul mate

🔊 **Lead-in**

1 Listen to three people talking about what a soul mate is and match each extract with the correct statement.

A soul mate is somebody who ...

a you get married to.
b is the same age as you.
c you can tell your secrets to.
d you don't have to see every day.
e is like a twin brother or sister.

Now it's your turn. Complete the following sentence. 'A soul mate is somebody who ...'

2 Fill in the following chart.

You too can find the perfect soul mate

1 My sex is male ☐   female ☐
2 My marital status is single ☐   married ☐   divorced ☐   widowed ☐
3 My age group is 13–18 ☐   19–25 ☐   26–35 ☐   over 35 ☐
4 I would like to meet people between the ages of _____ and _____
5 Tick those characteristics which best describe you. Are you more:

	(opposite)		(opposite)		(opposite)
☐ romantic	**unromantic**	☐ ambitious	_____	☐ outspoken	_____
☐ sensitive	**insensitive**	☐ practical	_____	☐ forgiving	_____
☐ rational	**irrational**	☐ loyal	_____	☐ flexible	_____
☐ quiet	**talkative**	☐ adventurous	_____	☐ good-natured	_____
☐ satisfied	**dissatisfied**	☐ secure	_____		
☐ mature	**immature**	☐ industrious	_____		

Vocabulary development: making opposites

1 In the first column of adjectives you will see six different ways of making opposites. What are they?

2 Complete the rest of the chart by trying to find the opposite of the words listed. You will have to use a prefix or a different word.

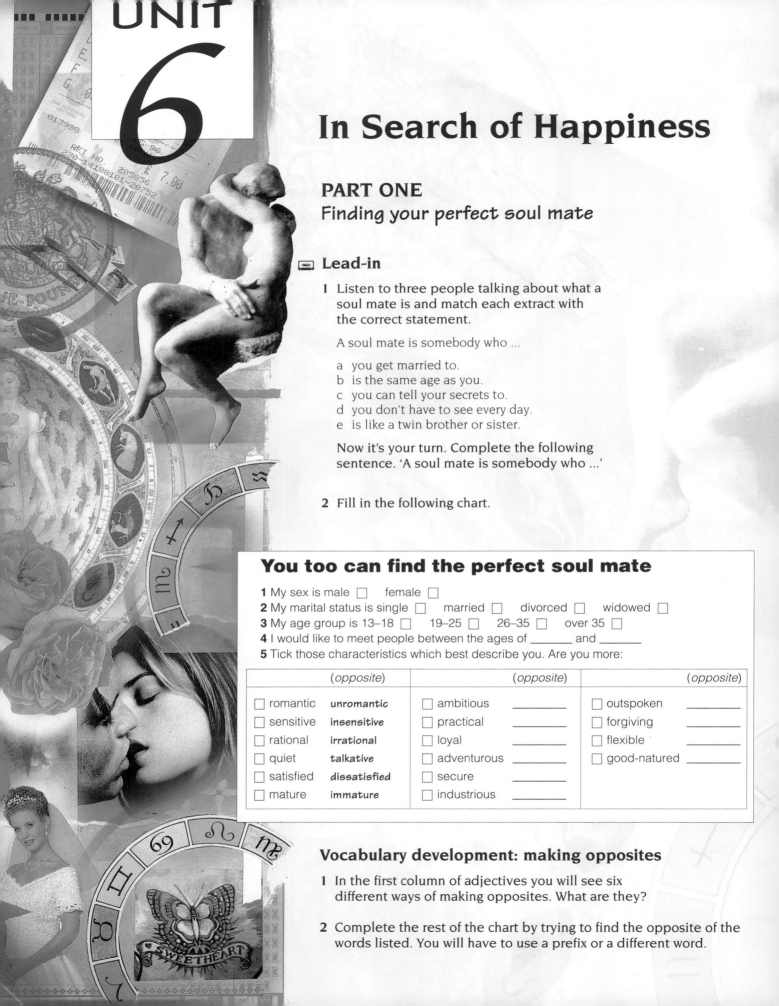

Reading technique: specific information

1 Is your ideal soul mate somebody who is like you or somebody totally different?

2 Work in pairs. Find out your partner's star sign. Student A, look at the article below. Student B, turn to page 150.

3 This is part of an article giving advice on finding your perfect soul mate by using star signs. Scan the article and make notes under the following headings:

- Your Sign
- Your Partner's Sign

4 Now share your information with your partner. Do you both agree with the information about you in the article? Think of reasons why and tell your partner. You might find some of the phrases below useful. Note that some of the phrases in italics often introduce a positive/negative quality.

negative qualities:
I *tend to be* a little selfish. For example ...
I'm *often accused of being* rather outspoken.

positive qualities:
I *like to think* I'm quite sociable.
People often tell me that I'm generally quite cheerful.

Leo: *July 24–August 23*
Sagittarians, who are warm, wonderful, witty and flexible, suit your rather inflexible nature. Geminis will offer you the passion you need, but they are not very loyal, which makes you insecure. Libra is rather too social, like yourself, so you would have no quiet time together. Aquarius is embarrassingly outgoing. Capricorn is socially mobile which makes you good together. Even Virgo will fit into your flashy world by following on behind you, taking care of the practical details. Cancer will provide you with a settled home but can be a little too possessive for you.

Aquarius: *January 21–February 19*
Another Aquarian is good news, as are Geminis, Sagittarians and sometimes Aries. You need a partner who is also a friend, who is never jealous, possessive or controlling and will allow you to keep up with your amazingly large circle of friends. Aquarians are sometimes too cool. You need a partner who will keep you in touch with your feelings. Virgo is ideal and so is Pisces. However, you should avoid Cancer and Taurus.

Pisces: *February 20–March 20*
Although you are emotional, you are also amazingly vague. Virgo is often your best match, since they look after your practical needs and are never bothered if you get lost in daydreams. Libra is tasteful and will leave you to enjoy your thoughts. Even Capricorn and Leo can work for you since they rush off to make money to keep you living in style. Aries gives you headaches. Aquarius can often make the ideal partner. Cancer is comforting, although Scorpio can be too demanding for you.

Taurus: *April 21–May 20*
You are marvellous with Virgo, who is flexible and helpful, although you need to stop them from working so hard and to cuddle more. Capricorn is also very good for you, although they can often complain that you're not working hard enough. Another Taurean is not good as you are too stubborn. Cancer is next favourite because they will make you a comfortable nest. Pisces is sweet, although not very tactile. Scorpio can prove to be difficult and power struggles are inevitable.

Gemini: *May 21–June 21*
Being a restless butterfly, it is quite possible for you to have several perfect partners at the same time. Sagittarius is probably your all-time favourite since you're both very talkative and share the same tastes in travel, adventure and books. Aries might interest you now and again. Virgo will help you be practical – not your strong point – and can be warmer than you might imagine. Even Scorpio is on your list because they share your need for excitement. With Libra you never run out of things to talk about.

Cancer: *June 22–July 23*
Female Cancerians like to be in charge as they age, while the male of the species sometimes searches eternally for the perfect partner, so tastes can differ with the gender. Pisces can be lovely since they are flexible. Scorpio can be jealous, and with both of you being sensitive and easily taking offence – even when none was intended – the combination can be quite volatile. Neither of you tend to be very forgiving. Capricorn often shares similar tastes. Aries and Aquarius are your nightmares.

Writing skill: describing a person

The magazine that you are reading has the following details of an essay competition that you have decided to enter. Write your entry in 120–180 words.

> Either:
>
> *A) Do you have a story to tell about a special friend in your life? Did you meet in unusual circumstances? Has your friendship lasted in spite of difficulties? There is a prize for the most interesting account.*
>
> Or:
>
> *B) Don't worry if you haven't met that special soul mate yet. Why not write and tell us about what a soul mate means to you and what qualities you would look for in this special person. You too could win a prize.*

1 Choose which essay you are going to write. Which of the following points would be suitable for including in your account?

Introduction:
a A soul mate is somebody who ...
b The person I'm going to tell you about is ...

Main part:
a The qualities I would look for in a soul mate are ...
b We met ... years ago and have been friends ever since.

c The reason we get on so well is ...
d Having somebody like this around would be great because ...

Conclusion:
a I hope we'll continue to ...
b If and when I meet this person ...

2 Write a first draft of your essay and show it to your partner. Ask your partner to give you marks out of 15 for:

● content (is it interesting to read?) – 5
● organisation (is it easy to follow?) – 5
● language (is the language mostly correct? did you use some of the adjectives from the Lead-in and Reading activities?) – 5

See Language awareness: conditionals (1)

PART TWO
The lottery

Lead-in

It's what many people dream of. You've won the lottery! All that lovely money! But would it make you happy? Try the following questionnaire, taken from a national newspaper, to see if you could cope with a huge win. Be prepared to defend your choices.

If I won the lottery I would stop working.	Agree A ☐	Disagree B ☐
If I won the lottery I would keep it secret.	Agree B ☐	Disagree A ☐
If I won the lottery I would take revenge on my enemies.	Agree A ☐	Disagree B ☐
If I won the lottery I would carry on much as before.	Agree B ☐	Disagree A ☐
A lot of money would solve practically all my problems.	Agree A ☐	Disagree B ☐
I hardly ever daydream about what I would do if I won.	Agree B ☐	Disagree A ☐
If I won the lottery I would enjoy other people's envy.	Agree A ☐	Disagree B ☐
Winning would not mean I was a special person.	Agree B ☐	Disagree A ☐
If I won the lottery I would go on a shopping spree.	Agree A ☐	Disagree B ☐
I (would) play the lottery mainly for the excitement.	Agree B ☐	Disagree A ☐

Speaking skill: sharing opinions

1 What were your reasons for selecting A's or B's? Before you look at your results, work in a group and compare your choices. Explain the reasons for your decisions. Who do you think would cope the best?

2 Now turn to page 151 to see your results.

EXAM FOCUS
(Use of English, Part 2)
open cloze

You are going to read a newspaper article about a man who won the lottery. For questions 1–15, read the text below and think of the word which best fits each space. Use only one word in each space. There is an example at the beginning (0).

Workers at a chemical factory near Blackburn, Lancashire, have not won the National Lottery, but they are hoping (0) *for* a share of the £17.9 million a fellow worker won in last week's draw. Rumours are flying (1) ...... Mr X – he has not been named even though everyone in his home town knows who he is – wants to share his good fortune with his workmates.

But the workers are blaming the bosses for making them lose out on their share. According to colleagues of (2) ...... 41-year-old Muslim father of three: 'He asked the managers on Sunday to work (3) ...... how many people were employed at the works, (4) ...... he could give the firm (5) ...... money for them to hand out £40,000 each for everybody.'

But his desire to give (6) ...... £8 million to his 200 colleagues met with a lukewarm response. It seems the managers turned (7) ...... down at first. 'They said he couldn't do it because it (8) ...... be too complicated with the tax and all that,' said one. (9) ...... that or managers were afraid that their workers (10) ...... be tempted to give up work – someone (11) ...... to keep the factory running.

Elders at Mr X's mosque (12) ...... also reported to have refused a donation earlier last week, saying (13) ...... was from the profits of gambling.

However, at least someone is benefiting from the good luck. The local paper (14) ...... run pictures of Dave Lowe, a barber '(15) ...... has cut the winner's hair' and a man who once employed the winner's wife.

(Guardian)

S T R A T E G I E S

1 Read the text quickly but do not add any words at this stage. Can you summarise the article in one sentence?

2 Fill in only those gaps where you are *certain* you know the missing word.

3 Of those that remain, which of these grammatical items have been deleted:

auxiliary verb
modal verb
pronoun
relative pronoun (who/that, etc.)
article/determiner
preposition
conjunction

4 Now you know what kind of words are required, try to complete the remaining gaps.

▶ Go to the Review page to record your performance.

See **Language awareness: articles**

Listening technique: understanding feelings or opinions

1 📻 You are going to hear five different people expressing their feelings about the lottery. For Speakers 1–5, choose from the list A–F which sentence summarises their feelings. You only need to use each letter once and there is one extra letter.

   A This person doesn't agree with the lottery.
   B This person wouldn't like to win because of all the publicity.
   C This person thinks the jackpot is too high.
   D This person thinks that they don't spend enough of the profits on worthwhile things.
   E This person thinks people who do the lottery are stupid.
   F This person's ambition is to win the lottery.

2 Check your answers with a partner. If you disagree, explain the words or expressions that helped you make your choice. Now listen a second time.

3 Do you agree/disagree with any of the points made by the speakers? Is there a National Lottery in your country? Have any of the points made by the speakers convinced you that it is or would be worthwhile having one?

Writing skill: a story

A young person's magazine is holding a competition for the most imaginative account of what it is like to win the lottery. Imagine you won the lottery yesterday. Give a description of what it was like to win and what you plan to do with the money.

1 You have been offered the following four sentences to start your story. Which one do you prefer?

   'Yesterday I won the lottery.'
   'What a difference a day makes.'
   'My life will never be the same again.'
   'Let me tell you what happened to me yesterday.'

2 You can often get ideas on what to write in narratives by asking yourself certain questions. How might the following help you? Pay attention to the tenses used in the questions as these will be useful in your story.

Yesterday:
When did you hear the result?
Where were you when you heard the result?
What were you doing at the time?
Who were you with at the time?
What had you been doing immediately before?
How did you feel when you heard the result?
What did you do for the rest of the day?

Today:
How did you feel/What did you do when you woke up this morning?
What does it feel like now?
What has been happening/What have you been thinking today?
Has it changed your life?
Have you got any plans?
Have you decided what you're going to do with the money?
Are you pleased you won?

3 Write your story using three paragraphs: yesterday's events, events so far today, what your plans are now.

4 When you have finished, compare your story with the one on page 162. Is yours more interesting and original?

PART THREE
Cults

Lead-in

1 Student A look at the photo below and
   Student B the photo on page 151. Describe
   your photos to each other. What do they have
   in common? How are they different?

2 What attention has the media given to cults in
   your country? Who usually joins cults and what
   reasons might they have for joining?

Reading technique: summary skills

Read the first two sentences of each section (A–D)
of this text about cults and give each section a
suitable heading. (Don't worry about understanding
every word!) When you have finished, compare your
choice with a partner to see who has the best
headings.

A

The origin of the word 'cult' is the Latin *cultus*, which means
anything to do with worship or ritual. It has now been given a
much wider meaning and is used for anything that has an
exclusive following (for instance, we talk about cult followings
5 for certain television shows). But being exclusive is not in
itself damaging.

   Ian Howarth, who runs the Cult Information Centre, believes
the definition of a cult is a simple equation: exclusive sect +
mind control = cult.

10 Christian Czurko, who runs a group with the aim, amongst
other things, of helping ex-members of cults, lays down four
criteria for his definition of a damaging cult:
   1. They recruit through inaccurate information.
   2. They inoculate their recruits mentally against any other
15   point of view.
   3. The group (or its leader) profits or benefits from the
       members, either directly by taking their finances or
       indirectly by making them work for nothing or for very
       low pay.
20 4. (a) ....

B

Cults are frequently accused of 'brainwashing' their members.
They don't; they use 'mind control' or 'thought reform'
techniques. Whilst brainwashing is usually temporary and
easily reversed, the mind control used by cults is more subtle;
25 the victim starts out willingly, and no coercion is necessary.
Individuals are deceived and manipulated, but not threatened
or bullied.

   When he or she joins a cult, the new recruit is given a lot of
attention and approval, known as 'love-bombing'. To keep this
30 approval, the victim has to conform. If they don't, the 'love' is
withdrawn.

   Cults also deprive their members of outside information.
Newspapers, magazines, radio and television are prohibited.
Instead members are exposed to cult literature, tapes, lectures
35 and study classes. (b)..

C

There are cult members of all classes, sexes and ages, but there are certain people more likely to join. Men are more likely to join than women, although this varies from group to group. Middle-class, well-educated people are more likely to join than
40 working-class people. Age varies, but religious movements are more likely to recruit among people in their late teens and early twenties.
(c) ....

A small number of cults deliberately target the elderly,
45 possibly in the hope of benefiting from bequests. But most live-in cults prefer the young and able-bodied, because of the physical demands of the work. Most cults have little time for sick members: there are stories of cults dumping members at a local hospital, or even sending them back to their families,
50 when they are too ill to cope with the workload.

D

Cults do damage. They damage health, finances, relationships, confidence, education, prospects. Many ex-members do manage to lead good and normal lives once they have recovered from their time in the cult, and this includes people who were in
55 cults for fifteen or more years. But the road to recovery is hard.

While they are in the cult, they run health risks through sleep and food deprivation.
(d) ....

The mental health of cult members is also under constant
60 threat. They often become paranoid about the rest of society, incapable of making their own decisions, and they may stop maturing at the point at which they join the cult. More seriously, some end up in mental hospitals suffering a range of serious conditions from nervous breakdowns to paranoid schizophrenia. Some commit suicide.

(Jean Ritchie: *The Secret World of Cults*)

Cult recruits were brainwashed

David Johnson in Manchester

FBI put blame on Koresh's control over cult members

Gillian James in Waco

Reading technique: text organisation ⓔ

1 Read the texts again and put one sentence into each of the gaps (a–d). There is one extra sentence that you do not need.

 1 In some cults, medical care is inadequate; this can lead to diseases going unchecked, and in a few extreme cases to death.
 2 Many cults actually recruit on college campuses, because they find them an easy place to recruit large numbers of people.
 3 People are hurt by them – and this can include the families and friends of members as well as the members themselves.
 4 Often the information given is totally false: for instance, the cult member standing on the street collecting 'for the poor' or for 'disadvantaged children' may genuinely believe that is where the money is going.
 5 If, initially, recruits voice rational criticism or question the teachings of the cult, they are told to wait a little bit longer and everything will become clear.

2 Check your answers in a small group.

Vocabulary development: similar words and opposites

1 In the text on pages 70 and 71 notice the way the writer uses different expressions with a similar meaning within the same paragraph.

Example:
Whilst <u>brainwashing</u> is usually temporary and easily reversed, the <u>mind control</u> used by cults is more subtle. (lines 23–4)

2 Read the text again and find:

a three other words which are used instead of 'members' (line 21). Which of these words are used emotively?

b another word for 'attention and approval' (line 29). What does the use of punctuation tell you?

c another phrase for 'cult' (line 32). Which of these two expressions is the most neutral?

d a word meaning the opposite of 'elderly' (line 44).

e two words used in contrast to 'able-bodied' (line 46).

f another word for 'physical demands of the work' (lines 47).

g two examples of 'serious conditions' (lines 63–4).

EXAM FOCUS
**(Listening, Part 2)
note taking**

You are going to hear an interview in which a young man called Ian describes his experiences with a cult in Germany. For questions 1–8, complete the notes which summarise what the speaker says. You will need to write a word or short phrase in each box.

Ian was in Munich for	1
He initially thought that the woman was a	market researcher 2
After answering her questions, he was asked to go to	3
The programmes were to help people be more	4
He phoned England twice: first, in order to say he was leaving	5
and then to say he was	6
Newspapers in England had printed a story about	7
When he arrived in England again he was relieved to	8

S T R A T E G I E S

1 First of all, you *must* read through the questions *before* you listen. This will help you understand the way that the information is structured.

2 Underline the key words in each question and listen carefully for these. They will give you a clue as to when you have to listen particularly carefully.

3 Listen to the tape once and complete as much as you can. Check your answers with a partner. Do you agree? Remember that your answers need to be brief and that there is some information which you have to disregard.

4 Listen again to check your answers or to fill in information you missed the first time.

▶ **Go to the Review page to record your performance.**

LANGUAGE AWARENESS
conditionals (1)

1 How important is appearance to you? Do you like to wear cosmetics or buy fashionable clothes?

2 Read the following statements and decide which of the things mentioned is:

a generally true or a fact about the person.
b imagining something that is likely to happen in the future.
c imagining something unreal or unlikely to happen in the present or the future.

1 If I wear make-up I come out in spots.
2 My mates won't talk to me if I don't get a tattoo.
3 If I had lots of money I'd buy bottles of expensive after-shave.
4 I look too short if I wear checked clothes.
5 If I don't get my ears pierced, I won't look fashionable.
6 If I had nicer knees I'd wear shorts more often.
7 I'll get a tattoo if it doesn't hurt.
8 If my mum would let me I'd get a nose ring.
9 If you don't wear fashionable clothes nobody notices you.

3 What tenses are used for categories 'a', 'b' and 'c'? Check your ideas in the Grammar Reference on page 169.

4 Complete the sentences below, using the verb in brackets in the appropriate tense.

a If everybody .... (speak) the same language, life .... (be) much simpler.
b If you .... (not pay) more attention, you .... (hurt) yourself.
c If I .... (not have) a TV, I .... (do) more homework .
d If you .... (arrive) late, ... (meet) me at the hotel.
e I .... (lend) you the money, if you .... (pay) me back.
f If I .... (be) you, I .... (see) a doctor.
g He .... (look) much better, if he .... (have) his hair cut more often.
h My tooth .... (hurts) if I .... (eat) ice cream.
i That cough .... (not get) better if you .... (not stop) smoking.
j He always .... (get) angry if we .... (not arrive) on time.

5 In which of the sentences in activities 2 and 4 can 'unless' or 'provided' be used without changing the meaning of the statement or sentences? Check your ideas in the Grammar Reference.

Example:
My mates won't talk to me unless I get a tattoo.
I'll get a tattoo provided it doesn't hurt.

6 Match the beginning of a sentence in box A with the end in box B. Then complete the sentences using a suitable modal verb (if necessary) and either 'if', 'provided' or 'unless'.

A	B
I/see you tonight	I/be your best friend
you/borrow the car	the ice/melt
the red light appears	I/retire
I/take up jogging	I have to work late
you/not do as you're told	you/not scratch it
you do my homework	switch the machine off
I/cook the dinner	immediately
I won the lottery	I/be you
temperature/rise	you/be in trouble
	you do the washing up

7 Now match each of the sentences with the following functions:

imagining   negotiating
instruction   persuading
conditional offer   warning
advice   conditional arrangement
describing a general truth

8 Write a sentence for each of the functions listed in activity 7. Try to write something that means something to you. Then compare and check them with a partner.

LANGUAGE AWARENESS
articles

1 Which of the following mistakes do you think is due to languages that:

a use the definite article with nouns with general meaning?

b use definite articles with proper nouns?

c don't use an article to describe somebody's profession?

d don't usually differentiate between 'a'/ 'an' and 'one'?

e have no articles?

I haven't got pen. (Russian)
I often drink the coffee. (French)
The John visited me last week. (Portuguese)
The English is a crazy language. (Greek)
He is architect. (Italian)
I heard funny joke yesterday. (Arabic)
I used to have one car. (Spanish)
I used to own small car before I bought this one. (Japanese)

2 Which of these mistakes are often made by English students from your country? How many of the sentences can you confidently correct?

3 Read the following newspaper article and decide which of the categories listed describe the nouns in italics. Then add the article which is used in each case.

An unemployed *teenager* who tried to keep his £2 million lottery win secret has finally admitted, 'I'm the *richest man* around.' The *youngster*, Graham Stein, 19, from Stamfield, finally announced the news in the *local paper*.

Graham, who worked as a *builder* before losing his job last year, explained yesterday, 'Actually, it was the worst kept secret in the world. Every time I went in the *pub*, the post office or just walked down the street, I could feel people's eyes on me. I finally decided *honesty* was the best policy.'

Graham, now a local celebrity, is overwhelmed by the reaction of his friends and neighbours. 'Money can often cause bad feeling – that's why I didn't want people to know I'd won the lottery. But the locals have been great. Everybody seems to be genuinely pleased for me.'

And one of those local people stands to benefit from the money. Graham opens a small builder's merchants soon and explained, 'I need somebody with experience to work as a sales assistant.'

Example: Article
mentioned before   *youngster*   (the)

a mentioned for the first time   ( )
b a proper noun   ( )
c there is only one of its kind   ( )
d describing somebody's profession   ( )
e with general meaning   ( )
f describing something shared by (therefore known to) the community   ( )
g a superlative noun   ( )

4 Can you find any other examples of articles used like this in the text?

5 How good is your general knowledge?

a Where is Lake Michigan?

b Where would you find: the River Thames, the Danube, the Ganges?

c In Europe it's the Alps, in Asia it's the_____, in S. America it's the _____.

d What is the biggest: the Pacific, the Atlantic, or the Indian Ocean?

e Which of the following take the definite article: mountain ranges, seas, continents, rivers and lakes?

f Why is it England, France, Greece, Spain but *the* USA, *the* Republic of Ireland? (Think about it!)

6 Examine the following sentences. Who is the criminal, the pupil, the religious person and the patient?

a Haven't you heard? Steve's gone to *prison*.
b The police went to *the prison*.

a Where's David? Is he at *school*?
b Where's your dad? Is he at *the school*?

a Ann goes to *church* every Sunday.
b Frank's gone to *the church* to do some repairs.

a Sam's in *hospital*.
b Mum's just gone to *the hospital* to visit Sam.

7 What is the difference in meaning when the definite article is used in this way?

8 ▣ Now turn to the tapescript of a news broadcast on page 183. Supply, *where necessary*, the correct article and then listen to the broadcast to check your answers. If your answers are different, try to justify your choices.

Your review of Unit 6

Vocabulary

Your selection:

Suggestion: How many of the words you have chosen can change their word class? Add them to the chart below.

noun	verb	adjective	adverb	noun	verb	adjective	adverb
happiness	–	happy	happily				

Exam skills

Complete the summaries by underlining the appropriate answer:

Use of English, Part 2, open cloze
- This question is a test of a) grammatical knowledge b) vocabulary or c) both.
- You fill in a) one word or b) more than one word in the gap.

Your score _____ /15
How well did I do?

Listening, Part 2, note taking
- This question tests a) general understanding b) specific information or c) both.
- You a) fill in the gap yourself or b) have a choice of four answers.

Your score _____ /8
How well did I do?

General

UNIT
7

The Natural World

PART ONE
Under the weather

Lead-in

Look at the following photographs with a partner.
How do they make you feel? Think of three or four adjectives
that best describe the mood they put you in.

Reading technique: prediction

You are going to read a text which describes the relationship between the weather and your health. Before you read, look at the chart below and see if you can guess any of the missing information.

What you may be feeling	Medical condition	Probable cause
low a) .... pressure, fall in body temperature, loss of b) .,.........................	hypothermia	c) ....
chest pains, breathing problems	d)	extreme cold
tiredness, sleepiness, depression, increased appetite	e)	lack of sunlight
red, f) ...., or g) .... skin	h)	exposure to sunlight
coughing, throat and i) .... irritation	j)	air polluted with ozone
sneezing, watery eyes, k) .... nose	l)..........................fever	m) ....
depression, headaches, painful joints, bowel problems	n)	o) .... ions in the atmosphere

Reading technique: scanning

1 Now read the text and complete the chart. Try to spend no more than five minutes. How much did you predict correctly?

Many experts as well as ordinary people think there is a strong connection between the weather and our health.

Even countries with a climate as mild as Britain's still experience the occasional drop into sub-zero temperatures. 'Most people think that fresh air is good for us,' says one professor, 'but in winter, that's not always true. It can kill.' Around 330 old people die every year from hypothermia, where the symptoms are a fall in blood pressure and body temperature and possibly loss of consciousness. However, research indicates that most deaths in winter aren't due to hypothermia, but to heart attacks sparked off by the extreme cold. Early warning signs of a heart attack are a severe pain in the chest and difficulty breathing.

But it's not just the elderly whose health is at risk during winter. Dr Josephine Arendt has done research into how light affects our mental and physical well-being. When the weather is cold we naturally spend most of our day indoors, but this means our bodies don't absorb enough bright light. The result? Tiredness, sleepiness, depression, and an increased appetite. Seasonal Affective Disorder (or 'SAD' for short) affects one in twenty people during the autumn and winter months.

Unfortunately, hot weather can also be bad news for our health. Too much exposure to bright sunlight on the beach, for example, can lead to the red, itchy or even blistered skin that characterises sunburn. In cities when summer temperatures reach the nineties, the air becomes polluted with ozone, a poisonous gas which causes coughing, throat and eye irritation. In addition, the summer also sees an increase in the number of hay fever sufferers, with symptoms similar to those of ozone poisoning, namely sneezing, coughing, watery eyes and a runny nose. This is caused by an allergy to pollen.

But it's not only things we can see on the weather map which affect our health. Some weather conditions are invisible to the human eye, yet can have a devastating effect on the state of our bodies – and minds. Changeable weather affects the electrically charged particles – known as 'ions' – in the atmosphere. When the ions in the air are negatively charged, we feel full of energy, but if there is a large amount of positive ions, there's a tendency for us to feel depressed, and to suffer from severe migraine headaches.

William Rea of The Environmental Weather Centre in Dallas took a group of 'weather sensitive' people and monitored them in windowless rooms so they had no idea whether it was rain or shine outside. Just before a thunderstorm – when there was a majority of positive ions – the weather sensitive group said they felt ill, with some complaining of painful joints, headaches and bowel problems. Many scientists, however, are not convinced by such evidence, and there is no medical name for this condition as yet. William Rea concludes: 'It's time for more research. It's a fascinating subject and there's a great deal yet to be discovered.'

(Top Santé)

e **Use of English: 'key' word transformations**

Rewrite the following sentences, using the key word given. You will find the correct version in the text you have just read!

1 Research indicates that the cause of most winter deaths is not hypothermia.
   due
   Research indicates that most deaths in winter .... hypothermia.

2 Dr Josephine Arendt has done research into the effect of light on our mental and physical well-being.
   affects
   Dr Josephine Arendt has done research into .... our mental and physical well-being.

3 The number of hay fever sufferers also rises in summer.
   increase
   The summer also sees .... the number of hay fever sufferers.

4 Some weather conditions cannot be seen by the human eye.
   invisible
   Some weather conditions .... the human eye.

5 We are likely to feel depressed.
   tendency
   There's .... to feel depressed.

6 They didn't know whether it was rain or shine outside.
   idea
   They had .... whether it was rain or shine outside.

7 Many scientists do not believe such evidence.
   convinced
   Many scientists .... such evidence.

Vocabulary development: weather words

1 Sort these words into three categories and put them in order of intensity.

   Example: warm   hot   boiling

   | wind drizzle sleet snow gale downpour breeze rain blizzard |

   Do you usually experience mild or extreme weather in your country?

2 Read the following letter and fill in the missing words from the box.

   On the whole, the a) _____ in Britain is fairly mild. Although there are four b) _____ – summer, autumn, winter and spring – many people say there are only two: cold and not-so-cold! The c) _____ today is around five d) _____ centigrade, although the weather e) _____ has promised sunny f) _____ . I can't wait! I suppose the weather g) _____ aren't bad for the time of year.

   | conditions spells seasons climate degrees temperature forecast |

PART TWO
It's your environment

Lead-in

1 Which of the following issues are taken seriously in your country?

energy saving in the home
purchasing 'green' products
environmentally friendly transport schemes
anti-pollution campaigns

recycling of waste material
organic gardening and farming
anti-litter campaigns
clean beach campaigns

2 Are there examples in your country/city where any of these policies are needed? Which ones would you prioritise?

EXAM FOCUS
(Use of English, Part 1)
multiple-choice cloze

For questions 1–15, read the text below and decide which answer A, B, C or D best fits each space. There is an example at the beginning (0).

Earth is the only (0)^{place} we know of in the universe that can support human life, (1) ...... human activities are making the planet less fit to live on. At the moment (2) ...... by a quarter of the world's people to (3) ...... on consuming two-thirds of the world's resources, and by half of the people (4) ...... to stay alive, are destroying the (5) ...... resource we have by which all people can survive and prosper. Everywhere fertile soil is (6) ...... built on or washed into the sea. Renewable resources are exploited so much that they will never be able to recover (7) .... We discharge pollutants into the atmosphere without any thought of the consequences. As a (8) ...... , the planet's ability to support people is being (9) ...... at the very time when rising human numbers and consumption are (10) ...... increasingly heavy demands on it.

      The earth's (11) ...... resources are there for us to use. We need food, water, air, energy, medicines, warmth, shelter and minerals to (12) ...... us fed, comfortable, healthy and active. If we are (13) ...... and use the resources carefully, they will (14) ...... indefinitely. But if we use them wastefully and excessively, they will soon (15) ...... out and everyone will suffer.

0	A place	B situation	C position	D site
1	A contrary	B still	C although	D while
2	A tries	B goes	C attempts	D moves
3	A continue	B carry	C repeat	D follow
4	A just	B already	C for	D entirely
5	A alone	B only	C individual	D lone
6	A rather	B sooner	C neither	D either
7	A completely	B quite	C greatly	D utterly
8	A development	B result	C reaction	D product
9	A lessened	B narrowed	C reduced	D lost
10	A doing	B having	C taking	D making
11	A natural	B real	C living	D genuine
12	A hold	B remain	C keep	D stay
13	A sensitive	B sensible	C brilliant	D able
14	A stand	B go	C last	D secure
15	A break	B run	C lose	D come

Check the Strategies box on page 80 before attempting this activity.

Use the word given in capitals at the end of each line to form a word that fits in the space in the same line. There is an example at the beginning (0).

Let's aim for a better world, where everyone can live (0) _comfortable_ ,	COMFORT
satisfying, secure lives, without the shadows of resource (1) .... ,	SHORT
polluted air and water, and (2) .... hanging over them. It's not	STARVE
impossible. We can stop (3) .... the earth and still have all the	USE
heat, light and food we need. We're just saying, as was said by	
Indian leader Mahatma Gandhi, 'the earth has enough for every	
man's need, but not for every man's greed'. We need to iron	
out the (4) .... so that everyone on earth leads a fulfilling	EQUAL
(5)	EXIST
Too idealistic? Too (6) .... ? Perhaps what you've just	PRACTICAL
read is both of these. But it's surely worth working for, (7)	SPECIAL
if you take into (8) .... what we have in front of us today. By	CONSIDER
growing your own food, (9) .... paper, planting trees and	CYCLE
campaigning for better public transport and for renewable ·	
energy sources, you can help towards this goal and also make	
other people aware that (10) .... exist.	ALTERNATE

1 Work in pairs. Student A should look at the first exercise, Student B the second. Read the text quickly and tell your partner what your text is about.

2 Now read your text again more slowly and look at the vocabulary you must supply. What are you being tested on? How could you organise your vocabulary learning on the course so that you would best be able to attempt this question?

3 Using a good dictionary, think about the most suitable words to complete your text and when you're ready, work with your partner and complete both texts.

▶ **Go to the Review page to record your performance.**

Listening technique: predicting

▱ You are going to listen to somebody giving suggestions on what you can do to cut down on waste and help conserve the world's resources. Look at the headings and the accompanying pictures. What do you think the suggestions are going to be?

Reduce waste

Endangered animals

Fighting pollution

Save energy

📼 Listening technique: specific information

Now listen to the interview and make notes under each heading. Share your ideas with a partner and listen again if necessary.

See **Language awareness: passives**

❷ Writing skill: a letter of complaint

You have recently been on a surfing holiday where you stayed at the Cove Hotel. Although the service at the hotel was excellent, the sea water was polluted and you became ill.

1 Read the documents opposite (and the notes that you have made) carefully. You are going to write a letter of complaint to the manager of the hotel about her misleading advertisement (up to 200 words).

2 Now make notes for your letter under these paragraph headings.

Dear Madam,
paragraph 1 – reason for writing
paragraph 2 – details of the problem
paragraph 3 – what action the hotel should take
Yours faithfully,

3 Write your letter, remembering that your tone should be fairly formal and not too direct (even though you are very annoyed!).

The Cove Hotel

Come and relax at this fine hotel, and enjoy splendid food and our warm, friendly service. Superbly positioned by a (safe) sandy cove. (Clean) beach nearby, (ideal) for sunbathing, water-skiing, surfing, etc.

water was brown

couldn't go surfing

litter everywhere

B E A C H W A T C H

Do you know that ...

☞ raw sewage is pumped into our seas every day?

☞ 100 kg of litter can be collected from the sea in just *one* day?

☞ the water should not be used for swimming or water contact sports?

Doctor's note
This is to certify that the patient is suffering from
.....an ear infection.... and will not be fit to attend
school/work for ....1 week..........

• spoiled holiday
• had to pay £5 for medicine

PART THREE
Out of this world

Lead-in

Imagine you were given two of these
photographs to talk about in the
exam. How confident would you be
that you would have something to
say? What do you think you could talk
about? Think of some questions you
might be asked. Then try them on
your partner.

Listening technique: global understanding

1   You are going to hear two students practising for Part 2 of the FCE
    Speaking paper. They are each asked to talk about two of these
    photographs. Which of the following do they do? Put a tick in the
    middle column of the box below.

compare and contrast the two photographs		
comment on how they feel about the holidays		
describe holidays that they have been on		
talk to each other		
talk about each other's photographs		
choose which holiday they would like to go on		

Listen again or turn to the tapescript on page 184. For each
activity listed above write down any useful phrases that the
students use in the right hand column of the table.

Speaking skill: giving and exchanging personal information

1   Work in groups of three. Student A should play the part of the
    interviewer. Turn to the tapescript if necessary to remind yourself
    of the kind of questions that were asked. Students B and C should
    choose two of the photographs to talk about.

2   Carry out the interview in the same way as the one you have just
    listened to. When you've finished, try grading each other on the
    following points:

    ● the range and accuracy of grammar and vocabulary used – 10 marks
    ● pronunciation – 5 marks
    ● fluency – 5 marks

EXAM FOCUS
(Reading, Part 3)
gapped text

You are going to read an article about tourism in space. Seven sentences have been removed from the article. Choose from the sentences A–H the one which fits each gap (1–6). There is one extra sentence which you do not need to use. There is an example at the beginning (0).

Out of this world

Some of us will soon be booking holidays in space! The idea may appear too fantastic to be true, but the space-tour operators of the future seem to regard it as a real possibility.

0 **E** NASA, America's space agency, and the Space Transportation Association, a group of 16 aerospace companies, are working on a detailed study 'with a view to establishing a US space tourism business'.

It has been reported that 2005 will see the start of mass tourism in space. By around 2010 at least one hotel will have been built, in which tourists could stay for up to a week. **1** There they will get a taste of 'weightlessness' for about two minutes and some spectacular views of the Earth. It will cost them around £400,000 each. The money would be used to help develop a fleet of vehicles and space hotels.

The next step would be to extend the up-and-down trips to orbital flights (probably two or three circles of the Earth, for as many as 20 passengers at a time), giving four hours in which to take pictures and enjoy some weightlessness games. **2**

In Japan, the Tokyo-based Shimizu Corporation has set a target date of 2020 for its orbiting space resort, to which it aims to shuttle parties of 64 tourists, eventually planning sightseeing trips to the Moon. **3** This will be followed by one 'Lunar Hotel' on the Moon. These two hotels, it adds, will be 'the basis for an entire space resort network'. **4** In less than an hour they will arrive at a large space station, and spend three days and two nights in rooms which will, 'provide artificial gravity so that everyone will be able to enjoy space travel without fully adjusting themselves to weightlessness.' **5** This rotation will produce an artificial gravity level which will allow guests to sleep, stand, walk and take showers as easily as on Earth.

Will there be much demand for such holidays? Well, when Neil Armstrong made his 'giant leap for mankind' in 1969, Thomas Cook had so many enquiries from potential space travellers that it set up a Lunar Tours Register. **6**

No plans are currently in progress to operate Thomas Cook Lunar Tours, but the company promises that 'when the idea does become a reality, every member of the list will be contacted and given first refusal'.

A   The room modules will be in a doughnut-shaped 140-metre-diameter circle frame that will rotate at 3 rpm.

B   It has grown enormously: today there are more than 6,000 names on the list.

C   The general plan, apparently, is to take passengers first to a height of 50 miles – the official boundary of space.

D   However, such a programme would depend on many factors.

E   They are not alone.

F   Guests will leave from the International Space Port, located in the Pacific Ocean.

G   By 2010, demand will have reduced the cost of a ticket to £4,000.

H   Its brochure says that a hotel will be constructed in space first.

STRATEGIES

1 Read through the whole text quickly for a general understanding.

2 Read the text again more carefully. Work with a partner and circle the words or phrases that create a link between information in the text and the extracts. Remember that pronouns usually refer *back* to something already mentioned.

Example:
Who does 'They' refer to in extract E?

3 When you've found all the obvious links concentrate on the extracts that remain. You may need to think about the overall meaning of the sentence in order to position it correctly. Remember that the extract may refer to information that appears *ahead* in the text.

4 Check your answers in a group, and try to justify your choice of answer.

▶ Go to the Review page to record your performance.

See **Language awareness: future (2)**

Writing skill: a story

You have decided to enter a short story competition. Your story must be based on the following pictures.

1 Work in groups of four. Each of you should choose two of the pictures and write one or two sentences about what is happening in your picture.

2 When you have finished, put your sentences together and concentrate on using linking words or phrases. You could use some of the following:

One day …
That evening/weekend …
The next/following day/week …
… when suddenly …
The next thing he knew …
Meanwhile …
Before long …
In the end …

3 Read your story to another group and ask them for their comments.

1 Read the following text and underline all the examples of passive constructions.

Experts have calculated that over one third of the food we produce is destroyed by pests. Locusts, for example, have been known to eat the weight of 1000 elephants in vegetation – in one day! By using pesticides, the number of locusts breeding can be controlled and precious food-crops are protected.

However, it has also been calculated that as many as 375,000 people will be poisoned by pesticides this year and that 10,000 of these will die. Even though people agree that chemical poisons should be used more carefully, the world-wide trade in pesticides is now $10 billion per year! Although some of the more dangerous pesticides have been banned, in many countries manufacturers still make them and sell them. In fact, last year, large amounts of pesticides were found in food imported from countries where the ban had not been enforced.

Spraying from the air allows large numbers of pests to be treated. But poison clouds can often drift out of control into areas where innocent plants, animals and people might live. Even more frightening, during tests in America, traces of pesticides were found in most of the people examined.

2 Find examples in the text of the following passive constructions:

present simple
past simple
past perfect
present perfect
future simple
infinitive
with modal verbs

3 We usually use the passive without 'by' when the agent is unknown, unimportant or obvious. How is this rule reflected in the passage above?

4 Who do you think did the calculations about the number of people being poisoned every year? Can you think of a situation where it might be important to know? Rewrite the following sentences in passive constructions beginning with 'It ...'. Which of the sentences might be more informative if kept in the active form?

a Police think the escaped prisoner has left the country.
b People have often said that life is becoming more stressful.
c The Government claimed yesterday that we are all better off than ever.
d A fire officer believes the fire was started deliberately.

5 Supply the correct form of the verb in brackets in the text below. You will need to decide whether it is active or passive and which tense to use.

Each year over 2.5 million people
(a) .... (die) from a disease called malaria which (b) .... (carry) by the blood-sucking insect called a mosquito. It
(c) .... (estimate) that before the use of pesticides, six million people (d) ....
(kill) by malaria every year. Now the spread of this disease (e) .... (control) by spraying the streams and pools where the insect breeds.

However, many scientists are worried about the effect of pesticides on our valuable wildlife. Insects which (f) .... (spray) are often food for other animals. Consequently, pesticides originally aimed at poisoning harmful pests
(g) .... (eat) by other animals and
(h) .... (pass) along the food chain.

We (i) .... (provide) with a rich variety of colourful fruits and vegetables when we
(j) .... (visit) the supermarket. In fact, unless tomatoes (k) .... (be) bright red and perfectly round many people
(l) .... (think) there is something wrong with them. Chemical poisons
(m) .... (use) to prevent pests from causing blemishes on fruits and vegetables which
(n) .... (make) them look unattractive.

6 When was the last time you ate a hamburger in a fast food restaurant? How do you imagine a beefburger is produced? In pairs, write a paragraph describing the process from the beginning.

Example:
The cattle are killed ...

LANGUAGE AWARENESS
future (2)

1 Look at these extracts from the article 'Out Of This World'. Which refers to (a) a completed action or the result of an action by a certain time in the future and (b) an action in progress at a future time?

By 2010, demand will have reduced the cost of a ticket to £4,000.
Some of us will soon be booking holidays in space!

2 ▱ It's the year 2025. Listen to the following conversation. Who's going on holiday, the man or the woman?

3 ▱ Complete the following sentences using the words the speakers use in the conversation. Which of the sentences refer to something that will be in progress at a certain time and which to completion of actions?

a This time next week I .... on the moon.
b By the time you arrive, you .... probably .... sick about 10 times on the journey!
c Just imagine! Next weekend I .... up there and .... at Earth.
d That's true. But you .... many post cards home by then.
e Just think. I .... a whole week in space by the time I get back.
f And I'm sure as soon as you get back you. .... us all your lovely photographs.

4 What do you think you'll have done in your life in: 1, 5, 10, 15 and 20 years' time? Share your ideas with a partner.

Example:
'In one year's time I'll have passed FCE.'

5 What do you think you'll be doing at the following times:

In two hours' time? This time tomorrow?
Next Saturday at 6.00? This time next week?

Example:
'This time next week I'll be on holiday.'

6 Complete the following dialogue using an appropriate future tense. You might need to refer back to the Language awareness section on page 61 as all the future forms appear at least once.

Boss: So what time (a) .... the train .... (leave)?
Secretary: 9.00 tomorrow morning.
Boss: And what are the arrangements for when I arrive?
Secretary: At 12.00 you (b) .... (meet) the shareholders. Then at 3.00 you (c) .... (play) golf with the Director.
Boss: Really? Well in that case I (d) .... (take) those new golf clubs I got for my birthday.
Secretary: (e) .... I .... (call) a taxi for you to take you to the station?
Boss: Yes, if you don't mind. I (f) .... probably .... (be) too busy packing tomorrow to remember. That reminds me. I've decided I (g) .... (spend) a few days visiting customers. Can you phone them and tell them to expect me?
Secretary: How many do you reckon on seeing?
Boss: Well, I'm hoping I (h) .... (see) all of them by the time I leave.
Secretary: It sounds like you (i) .... (be) really busy!
(j) .... I .... (forward) any important letters to you at the hotel?
Boss: Yes, good idea. I (k) .... (talk) to customers all day Tuesday and Wednesday so you might need to leave any messages at reception.

7 Now fill in a table like the one below with examples of each function from the dialogue.

Function	Example
intention	
arrangement	
firm prediction	
simple prediction	
timetable/calendar event	
spontaneous decision	
suggestion	
completed action by future time	
action in progress at a future time	

Your review of Unit 7

Vocabulary

Your selection:

Suggestion: Look back at the way you have recorded vocabulary in the last six units of this book. What method has worked best for you? Compare your ideas with other people in your class.

Exam skills

Complete the summaries by underlining the appropriate answer:

Use of English, Part 5, word formation
- This question is a test of a) grammar b) vocabulary.
- You a) add a prefix/suffix b) make compound words c) change the spelling.

Score _____/10
What I need to improve ...

Reading, Part 3, gapped text
- In this question you need to a) find the main ideas b) understand how texts are organised.
- There is/are a) one b) two extra sentences or paragraphs.

Score _____/6
What I need to improve ...

General

UNIT 8

Pastimes and Passions

PART ONE
Get the picture?

Lead-in

1 How good are you at drawing? Work in small groups and draw a quick sketch of someone else in the group. Compare your sketches to see who is the best (and worst!) artist.

2 If you are good at drawing, do you have any advice for those who are not?

Listening technique: global understanding

Don't despair if you're hopeless at drawing. Harriet Whitehouse is an artist and writer, who believes that anybody can learn to draw simple cartoons. Listen to her five tips on how to improve your drawing and one tip on what not to do. Match each tip (1–6) with the correct picture (a–f).

▱ Listening technique: comprehension and inference

1 Read through the following statements and see if you can remember if they were True (T), False (F), or whether Harriet Doesn't Say (DS).

Tip 1: Harriet is good at drawing both people and animals.
Tip 2: Drawing different facial expressions is very simple.
Tip 3: You should always try to draw facial features (eyes, nose and mouth) in the right place.
Tip 4: The body of a cartoon person is just as important as the head.
Tip 5: You should make actions look bigger than they really are.
Tip 6: You should use equipment to ensure your circles and straight lines are perfect.

2 Now listen to the tape again to confirm your answers. Correct any false statements.

Vocabulary development: words with similar meanings

Look at the following sentences and underline the more appropriate word in each case.

a   Oil paint is usually sold in tubes/pipes.
b   You can mix your colours on a tray/palette.
c   You should save empty jugs/jars for rinsing brushes.
d   The canvas/cotton has to be stretched before it is painted on.
e   Some artists like to have a model/figure to pose for them.
f   Shall we visit the art showplace/gallery today?
g   How much is the entrance cost/fee/price?
h   Which artists are holding exhibitions/displays at the moment?
i   Some people just don't appreciate modern/up-to-date art.
j   Do you take any notice of what the art guides/critics say?
k   Sometimes the surrounding/frame is more beautiful than the painting itself.
l   That caricature/satire picks out all her worst features.
m   That portrait isn't a very good similarity/likeness.
n   This painting shows a beautiful scene/stage.
o   Is this a correct/genuine Monet or a fake?

EXAM FOCUS
(Speaking, Part 2)
comparing two photographs

Candidate A's pictures

Candidate B's pictures

S T R A T E G I E S

1 Work in groups of three to practise for this part of the exam. Two of you will be Candidate A and B, and the third will take the role of the examiner. (Your teacher will give you instructions.)

2 When it is your turn to speak you will be asked to compare and contrast the two pictures, as well as giving a personal reaction of some kind. Remember that your task is not just to describe what you see in the photographs. Some useful phrases are:

This one is more/this one is not as ... as the other. (comparing)
This one is rather ..., while this one is more ... (contrasting)
On the whole/on balance I prefer this one. (giving a personal reaction)
I like both of them, but if I had to choose it would be ...
I definitely wouldn't choose this one.

3 Don't worry about the time because it is the examiner's job to stop you after one minute.

4 When your partner has finished, you will be asked to comment briefly on his/her pictures.

▶ **Go to the Review page to record your performance.**

PART TWO
Salsa fever!

Lead-in

1 Can you name the dance styles shown in these pictures? With which country do you most associate them?

2 Have you ever had dancing lessons? What kind of dancing would you choose to learn given the chance? Or maybe you hate the thought of dancing? Tell the rest of the class.

EXAM FOCUS
(Reading, Part 1)
multiple matching

You are going to read an article about a woman's passion for salsa. Choose from the list (A–I) the sentence which best summarises each part (1–7) of the article. There is one extra sentence which you do not need to use. There is an example at the beginning (0).

A　It's safe for a woman in La Finca.
B　Doing salsa regularly can make you a happier person.
C　Salsa has many influences.
D　You can have fun without spending a lot of money.
E　Salsa can be very tiring if you're not careful.
F　Some people are naturally good at salsa; others find it more difficult.
G　There is a range of ability in the people who learn salsa.
H　Every beginner wants to be an expert.
I　A woman's role in salsa isn't as easy as it seems.

Check the Strategies box on page 92 before attempting this activity.

Salsa Fever!

Salsa, lambada, merengue, *qué*? Pick a partner and learn the language of Latin American dance. You pay a small fee for a two-hour lesson with Maverick at The Finca Bar in London, followed by an evening of free dancing. Julie Parry decided to try it.

0	G

To begin with, I was a little nervous, but the joy of La Finca is that as long as you're keen then you don't feel stupid. No special clothes are required and beginners should wear shoes that are comfortable enough to dance in. The classes include a wide mix of people, from students to workers who've come straight from the office. The classes cater for all levels from beginners through to intermediate and advanced levels.

1	

For those of us who are new to salsa, our inspirations are the beautiful people who twist and turn and move their hips around the dance floor making it look effortless. They are mostly South Americans; the women wear little dresses, the men T-shirts and braces and they all look stunning. We watch with admiration and hope that one day we will be half as good as they are.

2	

The music of salsa (meaning 'sauce' in Spanish) is a mixture of African rhythm, East Coast jazz and Latin balladry. It can be slow or fast and wild. The roots of the music come from African slavery, and it was then carried over to the Caribbean, Cuba and Puerto Rico and on to the United States.

3	

Salsa has become very popular with black and white Britons, and clubs have been springing up all over England. The DJ, a guy called Ramiro, says: 'The Trinidadians and Jamaicans are really good at it because it is the same basic hip movement as their dance, soca. The English seem to find it impossible to loosen their hips. You have to find the rhythm. That is not something you can learn.'

4	

One of the hardest things to get used to in salsa dancing is that the man must always take the lead and the woman must follow. The men I danced with found this almost as hard to cope with as I did. I was told that for a woman the requirements are simple: to be graceful and flexible, to be sensitive to your partner, to be able to spin on the spot for hours and to always look and smile at your partner!

5	

To begin with, dancing salsa is both physically and mentally demanding. La Finca gets very hot indeed, and it is advisable to drink frequently – iced water is best – and to have small snacks to keep up your energy levels.

6	

Although the dance is very fast and sexy, the salsa scene is a family affair. People of different generations and communities come together to dance rather than look for romance. As my Chilean friend, Isobel, says: 'I don't mind if my fiancé dances with other girls, because I know it's not going to go any further than that.' Unlike the traditional nightclub scene of boy-meets-girl, the atmosphere here is very comfortable, particularly if you're a woman.

7	

Dancing is now the highlight of my week. It's a release from all the day-to-day pressures of sitting in front of a computer. I catch myself walking about the office with a huge smile on my face, and even having a quick practice in the lift! It's a better way to keep fit than jogging. It looks like I've got salsa fever.

S T R A T E G I E S

1   Read the text through once to get a general understanding. Don't look at the paragraph summaries yet.

2   Now read the text more carefully, and for each paragraph, try to work out what the main point of the paragraph is. Writing a short sentence next to it may help.

3   Compare your ideas with a partner and try to justify your summary sentence if your ideas are different.

4   Now go through the list of paragraph summaries given (1–7) and tick off the ones which correspond to your own ideas. With those that remain, read the paragraphs again and try to find a match.

▶ **Go to the Review page to record your performance.**

Listening technique: following instructions

1 You are going to hear Maverick, the teacher at La Finca, explaining how to salsa. Listen to his description of the eight basic steps and look at the pictures opposite. The first four are in the correct order. Listen and order the remaining steps correctly.

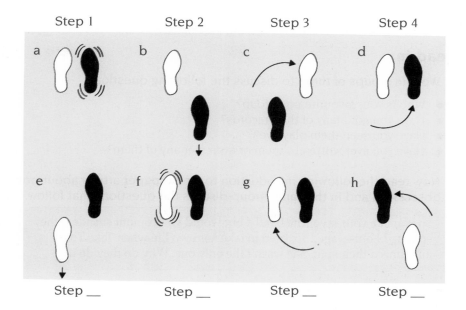

2 Listen again and see if you can find three occasions where Maverick contradicts information in the newspaper article on page 92. Check against the text and the tapescript on page 185, if necessary.

3 Now you know how to salsa, you can try the steps at home!

Writing skill: an account of a hobby

1 The newspaper which printed the article about Julie Parry on page 92 would like to hear similar stories from its readers.

2 First of all, decide what hobby/interest you are going to write about and then make notes under the following headings:

- what type of people do it
- special equipment needed (if any)
- what inspired you to start
- what makes it enjoyable
- what you find difficult
- the benefits to you since taking it up

3 Write your account from your notes. You could use some of the phrases opposite.

4 When you have finished, read your partner's account. If you were the newspaper editor, would you choose to publish it? Say why/why not.

5 Compare your accounts with the one on page 163. Whose is the best?

See Language awareness: reported speech

What's *your* special interest? It could be something as energetic as salsa, like aerobics or windsurfing. Or it could be something a bit more tranquil, like painting water-colours or stamp collecting. Write a short account (up to 180 words) for people who may be interested in taking up your hobby.

Mine's an unusual hobby for young people.

One of the most difficult things to master is ...

Since taking up aerobics, I've noticed that ...

You can hire the equipment instead of buying it.

I started because I was fed up of having nothing to do in the evenings.

It's a great way to relax.

PART THREE
The fans who go too far

Lead-in

1 Work in groups of three to discuss the following questions.

- Who is your favourite pop group?
- Have you got many of their records?
- Have you seen them play live?
- Have you ever written to them or even met any of them?

2 Now read the following introduction to a newspaper article about pop obsessions and in the same group discuss the questions that follow.

> So you like your favourite band – but would you commit suicide if they split up? Louise, aged 15, tried to take her own life when Take That announced their split. She wasn't the only one. Why do they do it?

- Why do you think some fans become so obsessed?
- What advice would you give to someone like Louise?
- Can/should top bands do anything to help the fans before they split up?

Reading technique: confirming your own ideas

Now read the rest of the text to see if any of the ideas you discussed in the Lead-in are mentioned.

> Louise's reaction to Take That splitting up may have been extreme, but she was by no means the only one to be affected. A helpline was set up to help young fans received a staggering 200,000 phone calls from distraught youngsters. Some of the callers were too upset to even speak out properly. Many callers were saying that the split had left a hole in their lives which they didn't know how to fill it. And it wasn't only teenagers who couldn't cope when the band split. Many calls they came from middle-aged women, university students and even the men.
>
> So why should a band splitting them up cause such unhappiness? Most people have heroes but don't take it much more further than that. But there are a few who don't have their own 'self-identity', and so fix on their favourite group. When the band splits up it's as like the death of a friend or relative. They also feel very angry that they weren't consulted about the split. Teenagers in particular feel a lot of so different emotions and are more likely to become obsessed. Psychologists think that fans can be helped if their band plays out a farewell concert, so that they are able to say a proper goodbye to the group.
>
> *(Bliss)*

e Use of English: error correction

Did you notice that some of the lines in the text contained a word that should not be there? There are ten extra words in all. Working with your group, cross out the ones you can find.

Listening technique: global understanding

1 You are going to hear five news reports about obsessed fans. Before you listen, see if you can guess which newspaper headline (1–5) goes with the appropriate pop star (A–E).

1
Angry fan attacks family of Jordy Chandler

4
Six-year-old girl suffers from 'depression'

2
Missing schoolgirl phones home at last

3
Tragedy of obsessed fan

5
Father rings helpline to say his daughters are 'out of control'

A Robbie Williams left Take That for a solo career

B Take That decided to split

C Michael Jackson – accused of child abuse

D Nirvana's lead singer, Kurt Cobain, shot himself

E Richey Edwards of Manic Street Preachers disappeared

2 Now listen to the reports and see if you were correct. Did any of these stories make the headlines in your country? Do you know of any similar stories?

Listening technique: finding the details

1 Listen to the stories again and, for each of the five news items, write down two facts from the story that are not included in the headline.

2 Compare your facts with a partner's and use the tapescript on page 185 to check if there is some disagreement.

Vocabulary development: music

1 Add suffixes or make compound words to describe the people who do the following.

Example:
Someone who ... plays music as a career – musi*cian*

Someone who:
a writes songs
b plays the drums
c plays the guitar
d plays keyboards
e plays the piano
f plays the bass

2 Write down five other musical instruments and the name of the person who plays them.

3 Test your knowledge of more musical vocabulary with this puzzle.

On tour!

Across
3 The person who looks after the band.
4 Posters, T-shirts, magazines, etc., are all examples of this.
7 An extra song played by the band at the end.

Down
1 A short word for a concert.
2 Where to write to if you need information about your favourite band.
4 The vocalist sings into this.
5 A guitar is plugged into this to make the sound louder.
6 What the band performs on.

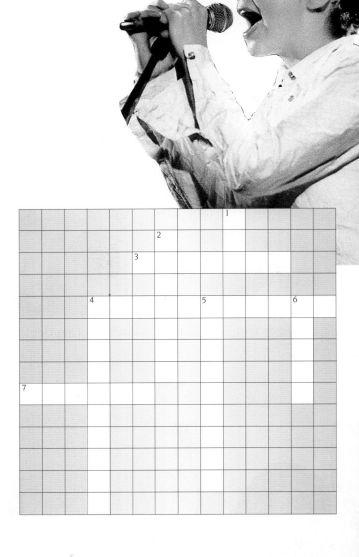

Writing skill: a letter of invitation

1 Imagine that your favourite band are coming to play a farewell concert in your home town and you have bought two tickets. Write a letter of invitation to an English-speaking friend of yours who is also a fan and who lives in the next town.

2 You have found an old book on writing letters of invitation. What do you think is wrong with these suggested phrases (opposite)? Study them and with a partner rewrite them so that they are more appropriate in style.

3 Write your letter giving details of the date, time to meet, and any other necessary arrangements in about 150 words.

***See* Language awareness: conditionals (2)**

I hope that you are in good health.

I am writing to invite you to a musical performance by ...

It would give me great pleasure if you were able to accompany me.

There is no need to concern yourself about the cost.

I will be able to accommodate you in my home after the concert.

I look forward to hearing from you soon,
Yours,

LANGUAGE AWARENESS
reported speech

1 ▭ Isabelle and Zoe recently spent an evening at the local disco and met two young men. Listen to Isabelle's report of what happened. Did she find her admirer interesting?

2 Turn to the tapescript on page 185. What did Steve actually say to Isabelle?

Example:
'I'm free now if you want to dance.'

3 What tense changes often happen when direct speech becomes reported speech? How do the following words change? Are there any other examples of words that change? Check the Grammar Reference on page 171 to confirm your ideas.

tonight   tomorrow   yesterday   next week   now   here

4 Read some more of the romantic comments made by Steve and turn them into reported speech.

'I live in the expensive part of London.'
'I've been driving around in a Mercedes since last Saturday.'
'I'm going to change it for a Rolls Royce next week.'
'I lived in America for a few years.'

5 ▭ Zoe's admirer was a little more interested in her than himself! Listen to Zoe and fill in the spaces in the following sentences:

a He wondered .... dancing.
b He asked .... from.
c He wanted to know .... again.
d He asked .... boyfriend.
e He wanted to know ....
f He asked .... romantic men.
g He wondered .... Chanel perfume.
h He wanted to know .... the following weekend.

6 Change the sentences into direct questions. What other changes take place when reporting questions?

7 Think of six questions to ask your partner about themselves. Each question must begin with the following words:

Where ...?   What ...?   How ...?   Do ...?
Can...?   Have ...?

8 Now tell somebody else which questions you asked and the answers you received.

Example:
'I asked him where he'd been for his holiday last year. He said he'd been to Spain.'

9 The following statements were made by people who heard about Zoe and Isabelle's romantic encounters. Match each statement with a suitable function below. There may be more than one correct answer depending on your opinion! Which was said by a friend and which by a parent?

advice   a command   a request   a warning

a 'Bring him home for dinner.'
b 'You should find a different disco.'
c 'Don't tell him where you live.'
d 'Treat him nicely.'
e 'Don't see him again.'
f 'He wants a wife!'
g 'You really should stop talking to strange men.'

10 Now turn each statement into reported speech using the following verbs. Refer to the Grammar Reference on page 171, if necessary.

warn   advise   tell   ask   suggest

Example:
Her mum asked her to bring him home for dinner.

11 Have you got any problems that you'd like your colleagues to solve? Think of a couple and then, in groups of three or four, take it in turns to listen to and then give advice on each problem.

Example:
'I always arrive late for class. What should I do?'
'Why don't you get an alarm clock?'
'Have you thought about getting up earlier?'

Who gives the best advice in your group?

12 Now report the problem and the best advice you were given to the rest of the class.

Example:
'I said I always arrived late for class. He advised me to stay in bed!'

LANGUAGE AWARENESS
conditionals (2)

1 Jane was desperate to see her favourite group perform in their final gig, but she had some problems. Read her letter to her friend below.

> so I told my boss I was sick and took a day off work. I was going to travel down to London by coach as it was cheaper. But then I heard the coach drivers were on strike, so I decided to go by train. I arrived at the station, bought my ticket and went down to the platform. Who do you think I bumped into at the bottom of the stairs? My boss! He sacked me there and then! I was really upset. A woman came up to me and tried to cheer me up and we ended up having such a nice long talk that I completely forgot the time. The next thing I knew I'd missed the train! She was so kind. She'd just dropped her friend off at the station and was driving to London and offered to give me a lift. But when we got to the car park her car had been stolen! She'd forgotten to lock it! It was then that I decided the gig just wasn't worth it and went back home. A few days later I read that the gig had been cancelled because the lead singer was ill!

2 How many hypotheses like the examples below can you make about the story? Get your partner to check your sentences.

Example:
If Jane had told her boss the truth she might not have got the sack.
If the coaches hadn't been on strike, she wouldn't have seen her boss.
She could have travelled by coach if there hadn't been a strike.

3 Work in two teams. One person from Team A should read the first half of a sentence. Somebody from Team B should try to complete the sentence logically.

Example:
(Team A) If Jane had caught the coach ...
(Team B) ... she wouldn't have got the sack.

4 Look at the following two comments. In the first, is Jane talking about the 'past in the past' or just the past? In the second, is she talking about the past or the present? Can you explain the use of tenses?

I wish I hadn't taken a day off work.
If only I still had my job.

5 Think of three things about your life now and three things about your life in the past that you'd like to change. Then explain the reason.

Example:
I wish/If only I could go home now! If I could go home now I'd get a video and relax in front of the TV.
I wish/If only I'd got up earlier this morning. If I'd got up earlier I could have revised conditionals.

6 Complete the following questions with the correct form of the verb in brackets and the appropriate modal verb. Refer to the Grammar Reference on page 172 to remind yourself of conditional structures.

a What .... you .... (do) if you .... (pass) FCE?
b What laws .... you .... (make) if you .... (be) in charge of this school?
c .... you .... (say) anything if somebody .... (push) in front of you in a queue?
d If I .... (telephone) you last night .... you .... (come) out?
e .... you .... (lend) me some money provided I .... (pay) you back tomorrow?
f Do you ever wish you .... (live) in another country?
g .... you .... (come) to the lesson today if you .... (know) we were going to do conditionals?
h Do you ever wish you .... (be) born at a different time in history?
i If you .... (can) be anywhere else now where .... (will) you want to be?
j .... you .... (rush) to school/work if you .... (be) late?
k .... you .... (do) my homework for me this week provided I .... (do) yours next week?
l If you .... (find) some money on the bus .... (will) you keep it?

7 Pick two people in the class who you think you know quite well. How do you think they would answer each question? Go and ask them and find out if you were correct.

Your review of Unit 8

Vocabulary

Your selection:

Suggestion:
Choose four of your favourite hobbies or interests and record any words that are associated with them.

Example:
Painting
  oil
  brush
  canvas
  paint

Exam skills

Complete the summaries by underlining the appropriate answer:

Speaking, Part 2, comparing two photographs
• Go back to page 51.

What I need to improve ...

Reading, Part 1, multiple matching
• In this question you need to a) find the main ideas b) understand how texts are organised.
• You have to a) fill in a gap in the text b) match one set of information to another.

Score _____ /7
What I need to improve ...

General

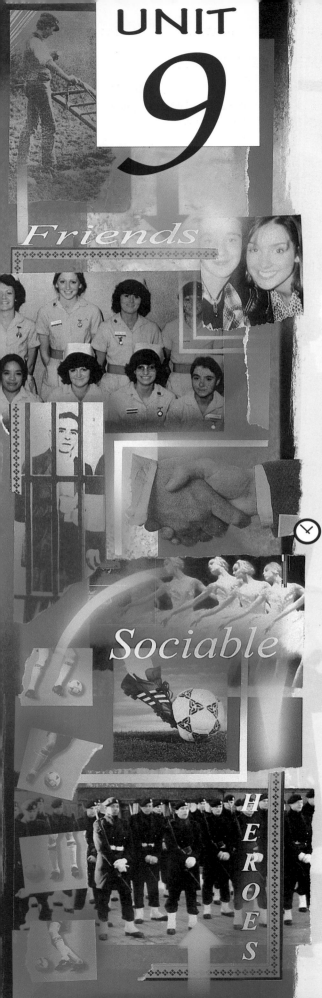

UNIT
9

The Things People Do

PART ONE
Getting on with others

Lead-in

1 Which of the following statements best describes your attitude to other people?

I work best alone rather than with other people.
I achieve more by working with a small group of people.
Being in a big group brings out the best in me.

2 Find others in the group who share your opinion and discuss why.

Reading technique: skimming

You are going to do a quiz to test your sociability. However, the headings for each section (1–5) have been removed. Skim read the questions in one minute and then choose the correct heading from the following list (A–F). There is one heading you do not need.

A friends
B relationships
C work
D school
E the future
F social life

Reading technique: comprehension

1 Just how sociable are you? Try the quiz to find out, starting with the questions on school. Follow the instructions carefully, as you may not need to answer all of the sections. You will find the conclusions on page 152.

2 Do you agree with the conclusion?

How sociable are you?

1

Teacher says you have to do a project in groups. What's your reaction?
A) Oh no! It gets on my nerves when someone else gets the credit for all my hard work.
B) Yes! I get more time talking to my friends this way.

Where do you usually do your homework?
A) At home by myself – it's much quicker that way.
B) At a friend's house – two heads are better than one.

You hear a hint about an exam. Who do you tell?
A) No one – I want to come top of the class.
B) All my mates – share and share alike.

Mostly A's: go to questions about the future.
Mostly B's: go to questions about your social life.

2

What's your ideal job?
A) Something where I'd be dealing with the public all the time, like a doctor or teacher.
B) Something where I could work with other people, like a journalist or TV researcher.

Where would you like to live in the future?
A) The big city where you can mind your own business.
B) In a small town or village where everyone knows each other.

Would you like to have a family when you're older?
A) Not much – I can't imagine being a parent.
B) I'd love a big family – at least two children.

Mostly A's: go to questions about relationships.
Mostly B's: go to social life questions.

3

Your friend is a bit down in the dumps. What do you do?
A) Spend hours on the phone cheering her up.
B) Gather some of her mates and go to her house.

A new person at school or work tells you they like your friend's partner. What do you do?
A) Tell them that he or she is off limits and keep a very close eye on them in the future.
B) Explain that he or she is taken and help them to find someone else.

Two of your friends have an argument. Do you?
A) Support the one who you think is in the right.
B) Keep your opinions to yourself and try to get them talking again.

Mostly A's: go to conclusion number 2 on page 152.
Mostly B's: go to conclusion number 3.

4

Who do you spend your Saturday nights with?
A) My closest mates – it doesn't matter where we go as long as we're together.
B) Anyone who happens to be around – I like to see as many people as possible.

What's your favourite keep-fit method?
A) Aerobics, running, tennis or badminton.
B) Volleyball, netball, football or basketball.

What's your idea of a perfect date?
A) A romantic dinner for two.
B) Going to a club in a foursome.

Mostly A's: go to conclusion number 2.
Mostly B's: go to questions about your friends.

5

What do you think of long-distance love?
A) I'd like it because I like having time by myself.
B) I couldn't cope – I would want to see the person I love more often.

Your perfect partner is:
A) someone who's always around when needed.
B) someone who I'm completely in tune with.

Do you fall in love easily?
A) Not really – it takes time to trust someone.
B) Yes, I fall head over heels in love straightaway!

Mostly A's: go to conclusion number 1.
Mostly B's: go to questions about your social life.

(*Bliss*)

Vocabulary development: colloquial language

1 Find and underline the following expressions from the quiz and match them with the definitions a–j.

1	(to) get on (one's) nerves	a	watch very carefully
2	two heads are better than one	b	completely
3	share and share alike	c	irritate or annoy
4	(to) mind your own business	d	sad and depressed
5	(to be) down in the dumps	e	beyond a certain limit
6	(to be) out of bounds	f	correct, with justice on your side
7	(to) keep a close eye on (sth)	g	it's best to share ideas
8	(to be) in the right	h	in agreement
9	(to be) in tune (with sb)	i	divide something equally
10	(to fall) head over heels (in love with)	j	concern yourself with your own affairs

2 Choose five of the expressions and write a sentence of your own.

Example:
People who put chewing gum under the desk really get on my nerves.

See **Language awareness: verb forms (1)**

Speaking skill: discussion and negotiation

1 You want to move into a flat with some friends. Put a tick (✔) next to those annoying habits that you would be likely to have. Put a cross (✘) next to the things that would get on your nerves if your flatmates did them.

Top 10 annoying habits:

1 smoking
2 playing music very loudly
3 leaving the washing-up or the housework
4 forgetting to pass on telephone messages
5 borrowing clothes from flatmates

6 having loud arguments with boy/girl friend
7 having phone calls late at night
8 spending a long time on the phone
9 getting in late at night
10 inviting friends to stay

2 Work in groups of four. Imagine that you are going to share a flat with the people in your group. Share your ideas to see how compatible you would be. How could you deal with any problem areas?

Listening technique: specific information

You are going to hear part of a radio phone-in which asked listeners to call in to talk about problem flatmates. As you listen the first time, make a note of which of the above problems are mentioned by each speaker. Write the relevant number next to the problem. (1 = speaker 1, etc.)

Listening technique: inference

1 Listen to the tape again. How did each of the speakers feel about their flatmates: a) when they first moved in? b) in the end?

2 When you have finished, turn to the tapescript on page 186 and underline the words that helped you decide.

PART TWO
Turning a blind eye

Lead-in

1 Here are some illegal things that people do. Do you approve or disapprove of the people who do these things, or doesn't it bother you?

2 Compare your answers in a small group. How far do you agree with each other?

- Stealing from a supermarket
- Stealing from a small shop
- Driving after drinking
- Keeping the change when the shop assistant makes a mistake
- Dropping litter
- Not paying the proper fare on the train/bus
- Watching 18-rated films under age

Vocabulary development: right and wrong

1 Read the paragraph opposite and fill in the missing words from the box below. Add another sentence to the paragraph using the word that you have left over.

witnesses	jailed	judge
convicted	proved	trial
jury	sentenced	evidence
accused		

The British Legal System

In a British court you are innocent until (a)_____ guilty. If you are (b)_____ of committing a crime the (c)_____ will take place in court. The 12 members of the (d)_____ listen to all the (e)_____ (including statements by any (f)_____) before they make their decision. If you are (g)_____, you may be (h)_____ to a period of time in prison by the (i)_____. - - - - - - - - - -

- -

2 Read these dictionary definitions and match them with one of the words in the box below. Write your own definition for the two words that remain.

a   *noun* person who attacks somebody in the street in order to steal their handbag, purse, jewellery, Walkman, etc.

b   *noun* person who asks for money in return for not revealing secrets

c   *noun* person who breaks into houses in order to steal

d   *noun* person who hurts somebody who is weaker than themselves

mugger	bully	thief	burglar
blackmailer	shoplifter		

What are the general nouns and verbs of all of the above words?

Example:
a mugger, mugging, to mug (somebody)

3 Read the advice sheet opposite and fill in the missing words from the box. There is one that you do not need.

security guard	first aider	guard
emergency alarm	traffic police	

How you can help

- You see somebody on the floor bleeding. Find a qualified (a) _____ .
- You are travelling on a train and some youths are causing trouble. Find the (b)_____ . If there is any sign of violence, use the (c) _____ .
- If you witness somebody shoplifting, tell the (d) _____ .

EXAM FOCUS
(Speaking, Part 3)
sharing opinions

Look at the situations shown in these pictures. In each one there is someone who might be in need of help or someone who is committing a crime. Talk to each other about three of the pictures and explain whether or not you would get involved and what action you would take. You have about three minutes for this.

▭ Listening technique: global understanding

You are going to hear an interview with Natalie, who talks about some research she did. Which of the pictures on page 104 and 105 refers to her experiment?

▭ Listening technique: specific information

1 Listen again and decide whether the following statements are True (T) or False (F).

   a Natalie carried out the experiment by herself.
   b The store manager knew about the experiment.
   c She wasn't afraid while doing the experiment.
   d The experiment was tried with all kinds of people.
   e Nobody reported her to the staff.
   f Her conclusion was that people were afraid to get involved.
   g Since doing the experiment, Natalie has changed her attitude towards real shoplifters.

2 If the experiment was tried in your country, do you think the results would be different? Tell the class.

Writing skill: a story

1 Choose one of the pictures from page 104. Imagine you are one of the people shown. What is happening? Why are you in this situation? How do you feel?

2 Build up a story around the picture by imagining what happened *before* and *after* the situation shown in the photograph.

3 Write a first draft of your story and ask your partner to read it for interest (10 marks) and language accuracy (10 marks).

See Language awareness: possibility and certainty

S T R A T E G I E S

1 Work with a partner and agree which three pictures you are going to talk about.

2 The best way to begin is to invite each other to speak.

   Example:
   What would you do in this situation?

3 Remember, it is not necessary to agree with each other. The discussion is more important than the conclusion.

4 Don't worry too much about the time: the examiner will stop you after about three minutes.

▶ **Go to the Review page to record your performance.**

PART THREE
Fallen heroes?

Lead-in

1 What do the following sporting heroes have in common?

2 Do you know of any other sportspeople who have done something wrong?

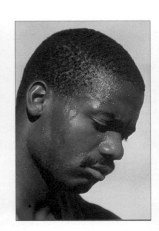

Use of English: finding the right word

Work in small groups, one group on Text A and the other on Text B. Read your text and answer the questions that follow.

Text A
Cantona the brave
In May 1996, Eric Cantona was crowned Footballer of the Year; it was the final *proof* of his rehabilitation with the English team, Manchester United.

Sixteen months *before* (1), the Frenchman had launched his infamous 'kung-fu' style attack on a supporter of the *rival* (2) team. Many people said Cantona was provoked by racist *comments* (3) made by the fan when Cantona was sent off the *pitch* (4). Even with his reputation for being a deeply passionate footballer, the action shocked the world. As a result, Cantona was *banned* (5) from playing football for eight months, and was ordered to spend 120 hours in the community. He *spent* (6) the time helping to instruct young boys and girls in the game.

His team, Manchester United, just wasn't the same without him. It was a lonely *time* (7) for the former Leeds United player, but his manager Alex Ferguson stood by him, even following him all the way to France to persuade him not to leave the club. He told Cantona: 'There's no reason to leave here. The supporters love you.' After his return to the team in October 1995, his playing was truly inspirational: he led Manchester United to a *dual* (8) victory – top of the Premier League and winners of the 1996 FA Cup. It was a fairy-tale ending.

Look at the words 1–8 in the text. Find *one* word in the list below that could replace the word in italics. Use your dictionary to help you.

Example:
... the final *proof* of his rehabilitation ...

   A showing   B <u>evidence</u>   C fact

1 A previously   B since   C then
2 A opposite   B enemy   C opposing
3 A words   B sayings   C remarks
4 A field   B grass   C area
5 A ordered   B prohibited C punished
6 A passed   B employed   C made
7 A period   B duration   C progress
8 A twice   B double   C second

Text B
Fighting back

Every newspaper carried the picture of Diane Modahl returning early *from* the 1994 Commonwealth Games after the announcement of a positive dope test, following her compelling victory in the 800 metres. The journalists (1) _____ waiting at Heathrow Airport to see this talented athlete get off the plane, now a sad figure in a yellow jumper and dark glasses. The media then camped outside her front door, turning her home (2)_____ a prison.

She found sanctuary at the home of one of her sisters but there was (3) _____ escaping the bewildering events of the next fourteen months, (4) _____ which the former Commonwealth 800-metres champion received a four-year ban from athletics. Modahl protested strongly that she was innocent ('(5) _____ were times when I nearly went crazy with rage and frustration') and she received strong support from fellow British athletes, (6) _____ as Linford Christie and Sally Gunnell, who both refused to believe that she had taken the drug testosterone. She presented her evidence – that a mistake had (7) _____ made in her test sample – at a trial in December 1994, but was (8) _____ guilty of drug abuse. During her time (9) _____ from athletics, the only bright spot in her life was having a baby girl, called Imani. She and her husband manager kept on fighting for an appeal, and new scientific evidence convinced the British Athletic Federation that the testing laboratory in Lisbon had indeed (10) _____ mistakes. The victory was sweet, but it had been a long time coming.

(Independent)

Fill in the gaps 1–10 with the correct word from the box below. There are some words that you do not need.

Example:

... returning early from ...

was	such	into	were	made	being	no	from	here
during	there	done	so	to		away	found	been

Reading technique: scanning and information sharing

1 Now read your text and find the answer to the following questions.

	Eric Cantona	Diane Modahl
sport		
previous achievements		
what they were found guilty of		
penalty		
media reaction		
how they spent their time away from their sport		
who they received support from		
how they regained their reputation		

2 Now work with someone from another group. What are the similarities and differences between the two cases? Were they treated fairly, in your opinion?

🔊 Listening technique: prediction

You are going to hear extracts from a documentary about the life of the footballer, Diego Maradona. See how much you can predict by guessing what the following points refer to.

30th October   slum   native Indian
magical   Barcelona   Naples
role model   the Hand of God
World Cup   triumph   cocaine
fame   drugs test
humiliation and disgrace
human rights   manager

℮ Listening technique: specific information

🔊 Listen to the tape again and fill in the missing information.

Family life:
Born a)............................ , 1960, in Argentina to an b)............................ mother and a c)............................ father. d)............................ brothers and sisters.

Career:
Made his international debut at the age of e)............................ .Played for Barcelona from f) ...., before moving to g) .... in 1984. 1986 World Cup was famous for the 'Hand of God' (handball) goal against h) .... Argentina went on to win the World Cup in the same year. Low point of career came in the next World Cup when he was found guilty of i)............................ . He then became a j) .... for an Argentinian football team. He is a strong campaigner for k) .... and social justice.

Relationship with the media:
Stormy! He has been called 'one of the greatest football players of all time'. In 1994, however, he fired an l) .... at a crowd of reporters who refused to give him privacy. It will be a long time before he is forgiven.

You see the following question in an international magazine.

> Who is your sporting hero? Have they achieved something great? Have they managed to overcome a problem? What contribution do they make to society? Let us have your nominations for Sportsperson of the Decade – male or female, any sport, any nationality. Let us know in 120–180 words who you would like to receive this honour, and why.

STRATEGIES

1 Choose your favourite sportsperson and give your partner clues to see if they can guess who it is. Talk about the following points:

- general information
- greatest achievements
- what the public/media think
- contribution to society
- character/lifestyle
- problems they have had to overcome

2 Begin your essay in the following way:

The person I would like to nominate for Sportsperson of the Decade is ...

and continue:

There are three things that make ... special in my opinion.

▶ **Go to the Review page to record your performance.**

LANGUAGE AWARENESS
verb forms (1)

1 Look at these extracts from Part One of this unit:

... *getting* in late at night
... *spending* a long time on the phone
... *playing* music very loudly
... *having* loud arguments

The verb in italics is in the gerund ('... ing') form. Change the following sentences using the gerund form of the verb instead of the infinitive + 'to'.

a It isn't a good idea *to borrow* clothes without asking first.
b It can sometimes be embarrassing *to turn* up at a friend's house without an invitation.
c It could be a little insensitive *to leave* the washing-up to your flatmate.
d It is a good idea *to smoke* outside if your flatmate is a non-smoker.

2 What rules would you like everyone who shared your flat to agree to? Work in a group and make a list.

Example:
Taking it in turns to do the washing-up.

3 Read the following newspaper article and then match the verbs in italics with the correct category below:

The police are *expecting* to see heavy traffic on the roads this weekend as holidaymakers *try* to head for the coast. Motorists have been asked to *avoid* using the M1 Northbound and *try* taking the alternative A route instead.

verb + 'to'   verb + '... ing'   verb + 'to' or '... ing'

Which of the following verbs take each of these patterns?

choose	enjoy	fail	finish	give up
hate	intend	learn	like	manage
mind	need	offer	prefer	put off

4 Complete the following questionnaire supplying the correct form of the verb in brackets. Then interview the people in your group.

Who:
a prefers (get up) early to (lie) in bed?
b has never learnt (swim)?
c always puts off (do) things?
d hates (eat) foreign food?
e needs (have) more than 8 hours' sleep a night?
f always offers (give) up their seat on a bus to an older person?
g doesn't intend (get) married?
h hates (be) the centre of attention?

5 In each case rewrite the second sentence below so that it has a similar meaning to the first. You must use the word given followed by a preposition. Use between two and five words. Do not change the word given.

Example:
Who was it who made all this mess?
responsible
Who's *responsible for making* all this mess?

a I'd really love to have more time to relax.
dream
I .... more time to relax.

b He said he was sorry he was late.
apologised
He .... late.

c I don't think it's a good idea to work too hard.
believe
I don't .... too hard.

d I don't care if I don't pass the exam.
worried
I .... the exam.

e The teacher said José had broken the window.
blame
José .... the window.

f I don't want to watch TV anymore.
tired
I .... TV.

LANGUAGE AWARENESS
possibility and certainty

1 🎧 Listen to the two people at the door talking about the poor man lying in bed. How many words are missing from each statement below? Write in the words.

  a He ...maybe... a stuntman.
  b He .... a serious accident.
  c He .... very comfortable.
  d He .... a little help at dinner time.
  e He .... home for a while.
  f He .... some kind of sport.

2 Underline the words in each statement that express degrees of possibility. Which ones mean 'sure', 'fairly sure', 'possibly'? Which statements refer to the past, the present and the future? Which form of the verb is used after the modal verb? Complete the following:

To make a present or future deduction with a modal verb use modal + ...
or ....
To make a past deduction with a modal verb use modal + ... or ....

3 Read the following report from a newspaper.

Sticky end for McDonald's man

Police had to lead a man through a McDonald's restaurant with a toilet seat stuck to his bottom yesterday after he fell victim to a joke involving superglue. The man went to the lavatory at the Dublin restaurant and found himself stuck to the seat which had been covered with the glue. Eventually the seat was removed, still attached to the customer, who walked – covered by police overcoats – to an ambulance.

Complete the second sentence so that it has a similar meaning to the first sentence, using the word given. Do not change the word given.

a He probably felt really embarrassed when he was leaving the restaurant.
  must
  He .... really embarrassed.

b You can be certain the operation was painful.
  will
  The operation .... painful

c I bet his bottom's feeling sore at the moment.
  must
  His bottom .... sore now.

d It will possibly be a long time before he sits down again.
  might
  It .... some time before he sits down again.

e He certainly didn't know the glue was on the seat.
  won't
  He .... the glue was on the seat.

f Surely the manager didn't ask him to pay for his meal.
  can't
  The manager .... him to pay for his meal.

g Maybe the practical jokers don't like McDonald's.
  might
  The practical jokers .... McDonald's.

h Perhaps the restaurant will offer a reward.
  might
  The restaurant .... a reward.

i I bet the police are still laughing about it now.
  must
  The police .... about it now.

4 Work in pairs. Can you solve the following puzzle?

A man is lying on the operating table and is just about to have an operation. All of a sudden he wakes up, jumps off the table and hits the surgeon. Why?

Your review of Unit 9

Vocabulary

Your selection:

Suggestion:
Dictionaries often give a sample sentence to show how a word is used. Why not write your own personalised sentence to help you remember the words you have chosen?

Example:
Eric Cantona is my sporting *hero*.

Exam skills

Complete the summaries by underlining the appropriate answer:

Speaking, Part 3, sharing opinions
• This part lasts around a) three minutes b) ten minutes.
• You speak mostly to a) the examiner b) your partner.

What I need to improve ...

Writing, Part 2, a descriptive composition
• In this type of question you have to a) discuss advantages and disadvantages b) tell a story
  c) give a description of a person, place, etc.
• The maximum number of words is a) 120   b) 180.

What I need to improve ...

General

UNIT
10

Transport

PART ONE
Getting from A to B

Lead-in

1 Look at these methods of travel for getting to school or work. Which ones are the most commonly used in your country?

2 Interview your partner to complete the following survey into attitudes towards various forms of transport. When you've finished, share the answers with the rest of the class. Did people have similar attitudes?

Transport questionnaire

	your partner	Amanda	Martin
Name:			
Age:			
Are you working/studying?			

Do you travel mainly to work/school by:
(Tick those which apply)

	your partner	Amanda	Martin
car	☐	☐	☐
bus	☐	☐	☐
train/underground	☐	☐	☐
taxi	☐	☐	☐
on foot	☐	☐	☐
bike/moped	☐	☐	☐
other	☐	☐	☐

What do you like about this form of travel?

What do you dislike?

What factors are important to you when deciding which form of travel to use?
(Number the most important ones 1–5, 1 = most important.)

	your partner	Amanda	Martin
beneficial to the environment	☐	☐	☐
good way to keep fit	☐	☐	☐
convenient	☐	☐	☐
comfortable	☐	☐	☐
speedy	☐	☐	☐
reliable	☐	☐	☐
safe (for you and/or others)	☐	☐	☐
good for longer distances	☐	☐	☐
stylish	☐	☐	☐
relatively cheap	☐	☐	☐
Average journey time:			
Weekly cost:			

Listening technique: specific information

1 Listen to two people describing their daily journeys to a market researcher. As you listen, complete the questionnaire by ticking the appropriate boxes or writing brief notes.

2 Listen again and decide what other forms of transport you would/wouldn't recommend to Amanda and Martin.

Vocabulary development: phrasal verbs

Choose the best verb or adverb/preposition in the sentences opposite:

Example:
The front wheel on my bike is starting to (<u>wear</u>/run/go) out.

1 Is your moped difficult to start (off/up/out) in cold weather?
2 No wonder the car won't start. We've (gone/run/come) out of petrol.
3 You were really lucky to be (let/told/got) off with just a fine for drinking and driving.
4 I was late because the taxi had broken (through/out/down) on the way.
5 What a pity! Was it (towed/pulled/taken) away?
6 If you set (up/down/off) on foot, you should get there by three.
7 Can you (take/pick/get) me up from the train station tonight?
8 We missed the train by seconds! We arrived just in time to see it (moving/going/pulling) away from the platform.
9 Could you fill the tank (in/out/up) with five litres of petrol, please?
10 This bus looks full – you'll never be able to get (in/on/out) if you don't get to the front of the queue.

Writing skill: a letter giving directions

1 Imagine a friend of yours is coming from Britain to visit you in your country. He has written to ask how to get to your home town from your nearest airport. The forms of transport he is interested in are:

- hiring a car
- catching a bus or coach
- travelling by train
- getting a taxi

2 Work out the most suitable option(s) for him and use the plan opposite to write your letter, in not more than 180 words.

3 Don't forget to include all the necessary information, such as approximate fares, length of journey, location of stations, and any dangers!

4 When you have finished, ask your partner to read your letter. How clear are your instructions? Did you follow the plan?

5 Compare the letters with the one on page 163.

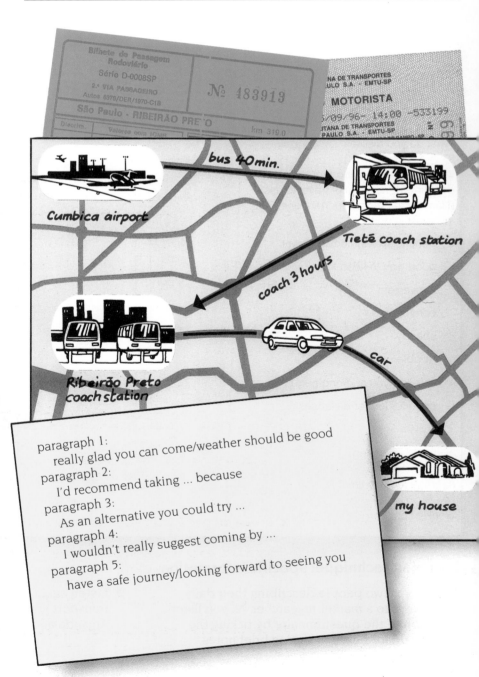

paragraph 1:
    really glad you can come/weather should be good
paragraph 2:
    I'd recommend taking ... because
paragraph 3:
    As an alternative you could try ...
paragraph 4:
    I wouldn't really suggest coming by ...
paragraph 5:
    have a safe journey/looking forward to seeing you

PART TWO
Young people's driving stories

Lead-in

In a recent survey about young people and driving British people strongly agreed with the following statements. How far do you agree with these views? Do you think similar views are held by people in your own country?

Seventeen is the best age to begin driving.
Parents shouldn't try to teach their own children to drive – they should be taught by a qualified instructor instead.
The driving test does not prepare you for real-life driving.
Most car accidents are caused by inexperienced teenagers within their first two years of driving.
Young people who drink and drive should go to prison for a minimum of four years.
Young people should be tested for drugs while driving, and not only alcohol.
Young men are worse drivers than young women.

EXAM FOCUS
(Listening, Part 3) multiple matching

🔊 **You will hear five young people talking about unlucky experiences with cars. For speakers 1–5 choose from the list A–F what the consequences were. Use the letters only once. There is one extra letter which you do not need to use.**

A	The friend's father was furious.	Speaker 1 ☐
B	Someone else was blamed for the accident.	Speaker 2 ☐
C	No one ever found out what had happened.	Speaker 3 ☐
D	The father was arrested and sent to court.	Speaker 4 ☐
E	The driver was asked to pay for the petrol used.	Speaker 5 ☐
F	The father needed time to calm down afterwards.	

S T R A T E G I E S

1 Make sure you read through the six statements before listening for the first time. In this particular example, you have to listen for the consequences. Where would you expect this information to be in the text? At the start or near the end?

2 Listen for the first time and complete as many answers as you can. Use the second listening as a chance to fill in the ones you missed, or to make a note of any phrases that helped you decide. Check them against the tapescript, if necessary, when you have the answers.

3 Do you know any similar stories to tell the class?

▶ **Go to the Review page to record your performance.**

Vocabulary development: on the road

1 Solve the following puzzle in five minutes if you can. You should find the name of a famous make of car when you have finished.

Clues:
1 You look in this to check if there are other vehicles behind you.
2 You have to pass this in order to be allowed to drive.
3 Every car has four of these.
4 The piece of glass at the front of the car is called this.
5 If you drive too fast you are guilty of this offence.
6 A word for people who are walking in the street.
7 You might receive this if you park in the wrong place.
8 You wear this while driving a car to protect you from accidents.

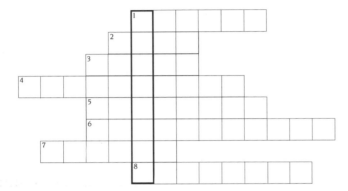

2 Form compound words by matching one of the words in Box A with one of the words in Box B. Some of the words can be used more than once.

A	B	
traffic	crossing	warden
car	park	limit
pedestrian/zebra	jam	alarm
parking	ticket	lights
speed	radio	fine
	horn	

3 Write clues (like those in activity 1) for some of these compounds and test the others in the class.

See **Language awareness: review of past tenses**

Reading technique: predicting

1 You are going to read two different stories about a skateboarder and a pizza delivery courier. Look at the following sentences and try to match them with the correct story:

a 'It is as dangerous as it sounds.'
b 'He was fined £50 for drink driving.'

 2 Skim read the texts on page 117 in two minutes to see if you were right.

Reading technique: comparing texts

Read the texts again more closely and discuss the following questions with your partner. Try to underline evidence in the texts.

1 How would you describe the tone of each text?
   a) serious   b) factual   c) amusing
2 The author's intention in each text is:
   a) to report an event   b) to entertain the reader
   c) to shock the reader   d) to criticise those in authority.
3 The author's attitude to those mentioned in the text is:
   a) sympathetic   b) indifferent   c) critical.
4 Which text are the following sentences taken from?
   a) There wasn't even a chance for a practice session before riding off in the rain and dark.
   b) 'I was coming across the driveway and they were just driving in.'
   c) He was also charged with failing to give police his name.
   d) ('my crash helmet was useless')
5 In your opinion, which text deals with the more serious issue?

Text A

A skateboarder, who drank a few glasses of rum before skating down the road to McDonald's for a hamburger, has been fined for drink-driving. John Forno, aged 19, pleaded guilty in court to driving a vehicle while under the influence of alcohol. Forno had a blood alcohol level of 0.153, which is three times the legal limit. He was fined £50 for drink-driving.

Forno said he had been drinking several glasses of rum at home, and about 10.30 p.m. he decided to skate to the local McDonald's for something to eat. 'I had drunk a fair amount of rum but at my age I'm allowed to,' he said. The skateboarder denied police claims that he had swerved all over the road and said he had pleaded guilty to the charges to 'get it over with'. But he added: 'I think it is very petty of the police to arrest me for this. The worst thing is I don't even drive a car.'

(Guardian)

Text B

Jonathan Green reports.

Home pizza delivery is one of the fastest growing sections of the fast food industry and teenagers short of money and looking for their first job can secure a position as a pizza courier earning a mere £2.90 per hour. But a loophole in the law enables young people who have never ridden mopeds to be used as professional dispatchers pressurised by a 30-minute delivery deadline. It is as dangerous as it sounds.

All the major pizza companies offer money back if the pizza is not delivered within 30 minutes of taking the order. Jason, 19, had never driven any type of vehicle on the road when he got his first job. 'The pressure was incredible. Sometimes the restaurant was so busy that it would take them 20 minutes to make the pizzas and we would then have 10 minutes to deliver them.' Jason's story is typical: no training, poor protective gear and eventually hospital after a serious crash.

Jonathan Green went undercover at one of the biggest pizza delivery chains in the world.

- Although a licence was asked for on the application form it was never checked.
- The crash helmet was too big and was already damaged.
- The waterproof trousers were split and had been stapled together.
- The gloves did not match – a woman's glove and a motorcycle glove.
- The moped had no mirrors.

(Big Issue)

PART THREE
Gridlock!

Lead-in

Is traffic congestion a problem in your country? If so, has the government tried to solve the problem? What solutions would you suggest?

EXAM FOCUS
(Use of English, Part 4)
error correction

For questions 1–15, read the text below and look carefully at each line. Some of the lines are correct, and some have a word which should not be there. If a line is correct put a tick (✔) at the end of the line. If a line has a word which should *not* be there, write the word at the end of the line. There are two examples at the beginning (0 and 00).

MOVIE CHASE

All week people sit in traffic jams. Sometimes, and on a Friday	0 _and_
night, they go to the movies. On the way they sit in more traffic	00 _✔_
jams, they miss the first part of the movie because of they can't	1_____
find a parking place. Then they sit in a dark cinema and watch	2_____
a man drive a car through a rush hour traffic, clear across a city	3_____
at eighty miles for an hour. If the man had turned into a	4_____
six-foot banana we would say it was a so stupid movie, but a	5_____
man driving a car through a crowded city at eighty miles an	6_____
hour we not only accept but remark at to each other how brilliantly	7_____
done the car chases were. Nothing can stop the hero by in his	8_____
car. If it meets to another car, he drives round it, or maybe over it, or	9_____
just possibly through it. He goes on the pavement, he crosses into	10_____
opposing traffic lanes, he hurtles down empty alleyways. His car	11_____
can jump, his car it can roll over, it is more like a performing dog	12_____
than a ton and a half of lifeless metal. If you offered it to a biscuit	13_____
it would probably sit up and beg. When the movie is over there,	14_____
everybody goes and sits in a jam again.	15_____

S T R A T E G I E S

1 Quickly skim read the text for a general understanding. Is the author in favour of cars or against them?

2 Now read each line carefully to find the mistakes. Look back at pages 53 and 94 to remind yourself of the types of errors you will find.

3 Check your answers with your partner before asking your teacher.

▶ **Go to the Review page to record your performance.**

Reading technique: predicting

1 You are going to read an extract from a novel by Ben Elton called *Gridlock*. (A gridlock is a massive traffic jam.) Before you read, imagine that on your way home today you become stuck in traffic. Would the consequences of your delay be serious or not too important? Share your ideas in a group.

2 What are the following things? Try to guess with a partner.

Beachy Head
Great Ormond Street Hospital
a Mini
the Highway Code

3 Now read the text to confirm your ideas.

1 Down on the ground, various human dramas were unfolding. Every car contained its degree of frustration, but some burned more agonisingly than others. The bride in the hired Daimler was assured by her father that it would be alright. He was wrong, it wouldn't be, and the unhappy groom would later get drunk and, in a foolish attempt to hang his silk wedding boxer shorts on top of the church steeple, would fall and break his neck.

2   Behind the Daimler was a fellow in a BMW who was rushing to meet a very important foreign client at Heathrow. His failure to do so put a black mark on his career ('You should have set off earlier.') which led him three years later to drive that same BMW off Beachy Head.

3   Nearby was a Mini in which was contained a beating heart, a beating heart that a small child lay waiting for in Great Ormond Street Hospital. That heart was destined to beat its last right there in the throbbing epicentre of the gridlock.

4   Beeping its horn at the Mini with the heart was an Escort van containing a plumber on his way to deal with a burst pipe that would now sadly destroy the entire lifetime's possessions of an elderly widow.

5   Behind the Escort, also beeping its horn, was a Mercedes containing three robbers who had just robbed a jewellery store near Harrods.

6   People's jobs, people's health, people's love affairs, people's futures were frozen in the traffic. A great lament rose above the smoke and the growling engines, wailing in sorrow for the losses of the day. It was the hooter's chorus. In the British driving test one is informed quite clearly what the car hooter is there for; it is there to inform other road users of your presence. Well, if that was what people were using their horn for around Hyde Park Corner on the day of the gridlock, then they were wasting their time. Everybody already knew everybody else was there, that was why no one could get anywhere. The truth is, of course, that, in the drama of the moment, people were forgetting the Highway Code and were not using their horns to say 'I am here' but were using them to say '*Why* am I here?'

(Ben Elton: *Gridlock*)

Reading technique: comprehension and inference

1 Read the text again without worrying about words you don't understand and then read the first five paragraphs more closely. As you read, tick the appropriate boxes.

2 Did you agree with the others in your class?

	Daimler	BMW	Mini	Escort	Mercedes
late for an important appointment?	☐	☐	☐	☐	☐
leads to the driver's death?	☐	☐	☐	☐	☐
leads to someone else's death?	☐	☐	☐	☐	☐
Who do you feel least sorry for?	☐	☐	☐	☐	☐
Who do you feel most sorry for?	☐	☐	☐	☐	☐
more than one person in the vehicle?	☐	☐	☐	☐	☐

Vocabulary development: word groups

1 Find and underline the following words that are in the text.

Daimler
bride
client
plumber
robbers
traffic

2 Can you find other words or phrases that are connected to these words?

Example:

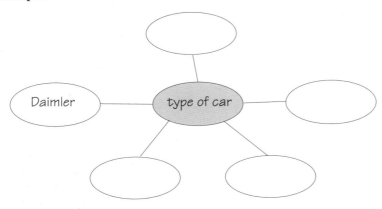

3 On your Review page write sentences of your own to help you remember them.

e Writing skill: letter to an editor

> Do you think the car is a force for good or evil?
> Write to the Letters Editor, Daily News,
> 3 Farringdon Street, London. Letters should be no
> more than 180 words.

1 Work in small groups, A or B. Group A should list all the advantages of the car, Group B should think of its disadvantages.

2 Work with somebody from the opposite group to share your ideas.

3 Before you write a first draft, think about the following points:

● Are you going to mention all of your points or be selective?
● What is the best order to put your points in?
● Are you going to give a balanced argument or argue strongly for one viewpoint?

4 Write a first draft of your letter and check it for language errors before you do a final version.

See **Language awareness: verb forms (2)**

LANGUAGE AWARENESS
review of tenses

1 Complete the following extract from the listening activity on page 115 by supplying the correct form of the verb in brackets. Then refer to the tapescript on page 188 to check your answers. Use past simple, past continuous, past perfect or past perfect continuous.

My dad (a) .... (teach) me to drive and I (b) .... (come) down a rather narrow road which (c) .... (have) cars parked on both sides. Suddenly, from nowhere there (d) .... (be) a young man on a bike coming towards us. I (e) .... (slam) the brakes on but he (f) .... (crash) into me, (g) .... (land) on the car and then (h) .... (roll) off. My father and I both (i) .... (jump) out of the car to see if he was all right. Fortunately, he (j) .... (stand) up and said he was OK, just a little shaken. My dad (k) .... (offer) to give him some money for the repair of the bike, and then an old lady (l) .... (come) along. When she (m) .... (see) what (n) .... (happen), she began shouting at my father, saying he (o) .... (drive) too fast, and it was a bad example to set to his young daughter. Poor old Dad (p) .... (not say) a word.

2 Can you remember the future structures you use for the following? Look back to pages 61 and 86 if you need a reminder.

Function	Form
intention	*going to*
arrangement	
firm prediction	
simple prediction	
timetable/calendar event	
spontaneous decision	
suggestion	
future action happening at specific time	
completed actions by a future time	

3 Read the following dialogue. How many mistakes can you find that Anna makes in the use of future tenses?

Miguel: So, are you looking forward to your trip?
Anna: Very much! The plane is arriving at Heathrow at 6.00 p.m. Jenny lives in London and she will meet me at the airport. She will take a sign so that I'll recognise her.
Miguel: What time do you think you'll arrive at the conference centre? I might phone you.
Anna: Jenny has never been to this conference hotel before but she guesses the journey will be taking about 30 minutes. So I suppose we're going to arrive about 7.00.
Miguel: Have you got to start work straight away?
Anna: No. The conference is starting on the following day. We will see a film that evening. Jenny has bought the tickets. Then after the conference I have decided I will spend a few days sightseeing. So this time Tuesday I will walk around London! Hopefully, by the time I leave, I will see all the main sights!
Miguel: Well, have a nice time and call me when you get back.
Anna: OK. The flight is leaving Heathrow on Thursday at 11.00. I don't think Jenny will have time to take me but I'm going to phone you when I arrive at the airport.

4 🔊 Listen to Jenny discussing the trip with one of her colleagues. Does her use of tenses correspond to the ones you have used? How many plans have changed or has Anna got wrong?

5 Anna has been told about the changes and has written to Miguel to tell him. Supply the correct form of the verb in brackets.

This is just to tell you about my new schedule. The plane (a) .... (arrive) at 6.00. Jenny (b) .... (wear) a bright red jumper so I don't miss her! She thinks the drive to the hotel (c) .... (take) about an hour because of the traffic. So phone at around 8.30. I (d) .... (recover) from the journey by then. By the way. We (e) .... (go) to the theatre not the cinema. I haven't seen a play for a long time so I'm looking forward to it. As I told you, the conference (f) .... (start) the next day. As you know, I (g) .... (do) some sightseeing. Jenny tells me there's a strike so it looks like there (h) .... (not be) any trains or buses. Jenny (i) .... (drive) me round.

   Anyway, by the time I see you next I (j) .... (see) the sights of London. I (k) .... (tell) you all about it when I get back. OK? Just think. In a few hours' time I (l) .... (sit) on the plane on my way to England!

   See you soon,

   Anna

LANGUAGE AWARENESS
verb forms (2)

1 How many examples of 'to' + infinitive can you find in the *Gridlock* text on page 119?

Example:
... a fellow in a BMW who was rushing to meet a very important foreign client ...

2 How many of these are examples of 'to' + infinitive to show purpose?

3 Make sentences using 'to' + infinitive to show purpose. Use one of the phrasal verbs below plus a word from box A and a phrase from box B.

Example:
He switched on the TV to see the film.

switch on	take up	go into	look up	pick up
look through	hand in	hang out	get in	put on

A	B
hospital	find a better job
jacket	get it dry
advertisements	see the film
essay	have an operation
TV	go to work
word	keep warm
exercise	have it marked
newspaper	find out the meaning
the washing	get fit
the car	do the crossword

4 ▣ Poor Petros has been working too hard ... he's lost his memory! Listen to the tape and answer the questions below.

a What is it Petros can't remember doing?
b He stopped Laura to ask her what?
c What has he stopped doing?
d What hasn't he remembered to bring?
e What's the difference between 'remember'/ 'stop' + 'ing' and 'remember'/ 'stop' + 'to'?

5 Check the Grammar Reference on pages 172–3 for examples of other words that follow this pattern and then supply the correct form of the words below.

a Do you always remember ... (send) your relatives a birthday card?
b Do you remember ... (be) punished as a child?
c Would you stop ... (learn) English if all British people spoke your language?
d Would you stop a stranger in the street ... (tell) them you loved their outfit?
e Do you go on ... (do) something if somebody asks you to stop?
f What will you go on ... (do) when you finish this course?

6 Pick somebody in the class that you know quite well. How do you think they would answer the questions in activity 5? Guess first, then ask them the questions.

7 You may want to look again at the Language awareness page 109 before doing the following exercise. There are several mistakes in verb forms in the accident report below. How many can you find?

GM Motor Insurers
Please give details of the accident
· ·

I was driving along the High Street and indicated turning left into James Street. It was difficult seeing clearly as a lorry was parked on the corner, and as I turned into James Street I had to brake quickly to avoid to hit an oncoming car. The vehicle behind had been driving too close for stop in time and hit the rear of my car. He denied to be too close behind me and accused me of drive dangerously, claiming that I had forgotten looking in my mirror. I decided not to phone the police as we were causing a traffic jam, so we exchanged names and addresses and I told him contact his insurers. Unfortunately, I didn't remember taking his registration number or making a note of the make and model of his car. I presume it will be easy enough for you find this out from his insurance company.

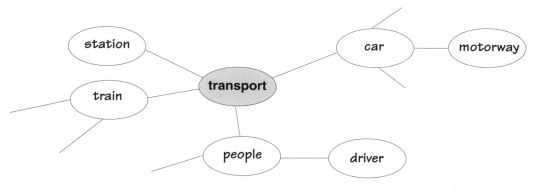

Your review of Unit 10

Vocabulary

Your selection:

Suggestion: Copy the mind map below on to a large sheet of paper and extend it with as much vocabulary as possible.

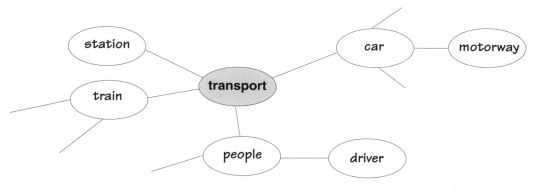

- station
- train
- transport
- car
- motorway
- people
- driver

Exam skills

Complete the summaries by underlining the appropriate answer:

Listening, Part 3, multiple matching
- You listen to a) some extracts on the same topic b) extracts on different topics.
- You have the chance to listen a) once b) twice to the extracts.

Score _____ /5
What I need to improve ...

Use of English, Part 4, error correction
- There is a mistake in a) every b) most lines.
- The error is a) an extra word b) a spelling mistake c) a wrong word that you have to correct.

Score _____ /15
What I need to improve ...

General

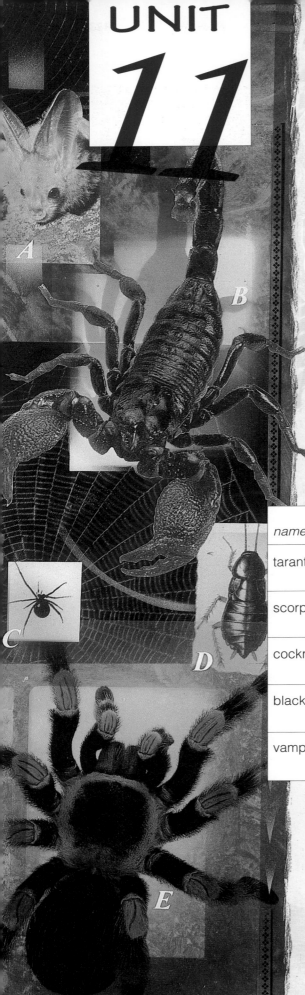

Dangerous Creatures

PART ONE
Small but scary

Lead-in

1 How much do you know about each of these creatures? Which of them would you *least* like to find in your bedroom one night?

2 Match each of them to the names supplied in the table below and then fill in the rest of the table (in pencil) with as much information as you think you know.

name	where found	maximum size	danger to humans	sting, bite or neither	prey
tarantula ( )					
scorpion ( )					
cockroach ( )					
black widow ( )					
vampire bat ( )					

3 Compare your answers in a group.

🔊 Listening technique: global understanding

You are going to hear an extract from an interview with a zoologist. As you listen for the first time decide in which order the creatures are being described. Write a number next to their names in the table on page 124.

🔊 Listening technique: specific information

Listen a second time and fill in as much of the table as you can. (You will not be able to complete every box.) Compare your answers with a partner and if necessary listen again. Were your original notes correct?

❸ Vocabulary development: words with a similar meaning

1 Choose one word from each of columns B, C and D which has a similar meaning to a word in column A. The first one is done as an example.

A	B	C	D
afraid (1)	population ( )	store ( )	manufacturers ( )
inhabitants (2)	frightened (1)	alien ( )	attitudes ( )
ideas (3)	save ( )	producers ( )	duration ( )
time (4)	overseas ( )	age ( )	citizens ( )
foreign (5)	builders ( )	residents ( )	immigrant ( )
delivered (6)	period ( )	beliefs ( )	nervous (1)
makers (7)	thoughts ( )	terrorised (1)	posted ( )
keep (8)	imported ( )	transmitted ( )	retain ( )

2 Using a good dictionary, if necessary, explore how the words in each group differ. Do they have slight differences in meaning? Are they always used in particular word combinations?

Example:
intensity of meaning

nervous   afraid   terrorised
                 frightened

⟶

usage
nervous + about/of sth.
afraid + of sth.
frightened + of/by sth., frightened + to death
terrorised + by sth.

e Use of English: multiple-choice cloze

1   Read the following text. How do the British differ from other nationalities in their view of spiders?

Huge, hairy and harmless

Britain is a fortunate country, at least in so far as spiders are concerned. No death has yet been caused by the bite of one. Being (1) ...... to death by a spider is more likely, however, for the British are notoriously arachnophobic. Each year, bees and wasps cause a handful of deaths, and about 120 people die from food poisoning. British spiders, by contrast, are virtually harmless and yet are feared, or at least disliked, by about half the (2) ....

   In eastern North America, (3) ...... towards spiders are different. There, spiders are not nearly as unpopular as cockroaches. In Amazonia, spiders can be a prized gastronomic treat. The Piaroa Indians hunt for the world's largest tarantulas by fishing them out of their burrows. They then cook them over a fire, a dozen at a (4)...... . The taste is said to resemble that of prawns.

   British arachnophobia turns to panic when (5) ...... spiders are found in fruit (6) ...... from countries such as Australia and Spain. Spanish grape (7) ...... report that only the British reject their consignments if spiders have been found in them.

   Britain has a national horror of the venomous Black Widow spiders and yet, in the southern states of America, they are accepted as neighbours and commonly live in outbuildings. However, if you want to (8) ...... one in Britain you must apply for a dangerous wild animal licence.

(Observer)

2   Read the text again and select the most appropriate word from the Vocabulary development activity for each of the gaps.

3   How about you? Are there any creatures that frighten you to death even though they're totally harmless?

See Language awareness: time conjunctions

PART TWO
Animal rights

Lead-in

1 Give each of the following statements a score of 1 to 5 (1 = strongly disagree, 5 = strongly agree). Think of reasons for your decisions.

> We shouldn't keep animals as pets.

> Keeping animals in zoos is perfectly justified.

> There's nothing wrong with using animals in a circus.

> Hunting for pleasure is barbaric and should be banned.

> Cosmetic testing on animals should be banned.

> Chimpanzees should have the same rights as humans.

> Animal experimentation for medical research is necessary.

2 How well can you argue your case? Share your views with your group and see if you can encourage the colleagues who disagree with you to change their scores.

3 Form two groups: Group A for people who see no problem with animal experimentation, Group B for those who aren't sure or who are against it.

ⓔ Listening technique: global understanding and note taking

1 💾 You are going to hear part of a radio talk on the subject of animal experimentation. As you listen for the first time decide if the speaker is for or against animal experimentation.

2 Now listen a second time and for questions A–J complete the notes with one word or a short phrase in each box. Compare your answers with a partner.

Vivisection has been defended by more than 1000	A
Before they can be sold there are laws that cover the testing of	B
and	
	C
For results to be accurate, the animal must not be	D
'Painless' animal experiments include	E
	F
and	
	G
A vet must be available to check on the animals'	H
Since 1976 the number of animal experiments	I
Numbers should hopefully drop even further due to	J

3 Has what you've heard made you or anybody else change their opinions? Can you persuade anybody else to join your group?

BUAV CAMPAIGNING TO END ANIMAL EXPERIMENTS

WHY IS VIVISECTION WRONG?
The BUAV was founded on the philosophy that inflicting pain, suffering and death on helpless animals during experiments is morally wrong. And for many the moral argument is sufficient reason to oppose vivisection.

But there is also a wealth of evidence to show that animal experiments are misleading and divert attention and resources away from more fruitful avenues of research.

The notion that results from animal tests can be directly applied to humans has been proved false time and time again:
- Aspirin causes birth defects in cats but not in humans
- Penicillin is toxic to guinea pigs and hamsters
- Morphine sedates people but excites cats
- Benzene causes leukaemia in humans but not in mice
- Saccharin causes cancer in rats but not in humans

There is always a real danger that, because of our reliance on animal tests, unsafe drugs and other products can be released into the marketplace for human use. An example of this was the heart drug Eraldin. Although the drug was thoroughly tested on animals, it had devastating side effects on human patients – including blindness and even death – before it was withdrawn from the market.

Many members of the scientific community agree with our views on animal testing.

"...the knowledge gained from studies in animals is often not pertinent to human beings, will almost certainly be inadequate, and may even be misleading."
Arnold D Welch, Department of Pharmacology, Yale University School of Medicine.

"...the sad reflection must be that the countless animals who have died in psychology experiments have died not only cruelly, but in vain."
Don Bannister, Medical Research Council external Scientific Staff, High Royds Hospital.

There are many alternatives to animal experimentation. Some of these methods, such as population and clinical studies, have been used successfully for years and some methods have been developed recently with advances in scanning and computer technology.

A great deal of research can be conducted in test tubes using human tissue cultures which have proved to be an extremely effective means of developing drugs and producing vaccines.

Unfortunately, research to develop non animal testing methods is seriously underfunded. To try and alleviate this problem the BUAV is calling for a Government-funded strategy to promote the use and development of humane research methods.

Animal testing causes needless pain and suffering to thousands of animals each day. It is of little or no value and can, in fact, produce dangerously misleading results. Relying on animal testing drains time and resources away from the use and development of more valuable research methods. Humane and superior research alternatives do exist. For these reasons, the BUAV is campaigning to end animal testing and stop the suffering of animals.

Vocabulary development: word formation

1 In the Exam Focus activity below, the word given at the end of each line forms a word that fits into the space in the same line. Look at the possible forms of the first word below.

(im)morality (n)   (im)moral (adj)   moralise (v)   (im)morally (adv)

2 Put the correct form of the word into the following sentences.

a The _____ of using animals for scientific research is often questioned.
b Some people argue that vivisection is _____ and should be banned.
c Scientists using animals for research argue that they are acting _____ .
d Would you _____ about the research that had gone into drugs if you needed them?

3 Using a dictionary, find all the possible forms for three of the other words in capitals in the Exam Focus.

4 Work in groups and write sentences like those in activity 2 for some of the different forms of these words. Test another group.

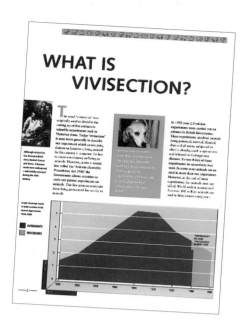

WHAT IS VIVISECTION?

EXAM FOCUS
(Use of English, Part 5)
word formation

You are going to read an extract from a text on vivisection. Use the word given in capitals at the end of each line to form a word that fits in the space in the same line. There is an example at the beginning (0).

Anti-vivisectionists claim that experiments on animals are (0) ..*immoral*..	MORAL
and (1) .... Peter Singer, author of *Animal Liberation,* believes	ETHIC
that those who support animal (2) .... are guilty of 'speciesism'.	EXPERIMENT
He writes that, while 'sexists violate the principle of (3)	EQUAL
by favouring the interests of their own sex, speciesists allow	
the interests of their own species to override the greater	
interests of other species.'	
Animal Aid, which has a growing (4) .... amongst the	MEMBER
young, also argues that animal research is 'bad science'. Its	
International Charter for Health and Humane Research dismisses	
it as an '(5) .... means of studying, treating and curing human	RELY
illness'. Animal Aid's (6) .... Mark Gold thinks high-tech	DIRECT
experiments carried out on animals divert attention, resources	
and funding from 'more reliable sources of (7) .... based on the	INFORM
study of humans'. He argues that 'the dramatic (8) .... in life	IMPROVE
(9) .... experienced by many countries in the past 100 years or	EXPECT
so is (10) .... due to improvements in nutrition, living and	MAIN
working conditions, hygiene and sanitation', not 'heroic'	
high-tech research.	

S T R A T E G I E S

1 Read the text quickly for a general understanding.

2 Try to work out which part of speech is needed in each case.

3 Working with a partner, supply the correct form of each word in the text.

▶ Go to the Review page to record your performance.

Writing skill: an article for a magazine

1 You have received the following letter from your
   friend in Britain.

*and last week at school we had a really interesting discussion
about the way humans treat animals. Some students were arguing
against zoos, saying animals shouldn't be kept locked up. Lots of
people didn't agree with circuses either, with some people saying
it's wrong to make animals perform just for our pleasure. A
friend of mine even argued that it was wrong to keep pets!*

*Anyway, there's a reason for telling you all about this. Do you
remember promising me ages ago that you'd write an article for our
school magazine? Well, you'd do me a BIG favour if you wrote one
on this topic. It only needs to be about 200 words long.*

*I think it'd be really interesting to collect as many views on the
subject as possible, so if you're not too busy, I'd really appreciate it.*

I'd better go now. Write back soon.

Take care,

David

2 Work in small groups to make a list of animal issues to write about.

3 Using the plan below, write the article for your friend's magazine. Use
   some of the points that were raised in the Speaking activity on page 127.

- **Introduction to the topic**
  The way humans treat animals is a really controversial topic ..

- **Situation in your country**
  What happens here in ... is ...

- **Your own opinion**
  I think this is a good/bad thing for reasons I will explain.

- **Reasons for**
  One reason I think this is ...
  Another is that ...
  And let's not forget ...

- **The opposing view**
  Of course, there are those who will disagree with this view,
  and say that ...

- **Conclusion**
  Nevertheless, I still believe ...
  In my opinion ...

4 Exchange articles with your partner. Do you think their report is
   good enough for the school magazine?

PART THREE
Living a lie

Lead-in

1 The following extracts appeared in a magazine article about a woman called Michelle. What do you think the story is about?

'Are you a vegetarian, too then?'
A year later Jack and I married.
After three months I couldn't bear it any longer.
I hate myself for giving in, yet I'm powerless to stop.
Jack would leave me if he knew what I do.

2 Work in small groups and invent a story that contains all the sentences above. When you've finished, compare your story to those of other groups.

Reading technique: skimming

Skim read the text as quickly as you can (three minutes). How similar is the real story to your own?

Everyone thinks Michelle is a committed vegetarian. But every single day she's living a lie ...

The dinner was nearly ready when the bell rang. 'I'll get it,' my husband Jack yelled from the dining room. As he let his parents in, I couldn't help feeling pleased with myself. I'd produced yet another fabulous Sunday lunch: lentil soup, nut roast, and a dazzling array of vegetables and rice. So why did I keep wishing that among our veggie food, I'd included a big piece of beef or lamb?

Everyone I know thinks I'm a dedicated vegetarian. But secretly, I crave meat. I just can't resist it. It all started five years ago when I moved to London. I didn't know anybody, but after a few weeks I went with the girls in the office to a bar after work. There were lots of friendly young people there, all around my age, and I soon noticed a man smiling at me from across the bar. He was tall with lovely dark hair and sparkling green eyes.

'I'm Jack,' he introduced himself. 'I haven't seen you here before, have I?' As we chatted, Jack told me that he and his friends were animal rights activists. They'd go on protest marches, sabotage hunts and hand out anti-meat leaflets outside burger restaurants. His eyes shone as he talked about the dreadful cruelty to animals that went on and I was horrified by what he told me.

'You agree with us, don't you?' Jack asked. 'Oh yes!' I said eagerly. And I did – then. We ordered some food and I heard myself saying: 'I'll have a veggie burger.'

'Are you a vegetarian, too, then?' Jack asked, delighted.

'Of course!' I replied, as he threw his arms around me.

'Great!' he said. 'I couldn't bear to go out with anyone who eats meat!'

At first, giving up meat was easy. I was in love, so food took a back seat anyway. My life became filled with dates with Jack and protest meetings with the group.

Sometimes we'd be hanging around outside a burger bar handing out leaflets to passers-by, when I'd suddenly get the urge to go inside and order the biggest burger on the menu. I knew Jack and my new friends would be disgusted, so I kept the urge to myself.

A year later, Jack and I married. We had a vegetarian meal at the wedding reception and everyone loved the menu – even my parents, who eat meat. For the first year I was very happy. And I was thrilled when I became pregnant ... but then the food cravings started. They weren't the usual cravings like ice-cream and pickles. I wanted hamburger and chips. After three months I couldn't bear it any longer. One Saturday I told Jack I was driving into town to meet a friend. Instead I drove to the nearest burger bar.

'A burger and fries, please,' I said nervously, feeling like a criminal as I sat down in a corner to eat it. When I got home, I rushed to the bathroom and cleaned my teeth vigorously. Afterwards, my longing for meat was twice as bad, and when baby Jonathan was born the craving just got stronger.

I became hooked on my secret visits to burger bars. It was like having a love affair – with meat.

I eat meat about twice a week now – pretending I'm on a shopping trip or a visit to a friend. I hate myself for giving in, yet I'm powerless to stop. Jonathan has been weaned onto a vegetarian diet and, at the age of two, he's a beautiful little boy. But I feel guilty about denying him meat when I love it so much myself. I feel like a hypocrite, but I'm trapped. Jack would leave me if he knew what I do.

Yesterday, Jack took Jonathan on his first protest march. I said I couldn't go because I felt ill, but I'd never felt better – I was 20 miles away in a burger bar.

(Bella)

EXAM FOCUS
(Reading, Part 2) multiple choice

For questions 1–6, choose the answer (A, B, C or D) which you think fits best according to the text.

1 Michelle was pleased with herself when Jack's parents arrived because

 A she knew Jack's parents were vegetarians.
 B she hadn't cooked meat for Sunday lunch.
 C she is good at cooking vegetarian food.
 D she enjoys eating vegetarian food.

2 Michelle pretended she was a vegetarian

 A because some of the girls in her office were.
 B so she could go to protest meetings with Jack.
 C as soon as she moved to London.
 D because she was concerned about animal cruelty.

3 The expression 'food took a back seat' means that food became

 A less important to Michelle.
 B something she enjoyed with Jack.
 C easy to give up.
 D a priority.

4 The first time she ate meat again was

 A six months after she married Jack.
 B during her pregnancy.
 C when she went to meet a friend.
 D after the birth of her baby.

5 Michelle eats meat now

 A when she goes shopping.
 B when she visits a friend.
 C when she is away from Jack.
 D while she is having a love affair.

6 What's the best title for the text?

 A Living without meat
 B My forbidden love
 C A strict vegetarian
 D Animal cruelty

STRATEGIES

1 For the first five questions here you need to find the appropriate section of the text, and read it very closely. (Don't be afraid to read it two or three times before you choose your answer.)

2 For question 6, you need to have an overall understanding of the text.

3 When you have finished, check your answers with a partner.

▶ **Go to the Review page to record your performance.**

Speaking skill: sharing opinions

1 What would you do in Michelle's situation?

2 Around one in six people in Britain don't eat meat or fish. Is vegetarianism as popular in your country? If you are a meat-eater is there anything that could lead you to give it up?

3 Which of the following would you be able to do for the one you love?

● miss an important sporting event or concert
● give up your last sweet
● miss your last bus home so you can spend a few more minutes together
● cheat on your best friend
● give up your warm jacket on a cold winter's day
● give up meat

See **Language awareness: expressing quantity**

LANGUAGE AWARENESS
time conjunctions

1 🎧 Listen to the following joke and then match the first part of each sentence (a–h) with the correct second part (1–8).

a   When the teams walked onto the pitch
b   The referee didn't start the game
c   The insects felt very depressed
d   When the second half started
e   After the centipede had spent two hours getting ready
f   The insects had played badly
g   The centipede had scored 16 goals
h   While the insects were celebrating

1   until the centipede came on.
2   the centipede played.
3   the two captains spoke.
4   until the teams had warmed up.
5   it went out to play.
6   the crowd started to cheer.
7   during the half time break.
8   when the referee blew the final whistle.

2 In pairs discuss the following questions:

a   What's the difference between 'during' and 'while'?

b   Is it possible to use past simple instead of past perfect or past perfect instead of past simple without changing the meaning of the sentences above?

c   Can any of the following connectors be used in the sentences above without changing the meaning?

before   once   as soon as   by the time   as

3 Most, but not all, of the following sentences contain mistakes. Correct all those that you find.

a   When they will arrive I'll start the dinner.
b   I'll pay you back once I get paid.
c   Hurry up! By the time we will get there it will have closed.
d   You're not going out until you will have tidied your room.
e   I'll give you the newspaper once I'll have finished reading it.
f   I just check the doors before I will go to bed.

4 Read the following extract from a letter, using any of the time connectors below in each space a–k. Several of them can be used in more than one position. Put the verb in brackets into the correct form.

during	after	by the time	until	after
when	while	as	before	once	as soon as

Anyway, the exams are over and it's great to be on holiday!

College finished last month. (a) _____ I _____ (have) a few days' rest I decided to go to the coast for a week – it's only about half an hour from here. I arrived at the hotel early in the morning and (b) _____ I _____ (unpack) I went straight to the beach and had a swim. It was great. In fact the whole holiday was fantastic.

(c) _____ the day I went to the beach or just walked around town. I even met a fella! One day, (d) _____ I _____ (sit) in a café having lunch, this good-looking bloke came over and sat at my table. We got into conversation and ended up talking for ages. (e) _____ I _____ (get up) to leave he asked me for a date! Of course I said yes! I had to go home later that day and (f) _____ I _____ (walk) through the door the phone rang – it was him! Anyway, to cut a long story short, we've seen each other three times already. (g) _____ you _____ (visit) me next I'll introduce you.

What else? Oh yeah, (h) _____ you _____ (receive) this I'll have started my summer job as a waitress. It's good money – the only problem is I won't get paid (i) _____ I _____ (work) there for a month. Still, (j) _____ I _____ (get) the money I'm going to spend it on some nice clothes. (k) _____ I _____ (forget), I'll give you the name of the restaurant – maybe you can come over one evening and I can serve you dinner!

5 Make a list of all the things you did from the moment you woke up this morning to the time you left your house. Then join those ideas together in a paragraph using as many of the connectors in activity 4 as you can.

LANGUAGE AWARENESS
expressing quantity

1 Look at these words which appeared in the magazine article on page 131. Which of the words are countable (can be preceded by a number) and which ones are uncountable?

nut rice beef lentil lamb vegetable

2 In pairs, decide if the following words can be used with countable nouns (C), uncountable nouns (U) or both (B). Refer to the Grammar Reference section to clear up any disagreements.

many ( )   much ( )   (a) few ( )
(a) little ( )   each ( )   every ( )

both ( )   a lot of ( )   lots of ( )
plenty of ( )   enough ( )   several ( )

none of ( )   some ( )   any ( )
no ( )   either ( )   neither ( )

3 Turn to page 152 and study the street scene for one minute. Then turn to page 153 and study a similar scene. There are several differences between the two scenes. Describe the differences using the words above.

4 Match a countable noun from column A with an uncountable noun from column B. Then complete the following sentences with one of the words.

A	B
information	journey
luggage	table
work	word
traffic	suggestion
time	suitcase
money	job
advice	minute
vocabulary	car
research	dollar
furniture	experiment
travel	fact

a So, you want some ideas to give up drinking? Well, I've got a few _____ .
b There are few _____ on the road better than a Mercedes.
c We've got a little _____ before we leave. Let's have a coffee.
d Little _____ has been carried out on the effects of the new drug .
e I'm not taking much _____ on holiday. I don't want to have to carry too much.
f Reading English newspapers is hard. There are so many difficult _____ .
g I had several _____ before I finally became a teacher.
h Almost every _____ in the news report was wrong.

5 Look again at sentences a–d. What's the difference between 'a few' and 'few', 'a little' and 'little'?

6 How good is your memory? Listen to the tape and decide if the statements about the creatures on page 124 are true (T) or false (F).

a( ) b( ) c( ) d( ) e( ) f( ) g( )
h( ) i( )

7 Listen again or turn to the tapescript. Answer the questions below about the words in the box. For more detailed information see the Grammar Reference.

both	every	each	all	none
no	neither	either		

a Which words take a singular/plural noun?
b Which words refer to *two* people or things?
c Which words refer to *two or more* people or things?
d Which words refer to *three or more* people or things?
e Which words can/must be followed by 'of'?

8 Look again at the sentences you wrote in activity 3. Are there any that you want to correct?

Your review of Unit 11

Vocabulary

Your selection:

Suggestion: The theme of the final section in this unit was vegetarianism. Make two lists of food (one for vegetarians and one for meat-eaters).

Exam skills

Complete the summaries by underlining the appropriate answer:

Use of English, Part 5, word formation
Go back to page 87.

Score _____ /10
What I need to improve ...

Reading, Part 2, multiple choice
• You have to choose the correct answer from a choice of a) three b) four.
• You have to a) read the text closely b) skim read the text.

Score _____ /6
What I need to improve ...

General

Skills and Abilities

PART ONE
The kiss that can save a life

Lead-in

1 There are twenty words that describe parts of the body hidden in
   the word square. How many can you find? The words go across,
   down and diagonally.

e	y	e	l	a	s	h	s	h	e	e	l
y	n	l	f	p	n	q	r	i	t	u	t
e	k	b	n	o	t	k	b	p	a	y	o
b	n	o	r	o	r	n	l	s	v	e	e
r	e	w	p	r	s	e	o	e	j	a	w
o	e	t	m	t	t	a	n	t	j	i	
w	l	l	s	c	h	n	r	r	s	b	r
t	a	i	c	h	i	n	c	i	m	h	k
p	r	d	z	e	g	b	l	u	l	e	l
w	x	s	y	e	h	k	h	b	t	g	i
b	n	e	c	k	j	t	f	v	u	g	p
c	a	l	f	f	g	s	h	i	n	k	s

2 Organise the words you found into the following categories:

   a head and shoulders   b arms and hands   c legs and feet

3 Can you add any more words to each category?

4 Which of the parts you have listed can be:

   sprained   twisted   fractured   swollen
   grazed   bruised   pulled

5 Which of these injuries have you suffered? Who's the most
   accident-prone person in your group?

Reading technique: global understanding and specific information

 1 The questionnaire below will show you how well you could cope in a medical emergency. Match each question with the appropriate set of answers (for example, 1=F, etc.) You should try to do this in no more than three minutes.

Can you cope in a crisis?

Could you cope with a medical emergency? Test your knowledge with these simple questions from St John Ambulance.

1 **An open top car crashes and catches fire in front of you. It rolls over, throwing out three occupants. Who would you go to first?**

2 **Two pedestrians walk into each other. One suffers a bad nose bleed. What do you do?**

3 **You are eating a picnic when all of a sudden your friend screams. There was a wasp in her sandwich and she has been stung in the back of the mouth. What do you do?**

4 **A workman drills through an electric cable and is electrocuted. Which is the first thing to consider?**

5 **Your friend cuts her arm. You bandage it. Her skin becomes pale and blue-grey in colour. It feels cold and she complains that her hand is numb and tingling. What has happened?**

6 **A colleague bangs his head on a door and is knocked out for five minutes. What advice would you give?**

7 **A young child swallows a bottle of weed-killer. What do you do?**

A
a Tilt the head backward and pinch the soft part of the nose.
b Tilt the head backward and pinch the bony part of the nose.
c Lean him/her forward and pinch the soft part below the nose.
d Lean him/her forward and pinch the bony part of the nose.

B
a Put an ice pack round her throat, go to a cool place and leave her alone to rest.
b Get her an ice cube to suck or keep rinsing her mouth with cold liquid, checking for swelling or breathing difficulties, and go for immediate medical aid.
c Get her to lie down with her feet above her head, check pulse and if it speeds up, give aspirin and salt in warm water.
d Rub the infected part with a cut onion until the pain subsides.

C
a Severity of shock.
b Extent and depth of burns.
c Risk of the heart having stopped.
d Possibility of internal injury.

D
a Tickle the throat to encourage the child to be sick.
b Give water or milk to drink.
c Send him/her to hospital.
d Walk him/her around to keep awake.
e Give strong coffee to drink.

E
a To rest for one hour before returning to work, providing no ill effects are felt.
b Go home and rest provided they have no headache.
c Make an appointment to see the doctor.
d Drink strong coffee to stay awake.
e Be taken to hospital at once.

F
a A man lying still on his back.
b A woman lying still on the floor on her side.
c A child calling for help to stop blood dripping from her arm.

G
a There is an object inside the the wound.
b Nerves have been cut through.
c There may be a fracture underneath.
d Circulation of blood has been cut off.

(Guardian)

2 Can you find the correct answer to each question? Share your ideas in groups. If there are differences of opinion, try to argue your viewpoint. Finally, see who's correct by checking the answers on page 153.

🔈 Listening technique: global understanding

The words or phrases below are mentioned in the following reports of how two lives were saved by family members. Listen and put them in the correct section. Make a note of other key words from each report.

bath   garden   living room   bike

Jamie and Tim   Ken and Stephen

🔈 Listening technique: specific information

1 Listen to the interview again to get a better understanding of the context in which the above words were used.

2 Write five facts from the reports that you are completely confident are correct. When you're ready work in teams. The members of each team should compare facts and devise eight questions to test the other team. Your teacher will give you the rules for scoring.

Writing skill: a magazine article

1 You have decided to write an article for your school/work newsletter to campaign for a first aid training course.

2 Start your article by describing an emergency and asking the reader what they would do.

3 In the second paragraph spend a little more time explaining why doing such a course would be so useful.

4 In the final section encourage your colleagues to put pressure on the institution to run a course. Make reference to the information in this leaflet opposite.

5 When you have finished, compare your essay with the one on page 164. Whose is the most persuasive?

'The Breath of Life'

St John Ambulance is launching a campaign, 'The Breath of Life'. Free two hour courses will be available from November 1 to May 30. St John also runs longer courses. For details contact your nearest branch.

PART TWO
Human achievement

Lead-in

1 Look at the list of achievements below. Do you know the name of
the person responsible for each one?

  a The first person to walk on the moon.
  b The discovery of penicillin.
  c Splitting the atom.
  d The fastest 100 metres runner.
  e The pioneering heart transplant surgeon.
  f The first manned flight.

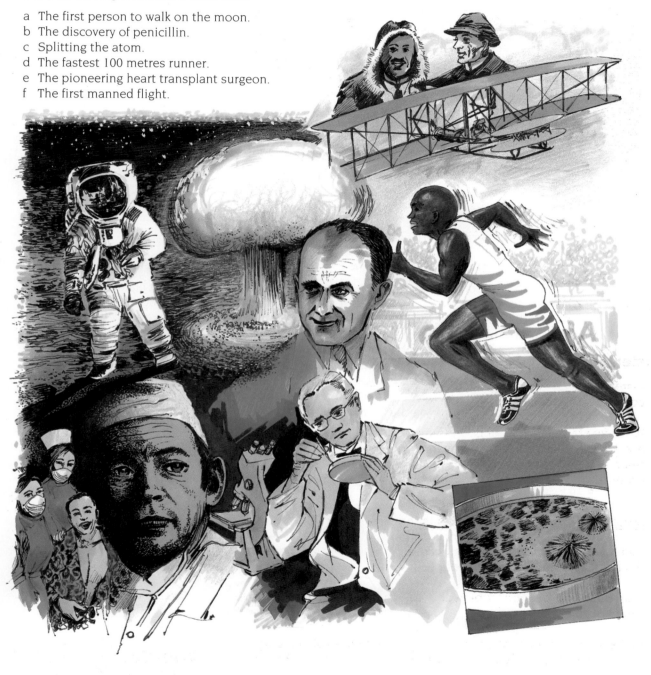

2 If you were asked to rank them in terms of what you consider to be
the greatest achievements, which would be your top three? Share
your ideas in a group. Would you add any others to the list?

EXAM FOCUS (Reading, Part 4) multiple matching

You are going to read some information about world records. For questions 1–15, choose from the extracts (A-G). Some of the records may be chosen more than once. When more than one answer is required, these may be given in any order. There is an example at the beginning (0).

Which record has been held the longest?

Which descriptions explain the type of skills required?

Which record holders have previously held records?

Which records were achieved in a single day?

Which records are held by people from more than one country?

Which single record is held by more than one person?

Which records are the most difficult to measure?

Which record led to someone else suffering?

Which description tells the reader how to do the activity?

0	G	
1		
2	3	
4	5	6
7	8	9
10		
11	12	
13		
14		

Record A: The most travelled couple are Dr Robert and Carmen Becker of New York, USA, both of whom have visited all 192 sovereign countries and all but 10 of the 65 non-sovereign or other territories. They met in her home town in France during World War II, when he was serving in the US army. He went on to Germany, and when the war ended he came back to marry her. Bob and Carmen have been running around together ever since.

Record B: Being able to run the 110 metre hurdles in 18.9 seconds is not bad for the average person although of course slow for top athletes. Doing so whilst juggling three balls, however, is something very different, and it is in fact the current world record. The record holder is Michael Hout of Ohio, USA, and he achieved his time, beating his own record of 20.0 seconds, on 24 June 1993.

Record C: The best recent claims for miniature writing come from India and China. Surendra Apharya of Jaipur, India wrote 1,749 characters (names of various countries, towns and regions) on a single grain of rice in May 1991. Xie Shui Lin of Jiangxi, China wrote 11,660 characters (speeches by Winston Churchill) within the size of a definitive postage stamp, measuring 19.69 x 17.82 mm. Finally, Pan Xixing of Wuxi, China wrote 395 characters, namely 'True friendship is like sound health, the value of which is seldom known until it be lost' on a human hair 2 cm long in April 1995.

Record D: Coin snatching is a skill which requires great patience, perfect balance, strength in an arm, fast hands and big hands! Build a stack of coins on your forearm near your elbow, bring your hands forward quickly and catch as many coins as you can in the same hand. Not easy, is it? Dean Gould of Felixstowe, England has caught 328 10p coins in this way, out of 482 placed on his forearm, setting his most recent record on 6 April 1993.

Record F: What constitutes a joke? How much does the audience need to laugh, if at all? Unfortunately, the more the audience laughs, the more difficult it is to tell jokes quickly - a comedian would not want to carry on if his audience cannot hear what he is saying. Working on the basis that a joke must have a beginning, a middle and an end, Felipe Carbonell of Lima, Peru told 345 jokes in one hour on 29 July 1993. Mike Hessman of Ohio, USA claimed 12,682 in 24 hours on 16–17 November 1992.

Record G: If being mean is measurable then Henrietta Howland Green (1835–1916), who kept a balance of over $31,400,000 in one bank alone, was the all-time world champion. Her son had to have his leg amputated because of her delays in finding a free medical clinic. She herself ate cold porridge because she was too thrifty to heat it. Her estate proved to be worth $95,000,000 (equivalent to almost $2 billion today).

Record E: The greatest number of storeys ever achieved in building a free-standing house of standard playing cards is 83, to a height of 4.88 m. It was built by Bryan Berg of Iowa, USA between 24 February and 3 March 1995. A lot of people who try to build a house of cards will be happy to manage two or three storeys. To the average person this is the extent of their ambition. But over the years record breaking attempts have required not only skill, a steady hand and patience, but also a head for heights.

S T R A T E G I E S

1 You should use a similar reading strategy here as you would if you were looking through a page of adverts for a particular item, or reading the TV page for a particular programme. Use the questions to guide your reading. Don't worry about reading and understanding every word.

2 Read the questions first, then skim read the article very quickly (three minutes) to get a general understanding of each record. If you read anything that connects with a question, for example any key words, mark where they appear for future reference.

▶ **Go to the Review page to record your performance.**

Vocabulary development: dependent prepositions and word formation

1 The following adjectives all refer to ability, but which preposition follows each one: 'at', 'of' or 'in'? (Some may take more than one.) Write the answers in the first column of the table opposite.

Adjective	Opposite	Noun
skilled _at/in_	unskilled	skill
talented _____		
gifted _____		
experienced _____		
trained _____		
capable _____		
competent _____		
accomplished _____		
qualified _____		

e 2 How do you form the opposite of the adjectives: with the prefix 'un' or 'in'? Can you also supply the equivalent noun?

3 Supply the correct words to complete the passage below. Two of the words from the table are not used and two are used twice.

I was sacked from my first job because the boss said I was (a) _____ of doing the simplest jobs. I wasn't very interested in the job and never really concentrated on what I was doing and kept making mistakes, which probably gave the impression that I was quite (b) _____ . Whenever anybody asked me why I'd lost the job I said I'd only been working in the industry for a few months and so was rather (c) _____ .

I'd lived in Paris with my parents for six months when I was younger and realised then that I had a (d) _____ for learning languages so I decided to get a (e) _____ in French. When I'd finished I got a job as an interpreter. I had to be (f) _____ in the various aspects of interpreting during my first year. Amongst other things, I learnt the basic (g) _____ needed when representing people from different cultures. Having completed the company (h) _____ programme, I've now (i) _____ in translating.

Speaking skill: asking questions

1 Everybody in the class should write down the name of a job or profession on a small piece of paper. Stick the piece of paper on somebody else's forehead without them seeing what you've written.

2 The object of the game is to guess your profession by asking yes/no questions to the rest of the class. For example, 'Does my job require a lot of skill?' 'Do I need qualifications?' 'Do I work with my hands?' You can continue asking questions until your question receives a 'no' response. It's then the next person's turn. If the class think your question is grammatically incorrect they can refuse to answer it. The first person to guess their profession is the winner.

See **Language awareness: ability**

PART THREE
Taking exams

Lead-in

1 Now you've come to the end of this course you should be well aware of what the FCE exam requires of you. How well do you and your colleagues know the format of the five papers? Work in teams. Each group should think of at least six questions to test other members of the class.

2 How well do you think you are going to do in the exam? Which of the papers is your most/least favourite?

Listening technique: understanding feelings or opinions

You are going to hear five different people who have all recently taken the FCE exam. For questions 1–5, choose from the list A–F. You only need to use each letter once and there is one extra letter.

Which speaker:

A didn't time themselves very well?   Speaker 1 ☐

B did lots of preparation before the exam?   Speaker 2 ☐

C used the questions to choose the best strategy? Speaker 3 ☐

D complained a little about another student? Speaker 4 ☐

E left the exam early?   Speaker 5 ☐

F was careful to fill in the answer sheet properly?

Use of English: open cloze

1 Read the following extract from a brochure giving advice on how to pass exams. Think of the word that best fits each space. By now you should be quite familiar with this exercise and know what kind of words are omitted. Work with a partner and share your ideas.

When the day comes give yourself plenty of time (a) _____ do everything: have breakfast (don't drink (b) _____ much, anxiety does funny things to you); go to the toilet; arrive on time, but not too early. Try not to talk about the exam before you go in.

   In the exam, settle yourself down carefully and lay out equipment. Read (c) _____ exam questions carefully and underline (d) _____ of the key instruction words that indicate (e) _____ the question should (f) _____ answered. If possible, start with the ones you (g) _____ do easily to give you confidence. Remember what you've learnt from practising questions and plan your use of time. Don't panic (h) _____ everyone around you seems to start writing furiously straight away and don't be tempted to follow (i) _____ example.

   Finally, after the exam, don't join in a discussion about (j) _____ everyone else did, (k) _____ you want to frighten yourself, and drain (l) _____ self-confidence for the next exam. (m) _____ of all, remember (n) _____ exams are not designed to catch you out, (o) _____ to find out what you know, what you understand and what you can do.

2 Which pieces of advice are you likely to take and which might you ignore?

EXAM FOCUS
(Speaking, Parts 3 and 4): exchanging information, exchanging and justifying opinions

Imagine that your school is holding the FCE listening paper. There are 30 candidates. Look at the diagram and decide where the exam should take place.

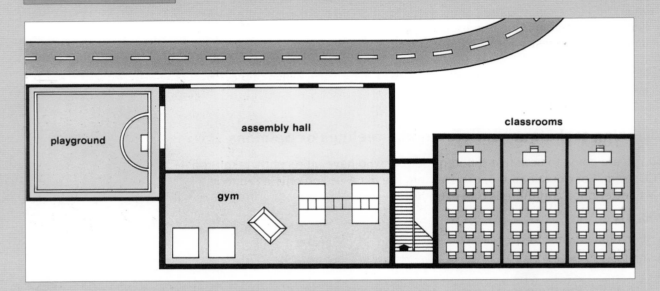

How do you usually feel before an exam?
Have you got any set procedures you follow before, during and after exams?
Which of the five FCE papers do you think is the most stressful? Why?
Does this stress affect your performance in the exam? How?
Are exams an important measure of academic success in your country?
Do you think exams are the best way of measuring ability?

S T R A T E G I E S

1 During Part 3 of the interview you will be assessed on:

   ● the range and accuracy of grammar and vocabulary used
   ● pronunciation
   ● fluency
   ● interaction with your partner

2 Before you begin discussing, look at the plan and work out the advantages and disadvantages of each room.

3 Remember it is not necessary to agree with your partner as long as you interact by taking turns, making suggestions, etc.

4 Now work in groups of four. Take it in turns to play the role of the examiner, the assessor (the person who assesses the candidates) and the two interviewees. The examiner should use the questions above to conduct Part 4 of the interview. When you've finished, swap roles.

▶ **Go to the Review page to record your performance.**

LANGUAGE AWARENESS
ability

1 Find out the following information from your partner:

  a How many languages can you speak?
  b Do you think you'll be able to understand this grammar point?
  c Have you been able to sleep OK recently?
  d Do you think it's important to be able to speak a foreign language perfectly?
  e Could you do anything when you were younger that you can't do now?

2 In which of the sentences above could you substitute 'can'/ 'could' with 'be able to' and vice versa? Can you explain why? Refer to the Grammar Reference on page 173 to confirm your ideas.

3 In one of the three sentences below 'could' cannot be used. Can you explain why? Which two sentences refer to the ability to do something on a particular occasion? What's the difference between them? Check the Grammar Reference on page 173 to confirm your ideas.

  a I couldn't/wasn't able to contact Sarah last night.
  b When the ship sank the survivors were able to swim to safety.
  c When I was younger I could/was able to swim quite well.

4 Which two sentences could be rewritten using 'manage to' and 'succeed in'?

5 Complete the following statements using the correct form of either 'be able to', 'can/could', 'manage to' or 'succeed in'. There may be more than one answer.

  a Did you .... find that square thing with the hole in it?
  b I've never .... putting them back together properly.
  c The owner brought it in because he .... get the radio to work.
  d I don't think I'll .... have this finished today.
  e I .... fix cars easily before they became so technical.

  f I thought I'd .... do it on my own.
  g I .... find the bit that makes the wheels go round.
  h I .... put my bike back together really easily last week.

6 Complete the second sentence so that it has the same meaning as the first. Use the word given and do not change its form.

  a Is there any chance that you can visit me next week?
     Will
     .... visit me next week?

  b Did you manage to understand the grammar point yesterday?
     able
     .... the grammar point yesterday?

  c I've always found modal verbs impossible.
     able
     I've .... to understand modal verbs.

  d I did that job you asked me to do.
     managed
     I .... you asked me to do.

  e The rescue team succeeded in rescuing the mountaineers.
     save
     The rescue team .... the mountaineers.

  f The window was open, so the burglar probably managed to get in there.
     able
     The window was open so the burglar must .... get in there.

LANGUAGE AWARENESS
grammar check

1 Read the following letter written by an English student. There are 40 mistakes. Work on your own. How many can you find?

2 Now share your ideas with a partner. How many can you find between you?

3 Make a note of all the mistakes you missed and, when you have time, look back at the relevant Language awareness sections.

Rua do San Miguel
Lisboa

Dear Nicole

How are you? I apologise for write so late. It's because I was very busy since I returned to Portugal. I'm still work at the same company, but now the work is more harder. I must to work from 6 in the morning until late at night. But guess what? My boss, who is really nice woman, she has offered me promotion to a new job last week. If I accept the new job I might be ask to travel abroad! I'd be able to visit you, hadn't I?

Because I work so hard at the moment I'm not studying so hard as I should. I'm not used to work full-time and study English. The FCE exam will take place in a few weeks. My teacher said me I should spend time to work on my essays. Often she tells us to do more work! I must to be crazy because when I will finish FCE, I'm going to start study for CAE. You've heard of it, have you? By this summer I'll have studied English for five years! Perhaps one day I could speak the English perfectly!

I'll go on holiday with my parents after the exam. If I would have the chance, I would stay at home. They go always to the same place! There's a little to do and there aren't much young people. I asked them if I could stay here but I didn't need to. I was already knowing the answer! So, this time next month I'll sit on the beach with my mum and dad. If you knew a good book that I can take it to read, can you tell me?

Anyway, the reason for I'm writing is to ask you if you want to come and visit me in Portugal. By the time I get back from the holiday I'll finish my exams and I wondered if you would like having a holiday here. I know you hadn't been to Portugal before and I could take you to sightsee. I promise the weather will be more nice than in England!

All the best

Teresa

Your review of Unit 12

Vocabulary

Your selection:

Suggestion: You've reached the end of the book. Well done! Are you pleased with the way you have recorded your vocabulary? Discuss with your teacher which of the suggestions have been most useful to you.

Exam skills

Complete the summaries by underlining the appropriate answer:

Reading, Part 4, multiple matching
Go back to page 39.

Score ____ /15
Have I improved?

Speaking, Part 4, exchanging and justifying opinions
• You are assessed a) individually b) on how you interact with your partner.

What I need to improve ...

General

Key

Unit 2

Reading technique: specific information (page 17)

1 Student A: read the following text and make notes on some of the following points.

- English used in advertising
- Everyday English
- English words with non-English spelling
- English words with different uses

Unless you heard them spoken, you might not instantly recognise *ajskrym, muving pikceris*, and *peda* as the Polish for ice-cream, the Lithuanian for moving pictures, and the Serbo-Croatian for payday. The Japanese are particular masters at the art of taking a foreign word and playing with it until it sounds something like a native product. Thus the *sumato* (smart) and *nyuu ritchi* (newly rich) Japanese person improves his or her conversation with *apputodeito* (up to date) expressions like *gurama foto* (glamour photo), *haikurasu* (high class) and *rushawa* (rush hour). *Sebiro*, for a suit of clothes, looks convincingly Japanese until you realise that it has been based on Savile Row, the London Street where the finest suits are made.

European languages also show a curious tendency to take English participles and give them entirely new meanings, so the French don't go running or jogging, they go *footing*. They don't take part in a spot of sun-bathing, but rather go in for *le bronzing*. A dinner jacket in French becomes *un smoking*, while in Italy cosmetic surgery becomes *il lifting*. A young person in Germany goes from being in his teens to being in his *twens*, a book that doesn't quite become a best-seller is instead *ein steadyseller*, and a person who is more relaxed than another is *relaxter*.

Sometimes new words are made up, as with the Japanese *salaryman* for an employee of a corporation. In Germany a fashionable dresser is a *dressman*. In France a *recordman* is not a disc jockey, but an athlete who sets a record, while an *alloman* is a switchboard operator (because he says, 'allo? allo?').

(Bill Bryson: *Mother Tongue*)

2 Now share your information with Student B.

Unit 4

Exam focus: (Speaking, Part 2) comparing two photographs (page 48)

a

b

c

d

Unit 5

Speaking skill: a panel discussion (page 54)

Headteacher (and chairperson)

You have received a gift of £100,000 to spend on school equipment. You would like to use the money to replace your existing computers. You are in favour of this because:

- your computers are old and cannot use the new software that is available, such as multimedia. (All the other schools in the area have invested in new technology and it is important that your school is not left behind.)
- using computers is good for motivating weak pupils.
- everybody needs to use a computer in today's technological world.

However, not everyone shares your view, so you will have to try to convince them.

Concerned parent

Your daughter's school has received a gift of £100,000. Her headteacher wants to use the money to buy 100 new computers. You are against the idea because:

- if your daughter uses the latest computers at school she'll want you to buy her one at home
- you have noticed that your daughter's handwriting and spelling has got much worse since she has started using a computer at school. What is she going to do in the exams if her handwriting is unreadable?
- you are worried that her eyesight is suffering as a consequence of looking at a computer screen for long periods.

You would prefer to see the money spent on new books for the school library.

Pupil

You are a pupil at a school that has recently received a gift of £100,000. Your headteacher wants to use the money to buy 100 new computers. You think this is an excellent idea because:

- you can get more up-to-date information from the Internet than from library books, which are usually old and become out of date quickly.
- you believe that computers are just a tool to help people. The people who are against them don't understand how they are used or are afraid of them.
- your school has a good pass rate in exams, so how can standards be falling, as some people claim?

You should support the headteacher's views.

Games teacher

Your school has received a gift of £100,000. Your headteacher thinks that the money should be spent on buying 100 new computers. You strongly disagree because:

- you believe that schoolchildren are becoming 'couch potatoes' (i.e. lazy and unfit) because they spend too much time working at computers.
- using computers encourages children to work in isolation and not in teams. As a sports teacher you believe that team work and co-operation are important skills.
- the more computers are used for work, the more they will be used in leisure. Look at the increase in computer games, for example.

You would like to see the money spent on new sports equipment.

Unit 5

Lead-in (page 55)

Unit 6

Reading technique: specific information (page 65)

STUDENT B:
This is part of an article giving advice on finding your perfect soul mate by using star signs. Scan the article and make notes under the following headings:

● Your Sign
● Your Partner's Sign

Aries: *March 21–April 20*
Sagittarians are ideal since they are flexible, good-natured and extremely cheerful. Another Aries can be quite competitive. Leos can be very passionate but can also become sulky when your frank nature upsets them. Geminis are wonderful mates since they share your need for excitement. Aquarius is almost as good, although they can be a little stubborn. Your worst nightmare is Scorpio, whose incredible need for passion damps your flame almost entirely.

Libra: *September 24–October 22*
As you are sociable, refined and very charming, you adore Capricorn, Leo, Cancer and Taurus, though the last two can be too possessive. Gemini and Aquarius are sometimes too embarrassingly outspoken or unconventional, although you will never run out of things to talk about with them. Aries adores your unselfish personality, but you find it very difficult to accept their overpowering approach to life and love.

Sagittarius: *November 23–December 22*
Sunny, sociable and rather cheerful, you are willing to try anything except passion. You hate being trapped. Aquarius, who is witty and adventurous, is your all-time favourite. Geminis are good, too, although they can make you a little nervous. Cancer, Taurus and Scorpio are not a good match as they will want to tie you down.

Virgo: *August 24–September 23*
Being a flexible sign, you are almost spoiled for choice. You tend to be a little restless, but Taurus will make you sit still once in a while. Both you and Capricorn often work far too hard. Pisces is often a favourite as they are charming, sensitive and rather artistic. Aquarius is a cool combination as their independence matches yours. Cancer can be too possessive. Two Virgos together would criticise each other to death.

Scorpio: *October 23–November 22*
Other Scorpios are your all-time favourites as both of you are very passionate. Cancer can be emotional and Pisces spend rather too much time daydreaming for your liking. Geminis, like you, are very adventurous and therefore make a good partner. Virgos are sometimes all right, but you and Taurus tend to be rather sulky. Capricorn is more attached to work than romance, which might turn you off.

Capricorn: *December 23–January 20*
Your ambitious nature often gets in the way of romantic happiness in early adulthood. Virgos can be quite flexible though they can also be rather too fussy. You often work well with Cancer, although you might have problems being together all the time. Libra and Leo share your love of the grand life. Pisces is a favourite quiet match. Aquarians are very rebellious and will therefore cause you problems.

(*Daily Express*)

Speaking skill: sharing opinions (page 67)

Discover your score by adding up the numbers of A's and B's you have ticked.

Seven or more B's:
Despite a big win you are likely to remain well-adjusted, secure and generally happy with the experience. Money will help buy you happiness, but in an unexpected way. It won't be the big house, fast car or foreign holiday which will change your life in a positive way, but the money will allow small, simple changes which bring much pleasure, like the ability to spend a little less time working and more time with loved ones.

Between five and seven B's:
Your generosity following a big win will bring you problems. Your expensive new car parked outside your old home may provoke jealousy from previously friendly neighbours, while expensive trips are problematic because your friends can't afford to accompany you to the exotic locations you now want to see – meaning holidays can now be more lonely affairs. On the other hand, your offer to pay for others to accompany you will create problems over who you choose and who you leave out. The main stress of a big win for you will be making sure your handling of the money does not create bad feelings from friends and relatives.

Between three and five B's:
You'll find you have problems working out who your real friends are following your win. Many you haven't heard from in years suddenly appear on the scene, while even dealing with those who were your genuine companions is not straightforward. When they are being kind or complimentary, can you ever be sure what is actually motivating their kindness? The stress of resisting emotional blackmail and manipulation from those around you will sharply reduce the pleasure of your big win.

Fewer than three B's:
While stopping work as you intend to may be initially appealing, the way work structures the day gives you purpose and provides a social network where you meet and make friends with similar people. These are all things you'll miss after many months of moping around your big new isolated house, and after you have become bored with the Ferrari. The largest part of your fortune could well be spent on lawyers' fees, protecting yourself from begging relatives, or on security devices, guards, the tennis coach and the therapist.

(*Daily Mail*)

Lead-in (page 70)

Unit 9

Reading technique: comprehension (page 101)

Conclusion 1
Two's a crowd. You're self-sufficient, hard-working and can easily motivate yourself. It's not that you don't like the company of others, but you don't need it to achieve your goals and often find other people's assistance more of a hindrance than a help. You might find things a bit easier, however, if you lighten the load on yourself by learning to trust other people more.

Conclusion 2
It takes two. You like to work in small teams with one or two other people in all the things you do, whether it's homework or going out at night. You tend to be quite protective of your small group. A small team means that your talents are more appreciated and you like to be acknowledged by others. Your team works well, but you could do even better by trusting people outside your group.

Conclusion 3
All together now. You are the definition of a team player. You like to be around other people and take all their abilities into account when you do things. You're very sociable, and take the wider consequences of your actions into account because you think about how they will affect everyone, not just yourself. Being in a big group brings out the best in some of those around you, but make sure others don't take advantage of your good nature.

Unit 11

Language awareness: expressing quantity (page 134)

Picture 1

Picture 2

Unit 12

Reading technique: specific information (page 137)

1F – a. The man lying still on his back: his airway may be obstructed.

2A – c. Leaning the casualty forward will prevent him from swallowing blood. The soft part of the nose, just below the bone, is the only place which will have the desired effect: stopping the blood flow.

3B – b.

4C – c. Death may follow very quickly without appropriate first aid.

5G – d. The bandage is too tight.

6E – e. Head injuries can have delayed effects. Victims should always be examined by a doctor.

7D – c. And do it very quickly.

Grammar Reference

Unit 5: Future (1)

3 The speaker has already ordered the salad.

Unit 5: Present perfect simple and continuous

1 They would be terminally ill.

Use of English Revision

Unit 2, Part 1, open cloze

For questions 1–15, read the text below and think of the word which best fits each space. Use only one word in each space. There is an example at the beginning (0).

Example: 0 by

Improving Your English
Do you realise that you can practise your English simply (0) ...... doing things you enjoy? Your cinema or local television service probably sometimes shows films (1) ...... English. Watch them if you can. Perhaps you can talk to friends in (2) ...... English club. If you can't find one in your area, you might start one. (3) ...... popular songs (4) ...... sung in English – if you can, find a singer (5) ...... words can be easily understood. If you often listen (6) ...... a song that you like you will pick up (7) ...... a bit of modern English in a very pleasant way. If you like writing letters (8) ...... will not be difficult for you to find a pen-friend to correspond (9) ...... in English; you could ask for (10) ...... through the pages (11) ...... an English magazine you enjoy or you could ask the British Council office in your country to suggest the address of a school you could write to. You can listen to the radio in English – (12) ...... to broadcasts of the BBC World Service or to those of The Voice of America. If you (13) ...... aerobics regularly, you could get a record (14) ...... cassette with instructions in English (15) ...... you to work to.

(English As A Foreign Language)

Unit 3, Part 2, multiple choice cloze

For questions 1–15, read the text below and decide which answer A, B, C or D best fits each space. There is an example at the beginning (0).

Example:
0   A opposite   (B) facing   C bordering   D fronting

Imagine this page was in a language you could not understand – yet you did not know until you had read this far. You would be (0) ...... a paradox. A paradox (1) ...... where a (2) ...... of statements interrelate with one (3) ...... in a way which means that they cannot all be true.

   However, one of the oldest paradoxes involves a single statement, (4) ...... by a philosopher, Eubulides, who lived in the 4th century BC. It involved a (5) ...... character, Epimenides, who came from Crete. Epimenides (6) ...... said: 'All Cretans are liars.' Assume that a liar is someone who always lies. Then (7) ...... the implication of what Epimenides was saying. He was a Cretan, remember. So in actual (8) ...... he was saying: 'I am a liar.' (9) ...... another way, he was saying: 'This sentence is false.' (10) ...... , is the sentence true or is it false?

   (11) ...... that 'This sentence is false' is true. In that case, the sentence is false, because it is a sentence which is true and that is what it says. (12) ...... the other (13) .... Assume that the sentence is false. But that (14) ...... that 'This sentence is false' is false – and that means it is true. Actually, it cannot be true or false. It is a simple, (15) ...... profound, paradox.

(Guardian)

1	A arrives	B presents	C occurs	D comes
2	A total	B quantity	C amount	D number
3	A another	B each	C both	D other
4	A arranged	B organised	C imagined	D devised
5	A false	B fictional	C imagined	D untrue
6	A plainly	B obviously	C simply	D clearly
7	A consider	B think	C debate	D inquire
8	A truth	B reality	C certainty	D fact
9	A Put	B Mentioned	C Made	D Spoken
10	A Certainly	B Well	C Really	D Factually
11	A Pretend	B Think	C Guess	D Suppose
12	A Try	B Achieve	C Undertake	D Do
13	A chance	B possibility	C condition	D ability
14	A spells	B expresses	C seems	D means
15	A yet	B however	C still	D while

Unit 4, Part 2, 'key' word transformations

For questions 1–10, complete the second sentence so that it has a similar meaning to the first sentence, using the given word. **Do not change the word given**. You must use between two and five words, including the word given. There is an example at the beginning (0).

0 Remembering these guidelines will ensure a happy stay.
follow
....If...you...follow..... these guidelines, you will be assured of a happy stay.

Host family accommodation – guidelines for students

1 The rent is currently £70.00 per week.
charged
You .... £70.00 per week for rent.

2 You should remember to pay your rent on time.
reminded
You shouldn't need .... to pay your rent on time.

3 For an absence of less than four days you must still pay full rent.
away
If you .... less than four days you must still pay full rent.

4 For longer absences you need only pay half the rent to keep the room.
have
For longer absences you .... pay half the rent to keep the room.

5 Tell your host family if you are having difficulties paying your rent.
difficult
Tell your host if you are .... pay your rent on time.

6 For breakfast you may be offered cereal or toast.
option
For breakfast you may .... cereal or toast.

7 During the week you will need to provide your own lunch.
not
During the week .... provided.

8 You should tell your host family if you are going to miss a meal.
needs
Your host family .... if you are going to miss a meal.

9 You must keep your room tidy.
obliged
You .... keep your room tidy.

10 Get permission if you want to have a guest to stay for the night.
put
Get permission if you want to .... for the night.

Unit 5, Part 1, error correction

For questions 1–15, read the text below and look carefully at each line. Some of the lines are correct, and some have a word which should not be there. If a line is correct put a tick (✓) by the number. If a line has a word which should not be there, write the word next to the line. There are two examples at the beginning.

Dear Sir or Madam

I am a student at a college which it has spent a lot of money	0	it
on computers and software. We now have three very large	00	✓
areas in the college in where the students spend hours every week	1	_____
sitting at computers rather than in traditional classrooms.	2	_____
Most of people would argue that this is progress and that we	3	_____
are lucky to have so much technology to work with it.	4	_____
However, I have noticed recently that not very little work is done	5	_____
by students in these rooms. Take the Internet, for example. The	6	_____
last time I used the computers, many students were using the	7	_____
Internet for to send messages to each other - in the same room!	8	_____
I have also noticed that we now have much less time in being	9	_____
taught by a teacher and much more time working on our own	10	_____
in the front of a screen.	11	_____
If they are used correctly, computers can be so extremely helpful.	12	_____
My writing has improved since I have started writing my essays on	13	_____
computers. I can to change the organisation or correct mistakes	14	_____
easily. But working alone on a computer all day is not education.	15	_____

Unit 5, Part 2, word formation

For questions 1–10, read the text below. Use the word given in capitals at the end of each line to form a word that fits in the space in the same line. There is an example at the beginning (0).

Example: 0 inventor

One person, the American (0) .... Thomas Midgely,	INVENT
created what are considered to be two of today's biggest	
(1) .... evils – CFCs and leaded petrol.	ENVIRONMENT
His inventions show how science can (2)	COME
practical problems but how (3) .... perfect	APPEAR
ideas can have (4) .... consequences.	DISASTER
After WW1, Midgely was searching for a chemical	
(5) .... to the problem of an irritating knocking sound	SOLVE
heard coming from car engines. This saw the (6)	DEVELOP
of leaded petrol. Nowadays, most (7) .... believe	SCIENCE
that lead causes (8) .... pollution and brain damage in	ATMOSPHERE
young children. Midgely then turned to the refrigerator	
industry in an attempt to make (9) .... to the cooling	IMPROVE
systems. He developed a substance known as CFC,	
which as we now know, is damaging the earth's ozone	
layer.	
In 1940, Midgely was paralysed by polio. He invented a	
pulley system to (10).................... him to get out of bed.	ABLE
Sadly, in 1944 he strangled himself while using it.	

(Guardian)

Unit 6, Part 2, open cloze

For questions 1–15, read the text below and think of the word which best fits each space. Use only one word in each space. There is an example at the beginning (0).

Example: 0 anyone

Does success equal happiness?
Happiness makes you feel young, your complexion glow and your eyes sparkle. But is it all a matter of luck or can (0) ...... achieve it?

(1) ...... our parents were happy then we can probably expect to be of a happy disposition, partly because of inheritance, but also because we have (2) ...... up in a happy home.

There's (3) ...... reason to believe that success always equals happiness. Studies show millionaires to be only slightly happier than others. What's more, many famous sportspeople said they were unhappy because of being envied, or being rejected by the media (4) ...... they gave a poor performance.

The greatest source of happiness (5) ...... far comes from one's partner, (6) ...... terms of emotional support and understanding when times are hard. However, young children (especially those (7) ...... the ages of three and five years old) can interfere with relationships. Parents tend to worry more (8) ...... childless couples.

Work can be a source of happiness for some – and not (9) ...... for the money it brings. The job satisfaction that people get (10) ...... their work is vital. However, for many people, leisure activities are (11) ...... satisfying than work.

So if you want to be happy, eat a well-balanced diet, look (12) ...... your health, (13) ...... time for friends and leisure, and be a good partner and parent. Happiness (14) ...... be guaranteed – it's clearly something that (15) ...... to be worked at.

(Ideal Home Magazine)

Unit 7, Part 1, 'key' word transformations

For questions 1–10, complete the second sentence so that it has a similar meaning to the first sentence, using the given word. **Do not change the word given**. You must use between two and five words, including the word given. There is an example at the beginning (0).

0 Scientists have conducted a lot of research into our beliefs about the moon.
   carried
   A lot of research *has been carried out* into our beliefs about the moon.

The moon and you

1 Neil Armstrong landed on the moon over 25 years ago.
   since
   It .... Neil Armstrong landed on the moon.

2 There are those who believe the moon has an influence on our lives and health.
   influenced
   There are those who believe that our lives and health .... the moon.

3 Births are said to increase during the full moon.
   be
   There is said .... births during the full moon.

4 Studies show that more murders occur when the moon is full.
   number
   Studies show a rise .... murders when the moon is full.

5 People say that there are more accidents, too.
   supposed
   There .... more accidents, too.

6 The highest number of hospital admissions occurs during the full moon phase.
   takes
   The highest number of hospital admissions .... during the full moon phase.

7 I asked a psychiatric nurse what she thought about all this.
   opinion
   I asked a psychiatric nurse .... all this.

8 She said, 'I see it happening all the time on the hospital wards.'
   occurred
   She claimed .... all the time on the hospital wards.

9 Scientists have carried out studies to prove whether this is true.
   undertaken
   Studies .... to prove whether this is true.

10 However, no conclusions have been reached yet.
    still
    However, conclusions .... reached.

Unit 10, Part 3, error correction

For questions 1–15, read the text below and look carefully at each line. Some of the lines are correct, and some have a word which should not be there. If a line is correct put a tick (✓) by the number. If a line has a word which should not be there, write the word next to the line. There are two examples at the beginning.

How to cut down on car pollution

Try not to use the car; make more greater use of public	0	more
transport or walk or cycle instead. If you must use the car,	00	✓
try car-sharing. Try to combine errands into one trip by the	1	_____
careful planning. If you must to drive, switch off the	2	_____
engine if you expect to be stuck for more than a few of	3	_____
minutes in a traffic jam. Try not to brake suddenly or	4	_____
to accelerate sharply. Do not warm the engine up more	5	_____
than you need to. Keep your engine be properly tuned	6	_____
and your tyres at the correct pressure. This will make it	7	_____
sure the vehicle is working as efficiently, save on petrol	8	_____
and reduce down pollutants. Do not park the car in direct	9	_____
sunlight whilst the engine is so hot if you can possibly	10	_____
avoid it. Use a garage or park in the shade. Avoid	11	_____
overfilling the petrol tank and spilling petrol. The	12	_____
spilled petrol evaporates which it releases hydrocarbons.	13	_____
If you will try these ideas you will save yourself money and	14	_____
also help to save the environment.	15	_____

Unit 11, Part 1, multiple-choice cloze

For questions 1–15, read the text below and decide which answer A, B, C or D best fits each space. There is an example at the beginning (0).

Example:

0 A across   (B) up   C down   D around

Midnight Creepers

They turned (0) ...... at midnight – thousands of giant insects, washed up on the (1) ...... of the River Thames. (2) ...... arriving for work in South London found factories and car parks swarming with the monsters that (3) ...... to have come from nowhere. About an inch-and-a-half long, they ran around everywhere, waving antennae (4) ...... front of them and even (5) ...... health inspectors to (6) ...... their breath. Workers, who initially thought the things were cockroaches, stamped on them to kill them. The bugs were (7) ...... as *ligia oceanica*, whose ugly looks hide their innocent nature. (8) ...... from invading London, they were desperately trying to return to the river (9) ...... from where they had come. Hundreds died (10) ...... the attempt. The mystery of the monsters from the deep was solved by Dr Jim Brock, who was brought a (11) ...... to identify. 'I can understand people being alarmed,' he said. 'They really do look like something out of a (12) ...... movie. But they are (13) ...... enough around coastal (14) ...... and will not go far from salt water, (15) ...... they cannot actually swim.'

(*Daily Mail*)

1 A flow	B stream	C tide	D way
2 A Commuters	B Travellers	C Walkers	D Trippers
3 A looked	B viewed	C thought	D seemed
4 A by	B on	C at	D in
5 A making	B causing	C doing	D having
6 A drop	B catch	C stop	D take
7 A explored	B discovered	C identified	D found
8 A Far	B Farther	C Way	D Away
9 A coast	B beach	C edge	D bank
10 A at	B for	C in	D on
11 A section	B sample	C pattern	D type
12 A shock	B fear	C horror	D terror
13 A common	B often	C routine	D regular
14 A lots	B spaces	C places	D areas
15 A although	B however	C still	D yet

Unit 11, Part 2, word formation

For questions 1–10 read the text below. Use the word given in capitals at the end of each line to form a word that fits in the space in the same line. There is an example at the beginning (0).

Example: 0 natural

Animal Concerns

Until recently, all farm animals lived fairly (0)	NATURE
lives on farmland. However, as the world's (1)	POPULATE
has increased, so has the (2) .... of food.	CONSUME
Factory farming methods and the (3) .... of	DEVELOP
genetically engineered (4) .... hormones are ways of	GROW
increasing food (5) .... But factory farming and drug	PRODUCT
(6) .... can cause animals a lot of distress. Many animals	TREAT
spend their entire (7) .... in one building. Many people	EXIST
(8) .... with the way this happens and argue that more	AGREE
emphasis should be given to (9) .... foodstuffs, like	ALTERNATE
cereals. They feel that, at the very least, more (10)	ENCOURAGE
should be given to farmers who use free-range methods,	
as this is both (11) .... and more humane.	ECONOMY

Writing Skills Development

Introduction

The aim of this section is to help you understand how your compositions in the FCE Writing paper will be assessed. You will also have the chance to look at some compositions written by students of the same level of English as you.

How is your writing assessed?

When the examiner reads your work, s/he is looking at the following points:

- **Content**: have you completed the question or have you missed out any important points? Is your composition interesting to read with good ideas of your own?

- **Language**: have you used a good range of vocabulary and grammatical structures? Is your language accurate, or do you use the wrong word or make a lot of grammatical mistakes?

- **Organisation**: have you organised your writing so that it helps the examiner to follow what you have written (writing in clear paragraphs, for example)?

- **Presentation and register**: is your writing clear and easy to read? Can you write in an informal way as well as a more formal way?

The overall effect on the reader (positive or negative) is also considered.

Use the key opposite to remind you of the above points.

Using the sample compositions

All of the following compositions have been written by FCE students. Read them and try the tasks below:

- compare your composition with theirs (is yours better, as good, or worse?)

- correct the underlined language errors, as in the first example (this is also good practice for the 'error correction' task in the Use of English paper)

- use the key to grade the compositions, giving each one a total mark out of 20

Content
5 – all points covered with original ideas
4 – all points covered with sufficient detail
3 – main points covered
2 – some points missing and/or not needed
1 – many points missing and/or not needed

Language
5 – wide range, with very few errors
4 – good range, mostly without errors
3 – adequate range, with some errors
2 – limited range, with errors causing problems in
      communication
1 – narrow range, with many errors

Organisation
5 – very clear
4 – effective
3 – adequate
2 – poor
1 – inadequate

Presentation and register
5 – very appropriate
4 – appropriate
3 – appropriate on the whole
2 – not always appropriate
1 – not appropriate

Task: a description of an important event in a book
(Unit 2: A good read, page 21)

Writing guidelines
Content/organisation: this account should give a clear description of one important event in the book, with sufficient background information to enable the target reader to follow the account easily. The title and author should be clearly stated in the first paragraph.
Language: the writer has a choice between using the simple past to narrate events or the simple present, which is more immediate. Interesting adjectives, like 'dramatic', 'compelling', 'poignant', etc., could be used.
Target reader: the reader would hopefully be interested enough to want to read the story him/herself.

(Usually,) I don't like reading poetry, but when I read 'The Iliad' (thought to be written by

Homer) I had to change my mind. It consists of 24 books and 12,000 lines, but although
                                                I didn't find it
it is the longest epic, it doesn't make me boring. There are many characters, for
                                                                        exciting? dramatic?
example, Achilles, Hector, King Agamemnon, Odysseus and others, and a lot of events.

   The most important event is a battle which takes place between Achilles and Hector.
            is angry
Achilles, who angrys about the death of his friend, Patroclus (killed by Hector), decides

to have a battle with Hector to get revenge. Achilles finally kills Hector, but that is not
                            mis
enough for him. He also (treats) badly Hector's corpse by tying it to a chariot and
                                                        filled me with horror
dragging it behind him. This part in the book made me horror.
                                                                        tic
   I have chosen this part of 'The Iliad' to write about because it is the most drama for

me; it tells us about passion, and feeling, and how someone feels when their best friend

has been killed.

By Joung Woo Choi

Comments:
You have answered the composition quite nicely and your work is organised into clear paragraphs. You use grammatical tenses effectively to describe the events in the story, but at other times you use some expressions which are not very clear (e.g. 'it doesn't make me boring' means something very different). Be careful with word formation, too (e.g. 'drama'/'dramatic').

Marks:
Content – 3
Language – 3
Organisation – 4
Presentation and register – 4
Total – 14/20

Task: a semi-formal letter to a host family

(Unit 4: Host families, page 45)

Writing guidelines
Content/organisation: this should be written in the form of a letter, with the appropriate layout (e.g. salutation and ending, but note that you are not required to include addresses in the exam). The letter should cover all of the points mentioned in the task (marks will be deducted if not).
Tone/style: the tone should be polite and the style reasonably formal.
Target reader: Mrs Smith should be fully aware of the writer's needs when she comes to stay; she should not be irritated or offended by the tone of the letter.

Dear Mrs Smith,

I am delighted to have the opportunity of coming to stay with you and your family. I am really excited about everything that I will experience in England. I would like to give you further information about me to be happy with each other.

First of all, I have got an allergic to potatoes, so would you mind if I ask you not to cook the meal which use potatoes. Also, sometimes cooking for myself is possible? Secondly, my English is very poor, so could you give me opportunities to practise English with you as often as possible? Thirdly, I have got an international driving licence, so I would like to use it. If I pay for everything connected with the car, would you allow me to use yours? However, if you mind me using your car I will not complain about that! Lastly, I have a difficulty staying with dogs, so I would appreciate it if you keep your dog away from me.

I apologise to you for asking so many things, but I would be grateful if you would do these favours for me. I would like to finish by saying that it'll be a pleasure to stay with your family.

Yours sincerely,
Kaori Inagawa

By Kaori Inagawa and Sun Ae Kim

Task: A story about winning the lottery

(Unit 6, The lottery, page 69)

Writing guidelines
Content/organisation: this essay should show clear organisation, i.e. a paragraph devoted to each stage.
Language: there is scope in this story to show a good range of tenses (for example, past continuous for setting the scene, simple past for general narration of events, present simple/continuous for explaining one's present state of mind, and so on). Key vocabulary could be: jackpot, prize, celebrity, dream.
Target reader: the competition judge should find the story out of the ordinary, and would not be impressed if there are too many language errors or if the meaning is not clear.

My life will never be the same again. Yesterday afternoon, when I was watching TV at home, my friend, Steven, who works for the lottery company called me. He told me that I had won the jackpot of £1 million. Having heard this wonderful news, I just couldn't believe it, not at first. However, after it was confirmed by the lottery company later on, I rushed to my wife telling her this incredible news. All of a sudden, I became a publicity. Hundreds of news agencies gathered in my house. Friends and relatives of mine called me and congratulated me. I had never been so important to them before.

Today when I woke up, I thought 'I am living in a world of dreams'. To buy a brand new Jaguar seemed to be an unreachable dream the day before, but now I can have as many as I wish. Maybe I would buy a mansion as well. And travel round the world, of course. My wife suggested me to donate a proportion of the money to charities. It is a good idea.

It is not easy to plan the ways to spend such a great amount of money, but I enjoy being a rich man very much so far.

By Tien-chih Yu

Task: an account of a hobby

(Unit 8, Salsa fever!, page 93)

Writing guidelines
Content/organisation: the account should give a full description of what the hobby involves in terms of equipment, how to get started, why you enjoy it, and so on. It should use paragraphs sensibly to order this information.
Language: if any specialist terminology is used, this may need to be explained.
Target reader: the reader should find the account interesting and enjoyable to read, and may indeed be encouraged to take up the hobby.

One of the most difficult things to find is something that you can enjoy doing by yourself. I think many people try to do hobbies that can be dangerous, for example, rock climbing or that can be expensive to do, for example, motor racing. I'm going to tell you about a hobby that is neither expensive nor dangerous. Fishing.

You don't need expensive equipment for fishing. You just need a fishing rod, a reel, a nylon line, a net and some food to catch the fish.

I usually prefer fishing on the river and if you want to go fishing you should go there early. In the morning it is easy to catch fish.

While you are fishing you should be patient because sometimes you might have to wait several hours. When a fish pulls at my hook it is difficult to explain how I feel. I think 'it is mine', it has come to see me. I keep quiet and wait. I pull the line slowly, take the fish and put it in my net. It is wonderful.

However, I have one difficulty. I can't put a worm onto the hook. I feel that worms are a bit sticky, that's why I usually use bread.

If you are looking for something exciting to do, I recommend you to try it. I'm sure you'll enjoy.

By Mehmet Akif Kutukcu

Task: a letter giving directions

(Unit 10, Getting from A to B, page 114)

Writing guidelines
Content: the letter should strongly recommend one form of transport over the others, and give a clear explanation of the cost, journey times and length, as well as any other useful tips about using this form of transport.
Style: the style of the letter can be fairly informal, and this can be achieved by the use of friendly salutations/endings.
Target reader: the reader should have no difficulty in reaching his/her destination.

Hello Sharon,

It's a pleasure to hear from you. I'm feeling very happy to meet you in Brazil and I'm sure you will enjoy a lot.

Talking about your arrival, I'd recommend taking a bus from Cumbica Airport to Tieté Coach Station. It takes about 40 minutes and costs approximately R$8. At the coach station, look for 'Cometa' Carrier. You must pay in the ticket office to get a coach to Ribeirao Preto Coach Station. There's one every 30 minutes. The journey lasts 3 hours and costs about R$15. Call me when you have arrived and I'll bring you.

I wouldn't really suggest coming by plane because it's more expensive and not so frequent.

Don't forget to change your money before leaving the airport. The rate is about £1 = R$1.56 (the Brazilian money is called 'Real'). Take my phone number and address everywhere you go. I'm looking forward to seeing you soon.

Lots of love

Gustavo

By Gustavo Rahal

Task: a magazine article

(Unit 12, The kiss that can save a life, page 138)

Writing guidelines
Content: the article should describe the benefits of doing a first aid course, firstly by addressing the reader directly and then giving more general reasons.
Style/tone: an informal style might appeal to students, although the topic of first aid and life-saving should be treated seriously.
Target reader: the reader should find the article persuasive enough to consider enrolling for a first aid course, and would have the information necessary to enable him/her to do so.

Imagine being with your best friend having a picnic at the countryside, and suddenly your friend falls ill because he or she has eaten a poisoned plant – what would you do? There's no telephone from where you can call the hospital. There's nobody else around to help you. It's just you and your friend, and your friend's life depends on you.

Unfortunately these things happen and more often as you can even imagine. Not just intoxications but a lot of sickness and sudden health problems – like a heart attack or a fit – and you have to be prepared for these situations. You can't rely on other people to solve these problems for you, because sometimes you could find yourself alone in a risky or dangerous situation.

So enrol as soon as possible to a first aid course and if you don't have that opportunity in your school or college, insist your institution opens one of these courses. Encourage your friends to do it too. If you're interested, please contact St. John Ambulance: The Breath of Life campaign. They are running free courses from November 1 to May 30. Always remember: 'Someone's life can be in your hands!'

By Paloma Atencia

Grammar Reference

Throughout the Grammar Reference explanations of structures are followed by examples. However, to help you remember these structures, you are advised to write your own examples in the spaces provided. These should ideally be sentences that mean something to you, as you are more likely to remember them if they are 'personalised'.

Unit 1: Present tenses

1 The **present simple** and the **present continuous** are the two tenses that are used to talk about the present. The present simple tends to be used for situations that are permanent or actions, like habits for example, that are repeated:

'I *live in London.*' (permanent situation)
'What *do you usually do at the weekend?*' '*I usually go to the cinema.*' (habit)

Your examples:

....
....

The present continuous is generally used to describe temporary situations or actions happening 'now':

'*I'm living with my aunt for the summer.*' (temporary situation)
'What *are you doing?*' '*I'm trying to find my pen.*' (now)

Your examples:

....
....

2 The present simple and continuous can both be used to describe the future. The present simple is often used to describe timetabled or calendar events, whilst the present continuous is used to describe future arrangements:

The tour starts at 9.00. (timetabled event)
....

I'm seeing the dentist this afternoon. (future arrangement)
....

3 The present continuous can also be used to describe situations that are changing:

The winters are getting colder.
Inflation is getting worse.
....

4 The present simple and continuous are often used when outlining the plot of a film or book. See the sample composition on page 21 for an example of this.

Unit 1: Adverbs of frequency

1 Generally speaking, **adverbs of frequency** follow auxiliary or modal verbs and the verb *to be* but come before other verbs:

We've never got milk in this house.
He can usually do it easily.
I'm usually busy at weekends.
He's always playing his music too loud.
I often go to the cinema.

....
....
....
....

Unit 2: Question tags

1 **Question tags** are normally formed using the modal/auxiliary verb or the verb *to be* from the main clause + the appropriate pronoun. As a general rule, we use a positive tag with a negative clause, and a negative tag with a positive clause:

We can't smoke in here, can we?
I've met you before, haven't I?
You aren't from around here, are you?

....
....
....

2 Sentences that contain 'negative' words like *nobody, nothing, never, hardly,* etc., take a positive question tag. The pronoun *it* is used after *nothing, they* is used after *nobody* or *somebody*:

He's never been to Japan, has he?
Nothing's happened, has it?
Nobody called while I was out, did they?

....
....
....

3 *Do* is often used in the question tag when the sentence does not contain a modal or auxiliary verb or the verb *to be*:

Manchester United played last night, didn't they?
You work in the city, don't you?

....
....

4 In the first person form, *aren't* I or *am* I is used in the question tag:

I'm next, aren't I?
I'm not very good at this, am I?

....
....

5 Question tags are used after statements, not questions. We **don't** say:

*Are you tired, are you?
*Have you been to America, have you?

6 When making a suggestion using *Let's* in the statement, we use *shall we* in the question tag:

Let's go to the cinema, shall we?

....

7 Intonation is very important in question tags as it is this that expresses the meaning behind the use of the question tag. Generally speaking, tags that act as real questions have rising intonation, whilst tags that have falling intonation are usually just asking for confirmation:

He wasn't here yesterday, was he? (question)

It's the 13th today, isn't it? (question)

He wasn't here yesterday, was he? (confirmation)

It's the 13th today, isn't it? (confirmation)

....

....

8 Question tags are very useful when making conversation, as they require the listener to respond to a statement. Try to practise them during conversations you have in class.

Unit 2: Past simple and past continuous

1 The **past simple** is used:

a to describe a sequence of actions in a narrative:

He went upstairs, got undressed and went to bed.
I arrived at school, went in the classroom, opened my book and fell asleep.

....

b to describe a past permanent situation or habit:

I lived in Brussels when I was younger.
I worked really hard before the exam.

....

....

c with the past continuous to express the idea that one action (past simple) interrupted or happened midway through another (past continuous):

I was having a bath when the phone rang.
She was waiting for the bus when it started to rain.

....

....

2 The **past continuous** is used:

a to describe something that was happening at a particular time in the past. Compare the following:

At half past six he had dinner.
At half past six he was having dinner.

....

....

b to give background information or to set the scene. It is often used at the beginning of stories to describe two or more actions happening at the same time:

He arrived at the station and looked around. People were queuing for tickets, an old lady was selling flowers and a young man was kissing a woman goodbye.

....

....

c to describe a temporary situation or temporary habit in the past:

I was living in Spain at the time.
She wasn't playing well due to a minor injury.

....

....

Unit 3: Comparatives and superlatives

There are many different ways of making comparisons in English; the following are a selection of some of the main structures:

1 *as ... as...* (equal comparison)
not as ... as   (unequal comparison)

He's as quiet as a mouse.
This isn't as hard as I thought it would be.

....

....

2 Generally, one-syllable and some two-syllable adjectives add *...er* and *...est* to the adjective to make the comparative and superlative form. Adjectives that end in *y* drop the *y* and add *...ier* or *...iest*:

Stephen is taller than me. John is the tallest in the class.
The blue bag is heavier than the grey one. I had to pay excess luggage for the heaviest bag.

....

....

3 Some two-syllable adjectives can take either *...er/...est* or *more/most*:

Her son was more polite/politer than her daughter.

....

....

4 Other two-syllable and longer adjectives use *more* or *most*:

The book was more interesting than I'd expected.
This is the most expensive holiday I've ever had.

....

....

5 One-syllable adjectives ending in a vowel + a consonant double the consonant in comparatives and superlatives:

hot	*hotter*	*hottest*
big	*bigger*	*biggest*

....

....

6 Superlatives usually take *the* before the adjective:

Everest is the tallest mountain in the world.

....

7 There are also several irregular words when used as comparatives and superlatives:

good	*better*	*best*
bad	*worse*	*worst*
far	*farther/further*	*farthest/furthest*
little	*less*	*least*
many/much	*more*	*most*
well	*better*	*best*

8 Comparatives can also be modified by using the following words:

Greece is <u>a lot</u> hotter than England.
He's <u>slightly</u> older than his wife.
She's feeling <u>a little</u> better today.

....
....
....

9 The comparative structure *the ... the* can be used to show the link between two separate actions or situations:

<u>The more</u> I study English, <u>the less</u> I understand.
<u>The quicker</u> we finish this grammar point <u>the happier</u> I'll be.

....
....

Unit 3: Defining and non-defining relative clauses

1 **Defining relative clauses** are essential to the meaning of a sentence. The relative clause gives information about the thing being described which cannot be omitted. A **non-defining relative clause** simply gives us extra information and could be left out without a breakdown in meaning. Compare the following:

Doctors, who work long hours, often suffer from stress.
Doctors who work long hours often suffer from stress.

In the first sentence, **all** doctors suffer from stress. The fact that they work long hours is extra information. If this information were omitted it would not change the essential meaning of the sentence. In the second sentence, the long hours cause **some** doctors to suffer from stress. This information is therefore vital to the meaning of the sentence and cannot be omitted.

2 In defining relative clauses *that* or *who* is used after people, *that* or *which* after things. *That* is preferable to *who* or *which* in spoken English. It is common for the pronoun to be omitted when it defines the object of the clause, especially in spoken English.

You know Carlos! He's the boy (who/that) I came to the party with.
It's a thing (that/which) you use to open bottles.

....
....

3 You cannot omit the relative pronoun when it is the subject of the relative clause.

You know Carlos! He's the boy who/that came to the party.
It's a thing that/which is used to open bottles.

....
....

4 In non-defining relative clauses *who* is used after people, *which* after things. It is not possible to use *that* in non-defining relative clauses and the relative pronoun cannot be left out. Commas are used to show that the information is extra:

Inflation, which has been rising slowly all year, is making the Government unpopular.
My brother, who lives in Ipswich, has three children.

....
....

5 Non-defining relative clauses are often used in written English but are rarely used in conversation.

6 In both defining and non-defining relative clauses, *when* is used after times, *where* after places and *whose* to show possession:

In England the evening is the time when most people have their main meal.
The bomb exploded in the town centre, where lots of people were doing their shopping.
She's the singer whose latest album went to number one.

....
....
....

Unit 4: Modal verbs of obligation

1 Note the following points about the general use of **modal verbs**:

a Modal verbs do not change their form like other verbs do. There is no s ending ...*ing*, ...*ed* or infinitive forms. Because of this we often have to use another verb when describing the past or the future:

The policeman told him he <u>had to</u> produce his documents at the police station. (not 'must')
You <u>won't be able to</u> do it unless you try. (not 'can't')

....
....

b Modal verbs are generally followed by the infinitive without *to*, apart from *ought to*, *need to* and *have to*.

2 *Must* and *have/has to* both express strong obligation. *Must* is used when the obligation comes from the speaker whereas *have/has to* expresses the idea that the obligation comes from an external authority. Compare the following two sentences:

Teacher: *You must tell me if you're going to be late for class.*
Student: *We have to tell the teacher if we're going to be late for class.*

In the first sentence, the authority comes from the speaker, whilst in the second, the student is reporting the teacher's rules. Write two of your own examples:

....
....

3 *Mustn't* is used to show negative obligation. *Do/doesn't have to, have/hasn't got to* and *do/doesn't need to* express absence of obligation:

We mustn't forget to pay the gas bill.
I don't have to/haven't got to/don't need to go to college today. The tutor's ill.

....
....

4 To express weaker obligation, in the sense of giving advice, *should* and *ought to* are used. If something was/wasn't done in the past giving rise to a negative result, *should have* is used:

You should/ought to see a doctor about that cough.
You shouldn't drink and drive. It's irresponsible.
You should have called to tell me you were going to be late. Your dinner's burnt.
He shouldn't have driven home after the party. It's his own fault he had an accident.

....
....

5 (Did) *not need* to is used to show that something wasn't necessary so it wasn't done. N*eedn't have*, however, shows that something was done unnecessarily:

We didn't need to reserve a seat. We knew the train would be empty.
Look! The train's empty! We needn't have reserved these seats.

....
....

Unit 4: Past perfect simple and continuous

1 Generally, the **past perfect** tense is used to refer to actions or situations that took place before another action/situation in the past. The time these actions or situations happened may or may not be mentioned:

I woke up at about 9.30. I felt absolutely terrible! There had been a lot of noise outside and I'd had an awful night's sleep.

2 The past perfect is used to show that one action was completed before another one began. Compare the past perfect in the first example with the past simple in the second:

We had eaten when they arrived. (When they arrived we had already eaten.)
We ate when they arrived. (When they arrived we started eating.)

....
....

3 As with all continuous tenses the **past perfect continuous** is preferred when we want to emphasise the duration, the repeated nature, or the temporary nature of the situation or activity:

I'd been living in Coimbra for almost a year when I finally left.
I was really surprised when he left Giggs out. He'd been playing really well.
She'd been acting really strangely before she went missing.

....
....
....

4 The past perfect continuous is used to highlight the fact that an action was unfinished or interrupted. Compare the past perfect continuous in the first example with the past perfect simple in the second:

When I fell asleep I'd been revising phrasal verbs.
When I fell asleep I'd revised the difference between 'do' and 'make'.

....
....

5 The past perfect is simply used to make the order of events clear to the reader or the listener. However, if it is over-used it can appear a little unnatural. If clarity has been achieved you can revert back to using past simple or past continuous. Look back at the inspector's report on page 50 and decide which, if any, of the past perfect tenses could be changed without creating any confusion. There are few 'right' or 'wrong' answers here: it's a matter of opinion.

Unit 5: Future (1)

See also page 171 for further future structures.

1 **Will** is used to:

a make a simple prediction (compare this with *going to* in **2a** below):

I think I'll do OK in the exam next week.
He'll probably be late for class. He was up till late last night.

....
....

b describe a spontaneous decision, one made at the moment of speaking (compare this with *going to* in **2b** below):

I think I'll have the Greek salad.
I'll give him a ring and see if he wants to come.

....
....

c Will and *shall* are often used when making offers or suggestions respectively:

I'll give you a hand if you want.
Shall I call you when I get home?

....
....

2 **Going** to is used to:

a make a firm prediction based on present evidence:

Look! The ladder's slipped. He's going to fall.
The referee has got the red card out. He's going to send him off!

....
....

b describe future plans or intentions that have already been decided:

Have you decided what to have? Yes. I'm going to have the Greek salad.
I'm going to have an early night tonight. (a decision I made earlier)

....
....

3 The **present continuous** is used to describe a future arrangement. The difference between this and *going to* (see **2b** above) is that the present continuous indicates that two or more people have reached agreement on a future plan, whereas *going to* refers mainly to the intention of the individual:

I can't come tonight. I'm seeing Carol.
We're meeting them outside the cinema.

....
....

Look again at the first example in **2b**. If the person had said *I'm having the Greek salad*, how would you explain the sense of 'arrangement'? (see page 153)

4 The **present simple** is used to describe future timetabled, scheduled or calendar events:

The lesson starts at 9 o'clock tomorrow.
My train leaves at 3 o'clock.

....

....

Unit 5: Present perfect simple and continuous

1 As a general rule, you should try to see the **present perfect** as a structure that links the past with the present. This link can be due to:

a experience, with the sense of 'up until now':

I've never met anyone famous.
Have you ever read any Shakespeare?

....

....

If the past tense were used in the examples above, the people would be in what state of health? (see page 153)

b a past action that is important now. Compare the following examples:

I've left my wallet at home! (I haven't got any money on me.)
I left my wallet at home, but my friend lent me some money.

....

....

2 The **present perfect continuous** is used, like other continuous tenses, to emphasise the duration, the repeated nature, or the temporary nature of the situation or activity being described. There are important differences in use between the present perfect simple and continuous. See the following examples:

I've been reading a really good book today. (focus on the action, maybe finished, maybe not)
I've read a really good book today. (I've finished the book)

....

....

She's been studying prepositions all afternoon. (duration, how long)
He's done three practice tests this afternoon. (completed activities, how much/many/often)

....

....

They've been playing really well recently. (temporary action or situation, they haven't always played this well)
They've always played well against us. (a permanent action or situation)

....

....

Unit 6: Conditionals (1)

See page 172 for further examples of conditional structures.

1 Conditional sentences refer to hypothetical situations. In a certain situation or under a certain condition, if 'x' does or doesn't happen, then 'y' does or doesn't happen. The choice of tense depends on whether we are talking about the past, present or future. The choice of modal verb (*will/can/might*), depends on how certain we are.

2 **Zero conditionals** describe a general truth or fact. They are also often used when giving instructions. The present tense is typically used in both clauses:

I get really annoyed if people ignore me.
If the light comes on, switch off the machine immediately.

....

....

3 **First conditionals** are used to describe a (possible/probable) future result in relation to a certain situation. They are often used to make a conditional arrangement/offer, to give a warning or to negotiate/persuade. The most common form uses present simple in the conditional clause and *will/might/could* in the result clause:

If you phone when you arrive, I'll come and pick you up.
If you drive like that, you could/might/will have an accident.
If you do my homework, I'll pay for the meal.

....

....

....

4 **Second conditionals** describe the (possible/probable) result of a less likely situation. To show that this situation is less likely there is a change of tense. They are often used to give advice or to daydream about changes to the present or the future. The past simple is used in the conditional clause, *would* or another modal verb (e.g. *could* or *might*) is used in the result clause:

I wouldn't do that, if I were you.
If I were the President, I'd give everyone longer holidays.

....

....

5 *If* is not always used in zero, first and second conditionals. It can be substituted with *unless* (= 'if ... not'), *in case* (= 'if by any chance') or *provided/providing/as long as* (= 'if'):

He won't pass unless he works a lot harder. (If he doesn't work harder he won't pass.)
I'll lend you the car provided you drive carefully. (If you drive carefully you can borrow it.)

....

....

Unit 6: Articles

The rules for articles are quite extensive; a brief outline of their use is offered here. See page 173 'Expressing quantity' for further examples of determiners.

1 *The*, or the **definite article**, is used generally to show that the noun being referred to is 'known' or understood. This can be due to the following reasons:

  a the noun has been mentioned before:

   I went into town and bought a pair of shoes and a jacket. The shoes are really nice but I'm not sure I like the jacket now.

   ....
   ....

  b the noun is the only one in existence:

   the sun, the world, the Pope

   ....

  c the idea of there only being 'one' applies to the use of superlatives, which take *the*:

   the best day of my life
   the tallest man in the world

   ....
   ....

  d the noun is something that is shared by people or the community and which is therefore known by everybody. The focus is on the institution rather than an individual example. Compare the following:

   I'm just going to the post office/the bank/the butcher's, etc.
   There's a post office/a bank/a butcher's in Humber Road.

   ....
   ....

   Similarly, compare the following two sentences. In the first example in each pair, the institution is being referred to, in the second, a particular one:

   John's in hospital. (he's a patient, which hospital isn't important at this stage)
   Steve's in the hospital. (as a visitor or employee in a particular hospital)
   Anne's at school. (she's a student)
   Carol's in the school. (she's visiting)

  e before the names of most mountain ranges, oceans and rivers:

   the Himalayas, the Rhine, the Pacific

   ....

2 *A/an*, or the **indefinite article**, refers, as its name suggests, to nouns that are not known by the reader or speaker. This can be because the noun has been mentioned for the first time.

   See **1a**. It is also used to describe someone's job:

   He's an accountant.

   ....

3 No article is used:

  a when we are talking about things in general. Compare the following:

   Garlic is supposed to be really good for you.
   The garlic I bought yesterday is still fresh.

   I've never been able to understand computers.
   The computer in my office isn't working.

   ....
   ....

  b with many proper nouns, for example people's names, the names of most countries, etc.

  c with the names of most lakes, countries and continents:

   Lake Ontario, Scotland, Africa

   ....

   The definite article is used before the names of certain countries because we are talking about 'one of a kind'. For example:

   The Republic of Ireland. (there are many republics in the world, we are specifying a particular one)

Unit 7: Passives

1 The **passive** is usually formed with the verb *to be* in the appropriate tense plus the past participle.

   Coffee is produced in many parts of South America. (present simple)
   Hamlet was written by Shakespeare. (past simple)
   She'd been arrested several times before. (past perfect)
   My car's been stolen. (present perfect)
   Trespassers will be prosecuted. (future simple)
   Examinations to be held in room 307. (infinitive)
   This product should not be re-heated. (with modal verbs)

   However, you will often come across examples where the verb *to be* is dropped, e.g. in newspaper headlines and in notices:

   Terrorists arrested
   Keys cut here

   ....

2 The passive is often used for the following reasons:

  a when the agent is people in general, obvious, unknown or unimportant:

   This product should be consumed within three days of purchase.
   My car's been stolen.
   The finished product is exported all over the world.

   ....
   ....
   ....

  b to create formality. Compare the following:

   We'll tell you our decision as soon as possible.
   You will be notified of our decision at the earliest possible date.

   ....
   ....

c when the agent wishes to avoid being held responsible. Compare:

My party has reduced inflation.
Taxes will have to be increased.

....
....
....

Unit 7: Future (2)

See page 168 for further future tenses.

1 The **future continuous** is used to describe an activity that will be in progress at a particular time in the future:

This time tomorrow I'll be flying to Brazil.
I'll be watching the film tonight, so come round when it finishes.

....
....

2 The **future perfect simple** and **continuous** are used to describe an action that will/won't have been completed by a particular time in the future. The continuous is used when emphasis is on the duration or the repeated nature of the activity:

I think I'll have had three children by the time I'm 35.
We'll have been going out together for a year next week.

....
....

Unit 8: Reported speech

1 Reported statements:

a The tense usually goes back one in reported speech:

'I live in Birmingham.' He told me/said (that) he lived in Birmingham. (present simple changes to past simple)
'The match was really exciting.' He told me/said (that) the match had been really exciting. (past simple or present perfect changes to past perfect)
'We're going away soon.' She told me/said (that) they were going away soon. (present continuous changes to past continuous)

....
....
....

b However, if the reporting verb is in the present tense or the original words spoken are still true, English speakers often leave the tense unchanged:

'I'm hungry!' He says he's hungry.
'Karen's going to be late tonight.' She said Karen's going to be late tonight.

....
....

c There are several words or expressions that change when we are reporting direct speech. Some examples appear below. Add others to the list as you come across them.

today – that day
tonight – that night

tomorrow – the following/next day
next week – the following week
yesterday – the day before
this – that
here – there
now – then .

....
....
....

d There are several verbs that can be used to report statements which follow the same pattern as 'say' and 'tell' but give us more of an idea about the speaker's or the listener's attitude. Add to the list any other verbs you find that are used like this:

'I didn't do it!' He claimed (that) he hadn't done it.
'I'll pay you back tomorrow.' He promised (that) he would pay me back the next day.

....
....
....
....
....
....

2 Reported questions:

a The same tense changes apply to reported questions as to reported statements. *Yes/no* questions are usually reported with *whether* or *if* . *Do/does/did* is generally omitted and the subject comes before the verb:

'Do you speak English?' She wanted to know *if/whether* I spoke English.
'Are you all right?' He asked him *if/whether* he was all right.

....
....

b Open questions beginning *What/Who/When/Why/How?* etc. usually retain the question word in the reported statement:

'What time is it?' He asked me what the time was.
'How will I do in the exam?' She wondered how she would do in the exam.

....
....

3 Reporting advice, commands and requests

These functions are often reported with the object plus *to* + infinitive. *Suggest* takes a 'that' clause or gerund:

'You should take up exercise.' The doctor advised her to take up exercise.
'Don't forget your homework!' He told me not to forget my homework.
'Could you close the window?' She asked me to close the window.
'Be careful on the ice!' He warned me to be careful on the ice.
'Why don't you go out for a walk?' She suggested that I *go/going* out for a walk.

....
....
....
....
....

Unit 8: Conditionals (2)

See page 169 for further explanation of conditional structures.

1 **Third conditionals** describe a hypothesis about the past. Because the focus is on the past, the hypothesis is impossible and therefore there is a further backwards shift in the tense used. The past perfect is used in the conditional clause, modal + present perfect is used in the result clause.

If I'*d known* you were coming, I *would have cooked* you something.
If he *hadn't gone* to Spain, they *might* never *have met*.

....
....

2 **Mixed conditionals**, a mixture of second and third conditionals, describe an impossible situation based on past and present time references. The past perfect is used when describing the past situation, would or another modal + infinitive to describe the present:

If we *hadn't bought* such an expensive car, we'*d have* more money now.
If you'*d remembered* to water the plants, they'*d* still *be* alive.

....
....

3 We can use *wish* and *if only* to hypothesise about situations that we aren't happy with or that we'd like to change. Because the situations are out of our control we go back a tense in the same way as in second and third conditionals:

I wish it *wasn't* raining. (now)
If only I *had* a million pounds. (now)
I wish I'*d worked* harder at school. (before)
If only he'*d scored* that penalty. (before)

....
....
....
....

Unit 9: Verb forms (1)

See opposite for further explanation of verb forms.

1 The gerund can be used as the subject of the sentence when describing a general activity. The *to* + infinitive structure is more often used to describe a particular occasion or event:

Learning to drive is pretty nerve-wracking.
It was great to hear from you.

....
....

2 Certain verbs follow one of these patterns: verb + *to*, verb + *ing* and verb + *to* or *ing*. Some examples have been supplied below. Add others as you find them:

I don't mind staying in if you need a baby-sitter.
She threatened to call the police.
I remember going to school for the first time.
He didn't remember to take his keys.

+ to	+ ing	+ to or ing
expect	avoid	try
asked	put off	hate
intend	....	prefer
learn	....	....
need	....	....
offer	....	....
....	....	....

3 The *ing* form is used after prepositions:

He was found guilty of dealing in stolen goods.
Sorry, but there's no excuse for being rude.

....
....

Unit 9: Possibility and certainty

For general rules governing modal verbs, see page 167 'Modal verbs of obligation'.

1 The following modal verbs are used to express degrees of likelihood or possibility. All are followed by the infinitive :

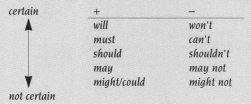

certain	+	−
	will	won't
	must	can't
	should	shouldn't
	may	may not
not certain	might/could	might not

2 If reference is to the past, add *have* + past participle to the modal:

John's late. He must have got held up in traffic.
He might have been working late.

....
....

3 All the above verbs can be used to express likelihood or possibility in the present or future, with the exception of *could not* which is not used with future reference:

You can't be 33! You don't look a day over 28.
She might not be coming in today. She looked quite ill last night.

....

Unit 10: Verb forms (2)

See opposite for further examples of verb forms.

1 *To* + infinitive is used to show the purpose or the reason why something is done:

I'm studying English to pass FCE.
We're going into town to do some shopping.

....

2 Certain verbs can be used in the gerund or the *to* + infinitive form but with different meanings:

Did you remember to call Peter? (a job that had to be done)
I don't remember saying that! (a memory)

....
....

Please stop tapping your fingers. It's driving me mad. (don't continue)
I stopped to get some petrol. (I stopped in order to do it)

....

....

The students went on shouting even though the teacher had a headache.
(continued shouting)
He went on to become the greatest footballer in the world. (later in his career)

....

....

Unit 11: Time conjunctions

1 Time conjunctions are not normally followed by *will*:

When they arrive I'll start dinner. (not 'when they will arrive ...')
By the time they arrive we'll have died of starvation. (not 'by the time they will arrive ...')

....

....

2 If you are talking about the past and want to show clearly that one action was the result of another or happened immediately after another, the past tense should be used in both clauses. However, if you want to show that one action was clearly finished before the second one began, the past perfect should be used when describing the first action. Compare the following:

When I got home my flatmate cooked dinner. (he started when I arrived)
When I got home my flatmate had cooked dinner. (it was finished when I arrived)

....

....

Unit 11: Expressing quantity

1 Countable nouns are literally nouns that can be counted and take 's' in the plural. **Uncountable nouns** refer to things or objects that cannot be counted and generally do not take 's' in the plural.

uncountable	countable
furniture	*chair*(s), *table*(s), *sofa*(s)
money	*pound*(s), *dollar*(s), *franc*(s)
....	....
....	....

2 Determiners (*much/many/a few/some/the*, etc.) can be used with countable or uncountable nouns or both:

     countable: *many/(a) few/several*
     uncountable: *much/(a) little*
     both: *a lot of/lots of/plenty of/enough/some/any*

3 A few is usually used with plural nouns, (*a*) *little* with uncountable nouns. Used with the indefinite article, *a few* and *a little* mean *some* and have a positive connotation. Without the article they indicate *not many* or *not much*:

A few people always do really well in the exam.
Few people believe in ghosts.

....

....

4 *Every, each, neither* and *either* are all used with singular nouns. *Both, all* and *no* are used with plurals. *Both* is used before two people or things, *each* before two or more people or things, *every* and *all* before three or more.

5 *Of* can follow *each, neither, either, both* and *all* with a plural noun, and must follow *none*.

Neither of the films were/Neither film was very good.
Both of my parents have given up smoking.
None of this makes sense.

....

....

....

Unit 12: Ability

See page 167 for general details on modal verbs.

Can, could and *be able to* are all used to describe ability, but there are important differences that you should be aware of:

1 *Can* is preferred if we are talking about something we know how to do or general ability:

Can you speak French?
I can't play the piano very well.

....

....

2 *Be able to* is normally used to refer to ability in the future:

I won't be able to see you tomorrow.
Do you think you'll be able to fix it?

....

....

3 In positive sentences, *could* and *be able to* are used to talk about general ability in the past. However, if we are talking about the ability to do something on one particular occasion, in the majority of cases we use *be able to, managed to* or *succeeded in*:

I could/was able to swim really well when I was younger.
The rescue team were able to/managed to save his life.
They succeeded in saving his life.

....

....

....

4 In negative sentences, however, *couldn't* can also be used to talk about inability to do something on a particular occasion:

She couldn't/wasn't able to/didn't manage to understand the question.

....

5 After modal or auxiliary verbs or *to* + infinitive structures, *be able to* is used:

We should be able to get there on time.
I've not been able to sleep well recently.
It's important to be able to carry out basic first aid.

....

....

....

Tapescripts

Unit 1

Part 1 Getting to know each other

S = student
D = Dimitris

S: Hello. May I ask you some questions?
D: Yes, of course.
S: OK. What's your name?
D: Dimitris.
S: Can you spell that please?
D: Yes. D–i–m ... no, 'm', not 'n' ... i–t–r–i–s.
S: And how old are you?
D: Sixteen.
S: Where are you from?
D: From Athens. I live in Athens .. in Zographou.
S: And how many brothers and sisters have you got?
D: I have one brother, Petros, and two sisters, Zoe and Poppy.
S: Do they all live with you?
D: Yes, with me and my mother and father.
S: You are single of course?
D: Yes.
S: How long have you been studying English?
D: Er ... for about three years. I study it at high school. I also study German. But I don't speak German very well.
S: Why are you studying English?
D: In high school everyone must to study English. I study English in evening class for FCE. Also, I want to study law in the university so English is important for me.
S: What things do you most like about yourself?
D: Mm ... that is difficult question. My friends say to me ... er ... I think I am good friend, I listen to their problems and, er, I try to help them.
S: OK. And what thing do you not like about yourself?
D: Oh ... that is more easy. I am very lazy, everybody says me this. And also I always spend money ... too much money. When I have money I spend it!
S: How do you think your friends would describe you?
D: Wonderful! Ha-ha. Very funny person. I go out often with my friends and I think I am a nice person to be with. Usually good company. But many times I am not these things.
S: OK. Last question. What is your ambition?
D: Well, I said you I want to be a lawyer ... to go to university. But really I like very much to play football and I would like to play ... to play for my favourite team, Panathinaikos.
S: Good luck!

Unit 1

Part 3 A candidate for FCE

One:
What about encouraging your students to correct each other's essays? Yes, I think this is a really useful idea. Firstly, it's interesting to see how someone else has written the same task. It's also good practice for Part 4 of the Use of English paper, where they have to correct a text with mistakes in it.

Two:
I would advise all learners to keep their own vocabulary records. Only you can decide what words it is useful to know. Think carefully about how you organise your vocabulary.

Three:
I do a lot of pair and group work in class. This is useful because it means that in each lesson all the students get the chance to speak English, and not just the loud ones. Secondly, it's good practice for the Speaking paper, which is done in pairs.

Four:
Doing past papers or practice tests is useful, up to an extent. It can teach you the skills of working quickly and keeping good time, and it can make you familiar with the format of the questions. You know what the questions look like so there are no surprises. However, it could be a little boring if all you did in class was practice tests.

Five:
Most people use a coursebook to prepare for the exam, and there are plenty of good ones on the market at present. A coursebook provides a structure for your exam course and you can carry it around with you easily.

Six:
Some people like to read papers or magazines in English. This will definitely improve your reading skills and also your vocabulary. Remember that in the Writing paper you have the chance to write about one of the books from a recommended reading list.

Seven:
You can develop your listening skills by tuning in to English programmes on the radio. You could listen to the news and write down the main stories of the day. Or you could record a short section of a programme – again the news would be useful – and transcribe a little bit of it.

Eight:
Finally, you could find an English-speaking pen-pal to practise your speaking or writing skills. Of course, your friend will probably be too polite to correct your language errors, but communicating in this way can be fun and it will give you confidence.

Unit 1

Language awareness: present tenses and adverbs of frequency
Activity 3

A: Hello, sir. I'm doing some market research. I wonder if you would mind answering a few questions?
B: Well, I'm trying to do some shopping actually.
A: What toothpaste do you use, sir?
B: Well, we usually use Cowgate, but at the moment we're using McGreens.
A: I see. Have you thought about trying Crust, sir? It cleans whiter than white.
B: No. My wife doesn't like Crust. She says it burns her mouth.

A: How often do you wash your hair, sir?
B: About twice a week. My wife washes hers every day. It costs us a fortune in shampoo!
A: And who chooses the brand?
B: My wife. She usually gets it in the supermarket. In fact, that's where I'm going now.
A: Really, sir. And what brand does she buy?
B: I don't know, to be quite honest. Have you got many more questions? It's getting rather late. The shops close in a few minutes.
A: Only a few more, sir. What perfume does your wife wear?
B: No idea. I never buy her any. Listen. I'm very sorry, but she's waiting for me at home. She's not feeling very well and the doctor's coming round this evening to have a look at her. Oh look! The man's closing the shop. I must go. Bye!

Unit 2

Part 1 Towards a global language

Question 1
Starting this week only in the *Sunday Telegraph*. You could get a hundred pounds off a canal holiday, giving you the chance to ... relax ... slow down ... mmm ... All you need to do is collect ten tokens. Get the first one in this week's issue. Plus, all the regular features, cinema and theatre reviews, and of course the magazine supplement, with articles and games for all the family. Only in the *Telegraph* this Sunday.

Question 2
Man: ... well, as soon as possible really ... Can't he see me sooner than that? ... Yes, it hurts so much I haven't been able to sleep ... I *have* been taking painkillers but they're not really working ... No, I've not eaten anything all day ... It's at the bottom, right at the back ... yes, he said it might have to be taken out the last time I saw him.

Question 3
Woman: ... by, er, running a summer school every year for young ... younger people.
Interviewer: Do you find it easy to make young people enthusiastic ... at the summer school?
Woman: Yes, I think so .. I think, yes because it's an appealing subject for young people, they see us play our instruments.
Interviewer: Yes, they're seeing you play or listening to it. It's wonderful, but seeing it as well that's even better, better than speaking about it in class.
Woman: Yes, I think the visual thing, you know, as I say it's really good to get up and perform and show people, you know, how much fun playing an instrument is ... and then form a group themselves and at the end of the course do a song or two themselves.

Question 4
Presenter: ... it's a special weekend this weekend. Tomorrow, that's the anniversary, was the beginning of Hollywood. Now we don't often do this, not on the BBC, but I'm sending four families to Hollywood. Yes! The hills of Hollywood are calling to celebrate one hundred years of the movies. Four families between now and eleven o'clock.

Hollywood, that's the prize, and also the subject of the question. I'm talking about, I'm looking for ... you can all guess this one ... a most unlikely movie star.

Question 5
Someone's walked away with my car. It's a Volkswagen Golf GTi 16 Valve .... GTi ... yeah, yeah, it's G243 MEP ... 243 ... Mike Edward Peter ... it's dark green with a stripe along the side ... from outside my house, just after I got home from work. It was broad daylight ... yeah, lots of people, but nobody saw anything ... 69 Green Lane ... yes of course I locked it ...

Question 6
Man: I would praise this man to the skies 'cos I think the pigeons in Trafalgar Square are absolute terrible, ghastly creatures and the more of them that are removed ... as painlessly as possible of course ... then ...
Woman: ... they're quite a tourist attraction though. You see loads and loads of tourists with them all over their arms and ...
Man: Nonsense! Think of all the diseases that they're taking away with them when they leave ... erm, I think they're ...
Woman: Parrots!
Man: ... they're terrible things. What?
Woman: That's parrots ... that carry diseases, isn't it?
Man: Well, don't they affect all birds? You're clearly an expert on these things!

Question 7
Woman: ... so no, I didn't really see the sights ... there wasn't much time. The hotel was, er ... the taxi ride to the hotel went through the city centre and I saw a few interesting places. But yeah ... it was a good couple of days ... the conference centre was wonderful, really good facilities, great sports centre we could all use, although I took it easy ... relaxed in the bar. The meeting went really well ... I think we've ironed out the problem at their end ... you'll get the report the end of the week.

Question 8
Woman: ... take Mars, for example, on ... Mars, well, er ... people say, 'Oh, we've been to Mars, we've sent satellites there and there's no life there.' But ... but ... if you imagine it the other way round, if ... if we were on Mars and we sent a rocket, er, satellite to earth, the chances are again it would land in the desert or in the sea ... you know, if you take a sample of soil from the desert there's not gonna be much in it, is there? But that doesn't mean there's no life here, does it?

Unit 2

Part 2 A good read

Student 1
Yes, our class ... we read a book in the lessons and for homework. The teacher decided on the book because all the students didn't agree about the same book ... we all liked different ones. But it, I can't remember the er ... *what it was called*, was very good. Also, we didn't have to study the coursebook every lesson so the lessons were more interesting. The teacher did a lot of exercise about *the people*

who were in the book ... we described them and er ... other things. There was many ... er ... *a lot of speaking in it* so we could do lots of speaking practice in the class. I didn't answer the book question for the er ... in the FCE. I couldn't remember many things. But it was still good to read.

Student 2
I wanted to study more grammar when I studied FCE and also the exam papers. We didn't have much time and I didn't want to read a book. Also it was *about a famous person*, but I can't remember who the person is ..., *about his life*. It was very boring for me. I think we shouldn't do books in class. If students they want to read a book they should do it for homework. All students like different things so not everybody can have a book they like ... so it isn't a good idea. Also, the book we studied was easy. It was made easy for the students ... I think this isn't real English. No. If you ask me, I say study the FCE, don't read books.

Student 3
I don't like to read in my spare time but the teacher ... asked to read a book I didn't want. But the book was very famous. I don't know *the person who wrote the book* but it was famous in my country. It was about a criminal and *it was very exciting* book. Also, it wasn't very difficult so we could read it fast and not look in dictionary all time. Sometimes we read in class but sometimes I read on my own before I went to sleep. It's necessary for us to study English grammar if we want pass the exam but also I think English is not only about FCE. I like learning about the culture and literature so for me reading is good. Also, we can know famous English writers. I think it must be ... must have a good story ... *what the story is about* must be interesting or students will become bored.

Student 4
Well there are good and bad points. First, everyone must read the book. If some students don't do the homework every student has problems. In our class only half read so other students must to explain what happened. I was good at grammar and the FCE exam was not difficult for me so reading a book was no problem for me. But some students they should practise more for the exam so for them reading is a problem maybe. In my school we studied only three months for FCE ... but when you study for one year, then I think the book is a good idea. I liked the book we read. T*he subject it was about* was politics, which I think is interesting. Also our teacher did grammar practice from the book and vocabulary exercises so we learnt a lot of English. So ... students don't only need a coursebook to study.

Unit 2

Part 2 Vocabulary development

a   the things that happen in a story
b   a story dealing with an imaginary world sometimes in the present but usually in the future
c   the sections of a book
d   a book that might give you bad dreams
e   a way of writing
f   you can usually read this very quickly
g   a word similar to plot

h   the main person in the story, sometimes somebody who is very brave
i   the person who writes a novel
j   the name for a type of book that doesn't have a hard cover and is usually quite cheap

Unit 2

Language awareness: question tags
Activity 1

a   We'd better be leaving, hadn't we ?
b   You're from Greece, aren't you?
c   Nobody called while I was out, did they?
d   Let's go to the cinema, shall we?
e   We hardly ever go out, do we?
f   I'm next, aren't I?
g   You don't speak English, do you?
h   You haven't got the time, have you?
i   We should be all right, shouldn't we?
j   We met at the sales conference, didn't we?
k   We have to turn left here, don't we?

Activity 3

a   You're probably studying for FCE, aren't you?
b   You've been studying English for at least a year, haven't you?
c   You can't speak any other languages, can you?
d   You think question tags are easy, don't you?

Activity 5

a   Who invented the telescope?
b   What language do people speak in The Netherlands?
c   Which side of the road do you have to drive on in England?
d   What month is your teacher's birthday?
e   In what year was John Lennon assassinated?
f   What will the date be this time next week?
g   How many times has the Brazilian football team won the World Cup?

Unit 2

Language awareness: past simple and past continuous
Activity 1

It happened when I was about 26 years old. I *often visited* my parents' house for the weekend while I was at university and I *was lying in bed* on Saturday morning *and thinking about getting up* for breakfast. I was suffering from a hangover and feeling terrible when all of a sudden I heard a strange scratching sound behind me ... like this. I thought it was the radio next to my bed, so I *turned over, reached out an arm and pulled out the plug.* But a few minutes later I heard it again. I opened my eyes, looked around the room ... and saw it! In the corner, lying on the floor with its back to me was this enormous rat! It looked like it was eating the wallpaper. I was absolutely petrified! I'd never seen a rat before, so to see one in my bedroom ... well you can imagine. So, I got out of bed, and feeling too scared to look back at the rat, walked very slowly to the door, opened it and ran downstairs. *Two relations were also visiting that weekend.* But I was so scared I just ran into the dining room wearing only a pair of underpants. M*y mum was just serving the breakfast* when I *screamed*, 'There's a rat in my bedroom ... a rat!' My mum thought I was absolutely mad and told everybody to ignore me. But I insisted that someone went upstairs to look. My brother led the way, followed by my mum, dad, the two relations and me. When we got to the bedroom door I pushed to the front, opened the door and without looking in, pointed to the place where I'd seen it. 'It's over there, can you see it?' My mum looked round the corner, shook her head, looked at me and said, 'You idiot!... a rat eh?' I looked round the door and there, lying on the floor where my rat had been, was the pair of socks I'd taken off and thrown against the wall the night before! You can imagine how embarrassed I felt. I never did learn my lesson. I'm still too lazy to hang my clothes up at night!

Unit 3

Part 1   A problem shared

Host: Good afternoon and welcome again to the programme that looks at issues affecting the youth of today. Here in the studio this afternoon we again have John Sissons (hello), a student counsellor, Mary Whiteworth, a secondary school teacher, (hello) and the agony aunt Jane Edmunds (hello). Now, John. I hear you've been doing some investigating.

John: That's right. If you remember, we had a letter last week asking about the differences in ages of consent around Europe.

Host: Any interesting findings?

John: Nothing particularly surprising, although there certainly is a bit of variety. Take schooling, for example. As you know, in England all children require schooling from the age of five to sixteen. This is much longer than in many other countries. In Sweden it's between seven and sixteen, in Italy between six and fourteen and in Greece between five and a half and fourteen and a half.

Host: What about crime? If I remember correctly, the letter was interested in the ages at which children across Europe are held responsible for committing a crime?

John: Yes, well again, it varies from country to country. It's ten in England. In Scotland it's eight and in Greece it's as low as seven years old. In France and Germany on the other hand you're free from legal responsibility until you're fourteen. There are also differences in terms of marriage. Generally speaking, girls are allowed to marry earlier than boys. In Greece it's eighteen for boys and fourteen for girls, although the girl needs her parents' consent until she's eighteen years old. In France the girl must be fifteen, the boy eighteen, whilst in England, as you know, it's sixteen for both the boy and the girl.

Host: So what about this letter from Kelly? Should she really be considering leaving school? Mary? You're the teacher. What do you think?

Mary: Certainly not! What is she thinking of? None of us likes rules or being told to do things, but it would be such a waste if she turned her back on education simply because she doesn't like wearing a school uniform.

Jane: Yes, listen, Kelly. I hated our school uniform! It was an awful green colour ... very unfashionable ... really horrible. But listen, dear. Can't you put up with it for just a few more years? As for being called by your family name, I like to think that your teachers will start treating you a little more like adults after your sixteenth birthday.

John: I totally agree. I think Kelly's teachers need to take a little responsibility for the way she's feeling. Honestly! If the teachers want respect from their students it's about time they started treating them with a bit more respect themselves. I hated being called by my surname at school. The teachers wouldn't like it if the students called them by their surnames, would they? Yes, Kelly. Try and ignore it. There aren't many jobs out there at the moment. Stay on and get your qualifications!

Host: Well, there you are, Kelly. The general opinion is stick it out. Now, what about this one from Carol? She really is in a difficult position, isn't she, Jane?

Jane: Yes. I get so many letters from people on this subject. My own opinion is that parents can be rather silly at times. We don't know the whole story of course, but if it is simply to do with school work I think they should deal with the problem a little more sensitively. Carol, try talking with your parents about this. Maybe you could come to some agreement. You promise to get all your homework or revision done before calling your boyfriend or going out to see him.

John: Be careful though, Carol. As you say, you don't want to upset your parents or do things behind their backs. Why not try and get them to meet your boyfriend? Invite him round for dinner and all sit down and talk about it.

Mary: Yes. I agree with John. As a teacher I'm often hearing complaints like this. Sometimes, attitudes like this can do more damage to the child's education than any boy or girlfriend. Why don't you try and get your parents to meet your boyfriend's parents. Try to build up a little trust.

Host: Finally, we have Steve's letter. Is this another case of parents over-reacting? Mary?

Mary: Not really, no. I can understand the parents' concern in this case. Motor bikes can be terribly dangerous. I certainly wouldn't allow a son or daughter of mine to own one. Sorry, Steve. I agree with your parents. Spend your money on something a little safer.

John: I totally disagree! The parents shouldn't promise something they're not prepared to do. Steve's carried out his side of the bargain, I think it's time for them to honour their side. OK. Bikes are dangerous. Why don't you agree to take some lessons, Steve? Show them that you're aware of the dangers and are willing to do something about it.

Jane: This is a difficult one. I agree with Mary. I really don't like motor bikes. But it's not really a good idea to break a promise, is it? This problem needs to be resolved or Steve could end up resenting his parents. Have you ever thought about a car, Steve? You'll soon be old enough to take driving lessons and in the meantime you could continue saving up. Why not see if your parents would agree to add a little more towards it?

Host: Yes, that's a nice idea, Jane. Well, let us know how things turn out, Steve. Now, we're now going to turn to the issue of ....

Unit 3

Part 2 Brain-teasers

The Plane Crash
Susan watched her husband get on the 8.15 p.m. flight from Toronto to Chicago. She then drove home from the airport and sat down to watch a movie. Halfway through the movie there was a news flash; the 8.15 p.m. flight from Toronto to Chicago had crashed and sadly there were no survivors. However, Susan was quite unconcerned and continued to watch the movie. Why?

The Lost Passenger
Little Billy was four years old and both his parents were dead. He was put on a train to send him to a new home in the country. Billy couldn't read or write and couldn't remember his address, so a message was hung round his neck showing Billy's name and destination. However, Billy never arrived at his new home. Why?

Unit 4

Part 1 A taste of Britain

When it's well cooked haggis is absolutely delicious. The main ingredients are lamb's liver and heart and, of course, you'll only find the best haggis in Scotland where it's usually served with 'neeps', a creamy mashed potato. A lot of people are put off eating it when they discover that it's wrapped in a sheep's bladder! But plastic bags are hard to find in the mountainous regions where it's made. For an authentic version try Charles McSween and Son, 130 Bruntsfield Place, Edinburgh.

Yorkshire pudding is popular throughout England where it's eaten as part of the traditional Sunday roast dinner. It's made from a mixture of milk, flour, eggs and cooking fat and baked in the oven. However, cheese and even sometimes beer is added to give it·extra taste. The Spurriergate Centre, York serves an extraordinary range of Yorkshire puddings.

You can travel the world but you'll never find anything quite as delicious as a Cream Tea. The best Cream Teas are found in Devon, home of the dairy industry that produces the famous clotted cream, which must, of course, be as fresh as possible when used. For home-made scones – a crumbly dry cake – topped with jam and cream and accompanied by a nice pot of English tea, go to the Old Forge at Totnes, Seymour Place, Totnes.

Originally, Cornish pasties were the basic food for the Cornish tin miners over 200 years ago. They look like a parcel made of pastry holding together a mixture of beef and vegetables. After a hard morning's work the miners would sit down to their lunch, but because of the nature of their job, their hands would be covered in poisonous substances. The design of the pasty enabled the miners to eat the meat and vegetables before throwing away the contaminated pastry. Try one at the Cornwall Patisserie, Lower Lemon Street, Truro.

Wales is famous throughout Britain for the quality of its lamb which is probably the sweetest, leanest and most tender in the world. The secret of Welsh Lamb Pie, a regional speciality, rests in the lamb being cooked very slowly for several hours in a saucepan with locally produced vegetables. The cooked meat and vegetables are finally topped with a covering of light crusty pastry. One of the best places to eat it is: Blas ar Gymru (The Taste of Wales), 48 Crwys Road, Cardiff.

Unit 4

Part 2 Host families

F = Friend
D = Dimi

F: Hi! May I speak to Dimi, please?
D: Hello! It's me. It's great to hear from you.
F: How are you enjoying your stay in England?
D: It's really OK. Mrs Smith and her family have made me very welcome.
F: Listen, before you tell me any more, can you give me your address so I can write to you?
D: Have you got a pen? It's 17 Stoke Road, that's S-T-O-K-E Road, London, England, of course.
F: So what's it like being with an English family? Do they have a nice house?
D: Well, the house is very big, but my room is a bit cramped. But at least I've got a desk in there so I can study at night.
F: And how's the food?
D: I'm afraid I don't like it much – it's so boring. We have potatoes all the time. If it's not chips, it's mashed or roast potatoes. I quite like their jacket potatoes though, that's potatoes served with the skin on. If I'm not careful, I'll turn into a potato!
F: Well, try not to get too fat. Are you going out much?
D: Yes, but not too often with my family. Whenever they go out, they are kind enough to invite me, and when I first arrived they had planned lots of social events, but really I prefer to see my own friends. I've made quite a few.
F: So your English will be brilliant now?
D: Not really. Mrs Smith and I are always so busy that we don't have much time to sit down and really talk to each other. It's a pity. But she's very helpful about practical things. For example, on my first day at college she took me to the bus stop, so I wouldn't get lost.
F: So everything's fine, more or less?
D: Sure. Oh, there's only one problem. They have this disgusting dog as a pet, and he must know I hate dogs because he always comes into my room in the morning and tries to jump on the bed! But apart from that I'm fine. The best thing is that the atmosphere is very warm and welcoming.
F: Well, I'd better go now. Take care.
D: Thanks for ringing and don't forget to write soon. Bye.
F: Bye.

Unit 4

Part 3 Out and about in England

I = Interlocutor
A = Candidate A
B = Candidate B

I: Now, I'd like each of you to talk on your own for about a minute. I'm going to give each of you two different photographs and I'd like you to talk about them. Candidate A, here are your two photographs. (Thank you.) They show different types of leisure activities. Please let Candidate B have a look at them. Candidate B, I'll give you your photographs in a minute. (Yes.)
    Candidate A, I'd like you to compare and contrast these pictures saying how you feel about leisure activities like these. Remember, you only have about a minute for this, so don't worry if I interrupt you. All right?

A: OK. In this photograph we have three women and one me... one man working out in a fitness centre. Mmm, they seem to be happy but er, quite er but er they are busy. We can see here most of them are women perhaps because they are pushed by their society to be fit these days. I don't know, you can see er, just a man here. These women are in different kind of machines. And in this other photograph er there's two girls er women er in a shop they seem to be happy as well er as is natural for women they want to, they want to... they like to go shopping. The women are looking at the window and er ... it seems to be a luxury shop ... a little bit er these girls, er it's different because in the shop there are things that I don't think the girls want to buy. But if you ask me which I do prefer I think I will prefer er the first one photograph because erm ... perhaps I ... it's because I like sports an' all that. But erm ... I prefer to er ... I don't know to make some sport outside, not in a fitness centre because it might be a little bit boring.

I: Thank you. Candidate B, could you tell us which leisure activity you would prefer, please?

B: Well, er there are women in a fitness centre and women who are shopping. Er ... I don't like the , er ... shop who are ... in which the women are shopping. I like shopping yes but I think I like shop to buy clothes or something like I can use every time. And I used to make body-building for er ... three years I enjoy, I enjoyed it very much at that time and I think I would like to be in the fitness centre more.

I: Thank you. Now, Candidate B, here are your two photographs. They again show people involved in different leisure activities. Please let Candidate A have a look at them. I'd like you to compare and contrast these pictures saying which activity you prefer and why. Remember, you only have about a minute for this, so don't worry if I interrupt you. All right?

B: I have two pictures. One of them is er being done in a restaurant, the other one in a house, I think. In the first picture there are three, four teenagers. Three of them are girls and one boy who are in a restaurant and um, they seem that they're enjoying their time very much. And they are so lifelike that er I er you can feel their happiness in the picture. In the second picture there are five mens, five very elder, very elderly mens who are playing poker. And er ... er ... although they seem that

they enjoy their time too, but I think it's poker is a very domestic thing, it's being made by people who er nothing to do at all so elderly people who are belonging to a club. And I think I would prefer to be with my friends in a er er restaurant and er enjoy myself. It must be a little bit music in something like that. In my country, Turkey, cards are not very common to er play in er in small society we are doing other things. We are talking about things or doing barbeques, barbeques are very popular when we are together. And we have very different kind of er enjoying our life. It couldn't be described as with playing poker.

I: Thank you. Candidate A, could you tell us which activity looks more attractive to you, please?

A: I think I will prefer playing cards. I don't know why. I really like to play cards and it's very common in Spain as well. But I like I like to play to er go outside to a restaurant and enjoy myself with my friends as well ... it's really good, but I think I like both. I can do them both easily.

I: Thank you.

Unit 4

Language awareness: modal verbs of obligation
Activity 1

S = Mrs Sproggit
C = Carlos
I = Isabella

Part One

S: Welcome to my house, Carlos. Let me start by explaining some important rules and regulations. I always say my guests are much happier when they know what's expected of them.

C: Yes, certainly, Mrs Sproggit.

S: Breakfast is served at 8.00. You should be out of bed by 7.30 to help me make it. My husband has to work late and so likes to lie in until late. You don't have to take him up a cup of tea in the morning but I'm sure he will appreciate it if you do.

C: Really?

S: Yes. Dinner is usually served at 6.00. You must tell me if you're going to be home late ... I do hate to see food going to waste, don't you, Carlos?

C: Yes, Mrs Sproggit.

S: Now, Carlos, I know what young men are like, always leaving their bedrooms in a mess. You mustn't forget to tidy your bedroom every morning. You needn't worry too much about dusting and polishing the furniture up there, although if you've got nothing else to do it might help pass the time.

C: Well, actually, Mrs Sproggit ...

S: My husband and I like to go to bed quite early at night. You needn't worry about going to bed as early as us, although we do like to see our guests tucked up in bed by about 9.30. Early to bed early to rise makes a man healthy, wealthy and wise, Carlos. Oh yes, that reminds me, you must let me know if you're expecting to be home later than 9.30. You ought to try and make sure you're never home later than that ... once I'm asleep it's impossible to wake me up.

C: Yes, Mrs Sproggit.

S: Finally, the bathroom, Carlos. You should tell me how often you take a shower so that I can calculate your share of the electricity bill. Is that clear? And I don't mind putting your clothes in the washing machine once a week, but you must help me with the ironing. If there's one thing I hate it's ironing. OK, Carlos?

C: But, Mrs Sproggit ...

S: Now, I made a nice pot of tea before you arrived.

C: Mrs Sproggit! You needn't have gone to so much trouble.

S: Not at all, Carlos. You wouldn't mind pouring it, would you? I feel quite tired all of a sudden.

Part Two

I: Carlos, I hear you are staying with a Mrs Sproggit. I told the college secretary that I wanted to stay with a host family and she recommended her.

C: Mrs Sproggit? Take my advice. If you want to enjoy your time in England, don't live with Mrs Sproggit! I have to tell her if I'm going to be home late for my dinner ... I have to tidy my bedroom every morning ... and I have to let her know if I'm going to be home later than 9.30 every evening! Last week I even had to help her with the ironing!

I: Oh dear. Maybe I should try somewhere else.

C: She went to visit her sister yesterday. It was great! I didn't need to tidy the bedroom or do any housework. I left a note to say I'd be late for dinner, but I needn't have bothered because she stayed out all night. She'll be back tomorrow, though. It's washing day so I suppose I'll have to help her again. I can't wait until September.

I: Why is that, Carlos?

C: I go back to Spain to join the army. It'll seem like a holiday after living with Mrs Sproggit!

Unit 5

Part 1 It doesn't add up!

I = Interviewer
Ms W = Ms Williams

I: Ms Williams, you are the headteacher of a local primary school and you believe that your young pupils should learn to use computers at a very early age.

Ms W: Yes, using computers is an essential skill these days, and if children can get used to them this is a good thing. Particularly so since, although many of their parents are starting to have computers at home, they don't really want their children to play on them, so at school all children can have the chance to try them out. At the moment we have started a project for our eight-year-old pupils where they write and publish short stories using the computer. It's very good indeed.

I: Surely one advantage is that the presentation of pupils' work is very good when it's done on a computer.

Ms W: Absolutely. They can change the layout and the size of the print very easily. Our only concern is that pupils must not forget how to write by hand. One drawback is that when they write with pen and paper,

their work has become more untidy. We constantly have to remind them that good handwriting is still important.

I: What about the children's stories? Have they become better writers?

Ms W: No, it wouldn't be correct to say that a young child will become the next William Shakespeare simply because of using a computer! However, I would say that generally our pupils find writing with computers very exciting and motivating. They aren't nervous about new technology in the way that many adults are. This is another point. I think that many parents are glad that their children are learning computer skills which are important in the real world, obviously not for all jobs, but many.

I: We hear many people say that using computers to write makes people lazy, about learning spelling for instance. Why bother to remember how a word is spelt if you can get the computer to check your spelling for you?

Ms W: I disagree quite strongly with this argument. What's the difference between using a Spellcheck on a computer and using an old-fashioned dictionary? There isn't any, apart from the fact that the first method is simply easier.

I: Computers are expensive to put in schools. Would it be better to spend the money on other things?

Ms W: Well, there are those teachers who would like to see every child at school with access to their own computer. At the moment we have one computer room with twelve computers. In a class of about thirty-five this means that pupils have to share, two or three to one computer. This is a good thing, in my opinion, because it helps children to work in a team and to share and co-operate with each other.

Unit 5

Part 2 Useful inventions?

Advert One

No need to get the vacuum cleaner out for a little piece of paper or a bit of dust. And don't go running to the cupboard to get the dustpan and brush! Make your life easier with the help of our mini Dust-away Slippers. Dust-away Slippers have a left toe-mounted mini-dustpan and a right toe-mounted mini-brush. Now you can deal with mess as you meet it! Just a walk around the house and the cleaning's practically finished. The whole family will be pleased to do a spot of housework with the help of your Dust-away Slippers. Don't delay! Send for your pair now while stocks last.

Advert Two

We all know what it's like! There you are sitting on the train after a hard day's work. There's some time to go before you reach home, your eyes get heavy, you start to doze when ... mmmmph ... your head falls forward and you're back in the land of the living, or perhaps you wake up to find yourself sleeping on someone else's shoulder ... perhaps you've even missed your stop! Thanks to our new Handy Helmet everybody can have a secure sleep on the underground. The Handy Helmet sports the message, 'I'm having a short nap. Could you please wake me up when I reach the stop written below.' The handy suction pad keeps your head firmly upright. An ideal way of saving your blushes and keeping your head off of your neighbour's shoulder.

Advert Three
Conventional umbrellas are ideal for keeping us dry from the knees up, but how many pairs of shoes have you ruined going out in the pouring rain? No matter how big the umbrella is we still seem to get the lower parts of our legs wet and have no protection right where we need it most – for those long-suffering shoes! Worry no more with our new Umbrella Shoe Protectors. The mini-umbrellas have a 30 cm diameter, and will keep the rain off the full front of the foot area. Take off the umbrellas when you get where you're going and your shoes look as good as they did when you put them on. If you're not totally satisfied with your Umbrella Shoe Protectors, return them within 21 days and your money will be refunded.

Advert Four
Are you, or any of your friends or family, an unfortunate hay-fever sufferer? Maybe somebody you love has one of those irritating head colds that never seem to go away. Are there never any tissues around when you need one? Having a cold or hay-fever is bad enough but running out of hankies turns misfortune into misery. The Hanky Hat offers you or your loved ones an all-day tissue dispenser. The hat supports a large toilet roll, big enough to deal with heavy blowing and constant sneezing from morning till night.

Advert Five
Here's an ideal gadget for the commuter. And just useful enough for you to be the envy of your strapless fellow passengers! You haven't got a seat on the underground, worse still all the straps are taken ... except that is for the one you keep in your briefcase! The portable Supa-strap comes with a plunger type sucker attached to one end that fastens securely to the roof of the train. The suction is just strong enough to take the weight off your feet, just weak enough to be removed with a firm pull at the end of your journey.

Unit 5

Part 3 Is Big Brother watching *you*?

There is nothing new about the use of surveillance cameras in this country. We have been using them for many years in the fight against crime. Traditionally, they have been used in shopping centres as a way of catching shoplifters, and cameras have been installed on many motorways as a way of discouraging people from speeding. Of course, we have always advised people (if they can afford it) to put a security camera outside their house – particularly if they have very large properties to protect from burglars. Another use in the past ten years or so has been to film people at large sporting events such as football matches, where small minorities of football hooligans can spoil the pleasure of the majority. All of these uses of cameras are a good thing as they make the general public feel safer and more secure.

You may remember the case, around five years ago, where a new baby was kidnapped from a hospital. A woman simply walked in and took someone else's baby. The problem is that hospitals are very open places – people come and go all the time. Since then, many hospitals have decided to use security cameras to monitor the movements of the general public, in order to prevent such a crime from happening again.

More recently, we have seen the introduction of cameras in public places such as car parks, where car theft is now decreasing as a result, I'm pleased to say. A new development has been the installing of cameras in educational institutions – schools and colleges – and in the workplace – in office lifts, for example. Again, the main aim is to prevent the theft of valuable equipment such as computers, and other crimes like vandalism and graffiti. I can understand, however, that people are becoming concerned about their rights of privacy, especially when they go about their daily business such as work or school. These are two areas we should be concerned about.

Unit 5

Language awareness: future (1)
Activity 3

Anna: Have you heard? Carl wants to come and visit me during the summer.
Cathy: That'll be nice. You know how much he likes you!
Anna: That's exactly why I don't want him to come! I've heard from one of his friends that he is going to ask me for a date!
Cathy: Wonderful news, I think I'm going to cry! I'm only joking. So when is he coming?
Anna: Don't say it like that. You make it sound as if it's all arranged! He is going on another walking holiday in Scotland with a friend. He gets back from there at the end of July. He wants to come after that.
Cathy: Well, I'm seeing Joanne then. We've already made plans to visit the coast.
Anna: But you can't leave me on my own with Carl! I'll go mad if I have to spend a week alone with him.
Cathy: Shall I phone Joanne and ask if you can come along as well?
Anna: Great idea! I'll write back now and tell him it's not possible.
Cathy: Poor Carl. He was saying on the phone how much he was looking forward to seeing you. He'll be really disappointed.
Anna: Not half as disappointed as I'm going to be if Joanne says I can't come!

Unit 5

Language awareness: present perfect simple and continuous
Activity 1

I've worked for the company for 25 years.
We've never met before, have we?
Have you ever had your name in a newspaper?
He's lived in the same house all his life.
I've lost my keys!
The Prime Minister's resigned.

Activity 5

Presenter: Students in the Midlands are divided over their college's decision to install closed circuit cameras in an attempt to cut theft and vandalism. The Student Union at St Martin's College claim that the college has been installing hidden cameras without any regard to privacy. As Mark of the Student Union explains …

Mark: We all appreciate the need for security, but the college are putting these cameras everywhere. They've even put one in the toilet! We've asked to speak to the Principal about this on several occasions but he refuses to discuss the matter.

Presenter: However, not everybody is against the idea. Here's Karen, a biology student …

Karen: We've been witnessing a lot more petty crime recently. I've been studying here for three years now. It never used to be like this.

Presenter: In a short interview yesterday the Principal stood firm …

Principal: The college has always acted in the interests of the students and will continue to do so. I will not tolerate such anti-social behaviour in my college.

Unit 6

Part 1 Finding your perfect soul mate

S1 = Speaker 1
S2 = Speaker 2
S3 = Speaker 3

S1: For me, a soul mate is a special kind of friend. It isn't someone you have a physical relationship with, or get married to, but more somebody who you always feel close to no matter how rarely you see them. It doesn't matter if you live hundreds of miles apart, because when you do get together, your friendship is just the same as always.

S2: I'm not sure I agree with you about that. I think that people spend all their lives looking for the perfect soul mate to spend the rest of their life with. I know that if I found my soul mate, I would marry her tomorrow!

S3: I think a soul mate is someone who is like yourself in every single way. You have the same interests and hobbies, the same hopes and dreams for the future, you like to do things together and you may even know what the other person is thinking! I guess it's like having an identical twin.

Unit 6

Part 2 The lottery

Speaker One

Yes, I suppose it'd be nice to win lots of money. But I don't think I could cope with all the pressures of being a winner. It would drive me crazy! Can you imagine all the reporters asking for interviews, having your picture in all the papers. When you win that much money you become a celebrity, don't you? The change in your lifestyle would be difficult to handle, wouldn't it? No, sorry, the money would be nice but only if you could keep it secret.

Speaker Two

If the government raised taxes by two or three pounds a week everybody would go mad. Yet everybody gets so excited about winning the Lottery they seem to completely forget they're wasting their money. They must be mad if they think they've got a chance of winning. You've got more chance of being hit by lightning or being invited to dinner with the Queen! OK, I know they spend lots of money on things like art galleries and sports facilities, which is the only reason why I agree with it, but winning the jackpot? No chance!

Speaker Three

It's just good fun, isn't it? It's most people's dream to be rich and never have to work again. And you wouldn't ever have to work again with so much money … can you imagine? Seventeen million pounds! I think they could share the profits out more fairly though. I heard a new opera house is going to be built and several museums are going to be given some money. But those kind of things are for the middle classes, aren't they? There are other things that would benefit poorer people like spending some on hospitals or schools. They could even build more houses. That's the only criticism I have.

Speaker Four

Every week I put all the numbers into my computer and try to see if there's any pattern, any numbers that appear more regularly than others. Numbers with three in them … 3, 13, 23, etc. … they're always in the jackpot line. I'm sure there's a way of working out the winning numbers and as soon as I've found out what it is, I'll be a jackpot winner. Some people say the jackpot's too high … they must be stupid, or jealous! You just wait. One day my name will be in all the newspapers holding a cheque for seventeen million pounds!

Speaker Five

Yeah, I do it every week … only two tickets, one for me and one for my wife. We only do it for fun really. We know we're never going to win the jackpot. In fact I don't think I'd want to win it. In fact nobody really needs all that money. They should make the top prize half a million pounds or a million pounds at the most. That way you would have more than one winner every week. But it's good fun, and really exciting. And at least you know your money is being spent on worthwhile causes.

Unit 6

Part 3 Cults

I was on holiday at the time in Munich, only for a fortnight. I was about 22 and travelling alone. During the second week I was walking along the street when a young woman stopped me and asked me if I'd like to answer a few questions. She was fluent in English – luckily – because my German wasn't that good at the time! I had nothing better to do so I thought 'why not?' I thought that she'd ask me questions about what toothpaste I used or something, like those market researchers do, but they were quite general questions. Things like 'Are you happy with your life?', 'Do you have a loving family?' and so on. When she'd finished she invited me to her office which was nearby, and asked me if I'd like to do a proper questionnaire. At the time, I wasn't suspicious at all and I went along with it quite happily.

Afterwards, one of her colleagues looked at my answers to the questionnaire and told me that they had some special programmes that could help me become a more confident and happy person. The programmes were quite cheap. What you have to understand is that the people involved were very friendly and welcoming, and they made me feel as though they really wanted to help me. By the end of the session I was so excited that I immediately phoned England to hand in my notice; it was a horrible job in an office, fairly well paid but boring.

That night, though, I also phoned my brother in England to tell him that I thought I'd found the answer to life, and I was staying in Germany. He reacted quite calmly at first, but when I told him why he went absolutely crazy. Apparently, the week before in England there had been a newspaper story about a similar organisation to the one I'd met in Germany. They were a cult group who operated by trying to get young, lonely people. You can imagine how upset and disappointed I was, but luckily when I got back to England my boss gave me back my job. I think I had a lucky escape!

Unit 6

Language awareness: articles
Activity 8

Good evening. Here is (...) Nine O'Clock News read by (...) John Stewart. (...) Prime Minister has arrived in (...) Washington and is due to meet (...) President later today. It is his first trip to (...) United States and both men are reported to be looking forward to discussing ways of improving (...) trade between (...) Britain and (...) America.

(...) fire has broken out in (...) centre of London bringing chaos to (...) rush hour traffic. (...) fire broke out in (...) factory overlooking (...) Thames at Greenwich and has been burning fiercely all afternoon. (...) factory is reported to be completely destroyed and firemen are still fighting to keep (...) fire under control.

(...) eighteen-year-old boy became (...) youngest ever winner of (...) World Snooker Championships in Sheffield today. Kevin Shields from Carlisle took (...) title and (...) cheque for £200,000 after (...) exciting seven-hour battle with last year's champion, Steve Williams. After (...) final his father, (...) fifty-nine-year-old bank clerk, said that he would now have to forgive his son for spending all his youth in (...) local snooker hall. 'Hopefully he'll treat me to (...) drink in (...) pub tonight ...'

Unit 7

Part 2 It's your environment

I = Interviewer
K = Karen Baker

I: I have with me in the studio Karen Baker, a leading conservationist. Karen, can we really make a difference as individuals to improve the environment and save resources?

K: Oh yes, quite a lot actually. People often forget that as individuals we have a lot of power whether as consumers

... buyers of goods ... or as people who together can make a difference through the actions we take. If lots of individuals work together they can often achieve a lot.

I: Could you give us some idea of what these actions might be?

K: Certainly. We're all shoppers, aren't we? Well, as shoppers we have tremendous power to influence manufacturers. I'm so often shocked by the amount of packaging ... wasted packaging that comes with the goods we buy. So an immediate action could be to buy goods that keep packaging to a minimum. Or if a shop assistant offers you a plastic bag you don't need, simply refuse it ... politely of course.

I: Yes, yes, I see your point.

K: Also as consumers, we can refuse to buy products made from animals threatened with extinction, ivory products or fur coats for example. Or maybe refuse to buy products that have required experiments on animals. If manufacturers don't supply this information ... write a letter and ask.

I: Yes, I suppose as customers we have a lot of power, don't we? You were talking about waste earlier. We have so many things in our homes, perfectly good things, that we don't use any more. Couldn't we make more use of these things instead of making even more waste?

K: Oh yes! That's a really important point. I personally never throw anything away. Especially things that other people might be able to use. You must have friends or relations that could do with some of these things ... maybe you could even swap them for things they have that you'd like. Remember, don't throw away your rubbish – recycle it!

I: Good idea. What about pollution? Is there anything we as individuals can do to clean up the environment? The problems of pollution are often so big that it's easy to feel helpless, isn't it?

K: I know. We often hear of terrible disasters on TV that require massive clean-up operations, but there are many smaller-scale problems that we can tackle. Get together with a few friends and make a study of pollution in your area. You could help to clear the rubbish from a local stream or river or even tidy up an area of wasteland. People can also join a campaign group, either a local or a national one, and get involved in action to improve your neighbourhood and to try and change people's attitudes.

I: Now, I know you're presently involved in a campaign to encourage people to save energy. What kind of tips have you got for the listeners that could help them do this?

K: Well, the car is here to stay and it would be foolish to ask people not to use them, but we could all try to avoid unnecessary car journeys. Go by bike or public transport sometimes or if you work in the same area as your neighbour, try car-sharing. Take it in turns to drive to work. And in the home, don't leave lights and other electrical equipment on. An enormous amount of energy is wasted this way.

I: Well, I'm afraid we've run out of time for now, but thanks for coming in to the studio. I'll certainly try putting some of your ideas into practice.

Unit 7

Part 3 Out of this world

I = Interlocutor
A = Candidate A
B = Candidate B

I: Now, I'd like each of you to talk on your own for about a minute. I'm going to give each of you two different photographs and I'd like you to talk about them. Candidate A, here are your two photographs. They show different types of holidays. (Oh!) Please let Candidate B have a look at them. Candidate B, I'll give you your photographs in a minute. (Yes.)

Candidate A, I'd like you to compare and contrast these pictures saying how you feel about holidays like these. Remember, you only have about a minute for this, so don't worry if I interrupt you. All right?

A: Here we have two pictures, one is from er er tropical beach. I assume this is in the Caribbean because the water is very blue. And the other one is er sightseeing, er, there is a cathedral and some people. Both of them are beautiful, I would like to do er er both of them I think. Er but one er the ... in of the er beach I think's better for summer and I think it's really romantic, so er I think it's good for er honeymoon or something like that. On the other hand in the other picture of this cathedral is really beautiful and the picture and the cathedral. And personally I really like sightseeing and I think I would enjoy both of them. Of course, this kind of holiday is better in the summer also, but if it rains you can always go inside somewhere. Perhaps if I have to choose maybe er I, I choose sightseeing because all my life I have been near the beach and perhaps I'm a little bit fed up of that, it's normal for me. But, as I told you, I like both.

I: Thank you. Candidate B, could you tell us which holiday you would prefer, please?

B: Er in my country we have the same scenes everywhere and er many times I have the occasion to go to beach or seaside and I think it's not exciting for me. Er in the other picture we have old cathedral and I'm, I'm really interested in history, I wanted to be a history teacher, now everywhere when I'm in a foreign place I try to go to places and take small pictures of old buildings.

I: Thank you. Now, Candidate B, here are your two photographs. They again show different holidays. Please let Candidate A have a look at them. I'd like you to compare and contrast these pictures saying which holiday you prefer and why. Remember Candidate B, you only have about a minute for this, so don't worry if I interrupt you. All right?

B: Er one of my pictures is I think from Africa safari holiday, one is backpacking. And er in the backpacking there are two men who are at the station and er are going on holiday. In the second there are, er there is a big car, er two men are on the car and they have their cameras, er they're staring on the elephant which I think it's very cruel because I er I don't, I can't imagine that any of the human beings can er would feel home if someone was staring at them and I think people are disturbing the domestic life of the peop ... er of the, of the animals on, in safari holidays. And er at the same time they're disturbing the nature, they leave, they're leaving lots of litter things who are killing the natural life of the animals. But er I think I, I've never been in backpacking holiday but I think I would enjoy it because it seems so freedom. You can do anything for ... er even if it's for two weeks, I think I would enjoy it. It's a whole freedom for two weeks.

I: Thank you. Candidate A, could you tell us which holiday looks more attractive to you, please?

A: Well, it's difficult for me to say which of them I prefer because I really like adventure and I think er being in Africa, I suppose this is in Africa because of because of the elephant and I really like that kind of holiday ... I haven't had the opportunity to do that. But on the other hand I have been backpacking and it's a great experience and it's a good holiday for a student because most of them they don't have enough money.

I: Thank you.

Unit 7

Language awareness: future (2)
Activity 2

Linda: So I hear you're off on one of your wonderful holidays soon.

Harry: I certainly am! This time next week I'll be walking on the moon! I bet you'd love to come, wouldn't you?

Linda: Not really, no. By the time you arrive, you'll probably have been sick about ten times on the journey.

Harry: Come on. You're just jealous. Just imagine. Next weekend I'll be standing up there and looking at Earth.

Linda: That's true. But you won't have sent many postcards home by then, will you? You won't find any post offices on the moon, I can tell you.

Harry: Yeah, yeah! Just think. I'll have spent a whole week in space by the time I get back.

Linda: Yeah. And I'm sure as soon as you get back you'll be showing us all your lovely photographs.

Unit 8

Part 1 Get the picture?

Tip one
First of all, if you want to be a successful artist, you should draw as much as you can, and as often as you can. Don't just draw the things you're good at. For example, if you're good at drawing animals, but bad at drawing, say, people, then you should keep practising people, until you improve. That way you will become good at drawing lots of different things.

Tip two
Being a cartoonist you have to be good at drawing different facial expressions. For example, look at this pair of eyes. I can make them look angry or annoyed by drawing two lines like this. By contrast, if I draw the lines in the opposite direction, I create an expression of surprise. I can make a mouth look sad simply by drawing it upside down. Remember that the most important elements in a face are the eyes and the mouth.

Tip three

My third tip would be to learn about proportion. Proportion means putting things in the right place. If I draw an oval shape like this – and call it a head – then the eyes would go approximately halfway down. Remember that you don't always have to follow the rules of proportion, particularly if you are a cartoonist, but they are useful to know in the beginning.

Tip four

When you are drawing people, the starting point is always the face. It is here that the character of the person is shown best. If you look at most cartoon figures, you will notice that the body is almost always very small in relation to the head. Here is a picture of a man with a classic cartoon body.

Tip five

When you are drawing somebody in action, exaggerate it! Here's this man running. Now look at the way his hair is flying behind him. Of course, in real life this doesn't happen, but in a cartoon we exaggerate everything. Look at the perspiration coming off his body as well, showing how hot he is. And by having this shadow underneath him I can create the illusion of him being above the ground, almost flying through the air.

Tip six

Now what about what not to do? Try to remember to be as simple as possible. Simple circles, ovals, dots and curved and straight lines are really all you need. If you try to draw eyes in the shape that you 'know' they have – that is, like two circles – you will kill the expression completely!

Unit 8

Part 2 Salsa fever!

M = Maverick
A = Anneka

M: OK, everybody, are you listening? OK, I'm going to teach you the basic salsa step. Anyone can do it once they know how. Now watch me first. Standing with your feet together, the first step is to tap the floor with your right foot like this. Now step back with the same foot. That's step two. Now for step three, bring the left foot across the right foot. No, no, ... Make sure you are in front of the right foot and not behind. OK? Now the fourth step is to bring your right foot back in line with the left. So, to sum up, step one is to TAP, step two is to go BACK, step three is to bring the other foot ACROSS, and step four is to bring your feet TOGETHER. So ... it's TAP, BACK, ACROSS, TOGETHER. Try it by yourselves for a while. OK, you should be looking at your partner, not at your feet, but don't smile. Salsa is a serious business! Now I want you to repeat the same movement on the other side. So it's tap with the left foot, that's step five. Then go back with the left foot. Step seven is to bring the right foot across, and step eight?
A: Bring the left foot in line with the right?
M: Exactly. Well done. Now let me see you practise. And ... tap, back, across, together, tap, back, across, together ... You can get the rhythm with plenty of practice.

Unit 8

Part 3 The fans who go too far

Report 1

German Take That fans are so upset at the news that Robbie Williams is leaving the band that a special telephone helpline has been set up for unhappy fans. One man has already contacted the helpline to say that his two daughters had thrown all the furniture out of the house and were now beating up their mother.

Report 2

It's not only teenagers who are devastated by the news that Take That are to split up. A six-year-old fan had to be taken to the doctor because she wouldn't stop crying at the news. Her mother told reporters that she had been given a ticket to see the band for her birthday, and has been hysterical ever since the news was announced.

Report 3

An obsessed Michael Jackson fan was so angry when her hero was accused of child abuse that she tracked down the family of Jordy Chandler, the 14-year-old boy at the centre of the case. She hounded them with late-night phone calls and then attacked Jordy's parents while they were out shopping. She escaped a prison sentence.

Report 4

A Nirvana fan has shot himself after lead singer Kurt Cobain killed himself in the same way. At the inquiry into the boy's death, his mother explained how he had idolised Nirvana and couldn't cope with the news of Cobain's death.

Report 5

A Manic Street Preachers fan, who was so shocked by the disappearance of guitarist Richey Edwards that she also went missing, has written to her parents to say that she's fine and is now living in London. Her father said that she was really upset when she heard that Richey had gone missing, and the next day she disappeared from the family home in Scotland.

Unit 8

Language awareness: reported speech
Activity 1

Isabelle: ... so I was standing there when this boy came over. I think he was more interested in himself than me! He came over and told me he was free at the time and if I wanted to dance ... can you believe it? He said his name was Steve. He told me he was really interested in jazz. He said he had seen his favourite band the day before. Then he told me how much he loved films and that he was going to see a film later that night. I don't know if he was inviting me. He never took the time to ask! He was so big-headed. He told me he had a really important job in banking. And what a snob! He said he thought the people at the disco were rather common and that he didn't usually go there. I finally decided to leave him standing on the dance floor when he told me he was thinking about getting his hair dyed the next day.

Activity 5

Zoe: Well, I got talking to a lovely boy. He was really sweet. He wondered whether I often went dancing. He asked me where I came from. He wanted to know if I would see him again.

Isabelle: Did he?

Zoe: Yes. And he asked me if I had a boyfriend. He wanted to know where I lived.

Isabelle: He sounds really serious!

Zoe: I know. He asked me if I liked romantic men. He wondered if I was wearing Chanel perfume. He wanted to know what I was doing the following weekend.

Unit 9

Part 1 Getting on with others

P = Presenter
S = Susan
G = Guy
A = Annabel

P: Welcome to today's programme in which we are asking you to tell us about the flatmates from hell! And our first caller is Susan from Lancashire. Hello, Susan. You've got a scary story to tell.

S: Yes. Two years ago I was living with a friend and we advertised for a third person to share our flat to help us with the rent. When Linda first moved in she was a model flatmate. We couldn't believe our luck. She always did the cooking and most of the washing up. I must admit we took advantage of her a little.

P: But then things started to change?

S: Yes. I noticed one day that my favourite dress wasn't in the wardrobe. I asked Linda if she'd seen it – she used to do my laundry sometimes – but she said she didn't know where it was. Then I found out she'd been telling lies about us to our friends. She used to take phone messages and then not pass them on. Then more of my clothes and jewellery went missing. I suspected Linda by this stage and in her room I found a photo of her at a party wearing my dress! When I confronted her about it she said she had only borrowed it and forgotten to give it back. By this stage I started to feel a bit afraid of her, so we asked her to leave.

P: Do you know what happened to her?

S: I've no idea. I'm just relieved not to be sharing a flat with her any more.

P: Now, Guy from London, you're having problems at the moment with your flatmate and his girlfriend. Does she live with you both?

G: No, she's got her own house, but she spends so much time at our flat she might as well be living here!

P: Oh dear, is that the problem?

G: Not really. The main problem is that they're always arguing, and not just quietly. The last time she starting throwing things down the stairs – like the Hoover and the ironing board. She also smashed the glass in their bedroom door. They're always shouting at each other and it makes it really difficult to relax once I get home.

P: Yes, I'm not surprised. Have you spoken to your flatmate about this?

G: Well, it's really difficult. When he first moved in I was a bit doubtful about whether it would work out – he's a very loud person and I'm more of an introvert – but we learned to put up with each other after a while. But when his girlfriend came along, well … She even phones him up at three in the morning to make sure he's there.

P: You must be feeling pretty frustrated right now.

G: Yes. They're driving me mad! I'm thinking of moving out just to get some peace.

P: Now let's move on to our third caller – Annabel from Aberdeen. Apparently, your flatmates are so awful that you're thinking of throwing them out. What's the problem?

A: They're absolutely disgusting. They never wash up the dishes after they've finished eating and I can't remember the last time they helped with the housework. I have to do it all myself.

P: Why don't you just leave it for them to do?

A: Because they won't do it, that's why! Last month I went on holiday for a week and when I came back the kitchen was so dirty we even had mice.

P: That's terrible. Mice carry all sorts of diseases.

A: I know! They hadn't even emptied the ashtrays for a week either. It's bad enough that they have to smoke in the flat – I'm a non-smoker myself.

P: Didn't you make any rules when you advertised for your flatmates?

A: Well, I asked for two non-smokers but these two were the only replies I got, so I was just relieved to find some people to help with the rent. But now I really regret letting them move in.

P: I hope you sort things out before the mice do. Thanks to all our callers today …

Unit 9

Part 2 Turning a blind eye

I = Interviewer
N = Natalie

I: Tell me about your project, Natalie.

N: For my project I decided to look at how far people would get involved if they saw a crime being committed. Three friends of mine also took part as observers to record the results of my experiment. We went to our local Boots store and asked the manager for permission to do some shoplifting.

I: So you wouldn't be arrested.

N: Yes, he agreed, because his shop had suffered a lot from shoplifters in the past. When I was ready to start stealing I felt terrible. My heart was beating really quickly and I even thought about not going through with the experiment. It was like I was actually committing a crime.

I: What did you pretend to steal?

N: A large bottle of bubble bath. The first time I did it I stood in front of a lady and made sure I got eye contact with her. Then I opened my bag and put the bottle inside. She definitely saw what I was doing. Then I walked out.

I: And?

N: The woman did nothing. I did the experiment again and

again. Still nothing. I went through the same routine in front of men and women, in singles and groups of two, three and four. Even a group of teenage girls. But they all said and did nothing.

I: Didn't anybody stop you?

N: It wasn't until experiment number 15 when I chose a middle-aged woman. I put the bottle in my bag and I thought she was going to grab my arm, but a man came between us. She did report the 'theft' to the manager but she was the only one out of a total of 22 people.

I: So what's your conclusion?

N: I think that people don't want to get involved in difficult situations. They think 'Well, other people are here, so why should I be the one to do something?' Or they may be afraid of making a mistake, which could be embarrassing. I was really pleased that the woman reported me.

I: Why?

N: Because if I saw someone shoplifting I wouldn't let them get away with it.

I: What about if you hadn't done the experiment?

N: Well, I'm sure I would've been like the rest and done nothing.

Unit 9

Part 3 Fallen heroes?

Diego Maradona, Argentina's most famous and controversial footballer, was born on 30th October 1960 in a slum area near to Buenos Aires. His mother was of Italian origin and his father a native Indian, and Maradona was one of eight children. Even from the age of nine he showed a remarkable, almost magical talent for playing football.

At the age of sixteen he played for his national team. In 1982 he began to play for Barcelona in Spain, and after two years he then transferred to the Italian team of Naples, where he achieved great success. Back home in Argentina, Maradona was becoming a role model for young boys. His reputation in England was less positive after Argentina's game against England in the 1986 World Cup. Replays of the match showed that Maradona had punched the ball into the goal. When questioned about this, he claimed it was the 'Hand of God'. The fact that Argentina went on to win the World Cup that same year made him even more unpopular with the English fans.

Maradona was by now a real celebrity. After the triumph of the World Cup his lifestyle became the subject of media attention. Whether he took cocaine to escape the pressures of fame, nobody knows, but after being banned from football for fifteen months after a positive drugs test in 1991, he was found guilty again of drug taking in the 1994 World Cup. He was sent home in humiliation and disgrace. More recently, Maradona has led a quieter life as the manager of a small Argentinian football team, and he is also renowned for his passionate concern about human rights and social justice.

His relationship with the media has always been full of ups and downs. After the disgrace of the World Cup in 1994 he was hounded by the media. In one famous incident he fired an air rifle at a crowd of reporters who were trying to get a photograph of him and his family. After a spectacular rise and fall the world waits for yet another comeback.

Unit 9

Language awareness: possibility and certainty
Activity 1

A: Look at that poor man! What d'you think happened?

B: I don't know. He might be a stuntman.

A: Yeah, maybe. He must've had a serious accident. He's in a terrible state.

B: Yes, isn't he? He can't be feeling very comfortable.

A: He might need a little help at dinner time.

B: Ha ha! That's true. He won't be going home for a while. That's for sure.

A: He could've been playing some kind of sport.

B: Yes, maybe. Elephant wrestling perhaps.

Unit 10

Part 1 Getting from A to B

I = Interviewer

A = Amanda

I: Hello there. Could you spare a few moments to answer some questions about your preferred form of transport?

A: Well, you'll have to be quick, I'm on my way to work.

I: Name?

A: Amanda Collins.

I: Age?

A: 22.

I: And how do you travel to work mainly?

A: I get the train usually, and then I walk from the station to my office.

I: And can you say what you like about this form of travel?

A: Well, it's cheaper than driving, on the whole. I have a car, but only use it at weekends. I can do work on the train, or read. In fact, it's quite relaxing.

I: And is there anything you dislike?

A: Obviously, if the train drivers are on strike, it's very inconvenient. Luckily, that doesn't happen too often. Sometimes, the train breaks down, and this means I'm late for work.

I: Can you look at the following list and tell me which five factors are the most important for you when deciding how to travel to work?

A: I suppose the first factor would be the cost. I don't earn a great deal so any form of transport mustn't be too expensive. Secondly, the train is pretty quick; it would take too long if I drove. Then I would say the comfort and convenience are the two next most important factors. Finally, I like the fact that I'm not polluting the environment, so that makes me feel good.

I: Thank you. Just two more questions. How long does it take you to get to work and how much do you spend a week?

A: About 40 minutes on a good day and an hour on a bad day. And weekly cost? I buy a season ticket which costs twelve pounds. If that's all, I really must go ...

I = Interviewer
M = Martin

I: Do you think I could have a few minutes of your time?
M: Sure.
I: What's your name?
M: Martin Henshaw.
I: Can you spell that?
M: Yes, it's H-E-N-S-H-A-W.
I: Are you still at school?
M: Yes, I'm fourteen.
I: And how do you get to school?
M: Well sometimes my dad takes me by car, but most of the time I go by bike.
I: I see. And what do you like most about the bike?
M: I don't know really; I'm just used to riding to school.
I: Is there anything you don't like?
M: Yeah, when it's raining. That's usually when I ask Dad for a lift.
I: Now can you look at this list and tell me the most important factors when choosing this form of transport.
M: OK. The name of the bike's important to me. I wouldn't ride any old make – it wouldn't be good for my image. Then I'd say ... it helps me keep in shape. I play a lot of sport and I need to be fit. It's cheap, of course, and providing I maintain it well it never lets me down, so reliability. Lastly, I suppose it's good for longer distances. My school is too far away to walk. By bike it takes half an hour.
I: And how much does it cost you in a week?
M: That's impossible to say really. Not much.
I: Thank you.

Unit 10

Part 2 Young people's driving stories

Speaker 1
I'd been taking lessons for a year before I passed my driving test at the age of eighteen, but my dad never gave me any help. Even after I'd passed he never let me use the car. So what I used to do was, I'd pinch the keys before leaving the apartment block where we were living and run round to the car park at the back where Dad left the car at night. He hardly ever used the car after getting in from work. I used to go and see friends or just drive around and then come back and leave the car in exactly the same place. One night though I got back at around ten thirty only to find that there were no parking places at all. I suppose because I went in and told the truth to my dad he was quite good about it, although he did take the cost of the fuel out of my allowance.

Speaker 2
My most unfortunate driving experience happened ages ago, before I'd actually passed my driving test. My girlfriend's father used to let her borrow his car whenever we were going to the cinema or something. Anyway, I'd just started learning to drive and I persuaded her to let me have a go. We took the car down to the beach on the sand where no one could see us and she let me take the wheel. We were having such fun that we didn't notice the tide was coming in until the car was actually swimming in water. We had to

leave the car where it was and catch the bus back to tell her dad. By the time the three of us returned, the car was almost covered in water. Needless to say, he was so cross he didn't let me go out with her again!

Speaker 3
My dad was teaching me to drive and I was coming down a rather narrow road which had cars parked on both sides. Suddenly, from nowhere there was a young man on a bike coming towards us. I slammed the brakes on but he crashed into me, landed on the car and then rolled off. My father and I both jumped out of the car to see if he was all right. Fortunately, he stood up and said he was OK, just a little shaken. My dad offered to give him some money for the repair of the bike, and then an old lady came along. When she saw what had happened, she began shouting at my father, saying he must have been driving too fast, and it was a bad example to set to his young daughter! Poor old dad didn't say a word.

Speaker 4
My advice about learning to drive would be to have proper lessons from a qualified instructor and never to let a friend or family member try to teach you. It's a guaranteed way to spoil a good relationship. Every Sunday (when the traffic was quieter) my father would pick me up and take me for a drive along the streets of our home town, and give me a lecture on how to drive, explaining everything he was doing and why. Eventually, it was my turn to have a go. My dad was so nervous that he panicked before I'd even started up the engine. He used to shout at the slightest mistake, and when the lesson was finally over, he'd come home and have a large glass of whisky to settle his nerves.

Speaker 5
I didn't start learning to drive until I was twenty-one. I had lots of lessons but I was a terrible driver, I must admit. The first time I took my driving test nobody expected me to pass. But after failing another four times the pressure was really on. I took my test for a sixth time and failed yet again, but I was too embarrassed to admit it to my family, so I just pretended that I'd passed after all. My family were delighted and my father went out and bought me a car the next day. I didn't know what to do, so I just got in and drove. I continued to drive – illegally – for three months. Fortunately, I was never stopped by the police, and the next time I took my driving test I passed.

Unit 10

Language awareness: review of tenses
Activity 4

Steve: So what time is Anna arriving?
Jenny: At six. I'm meeting her there. I was going to take a sign so that she could pick me out, but everybody carries them. So I've decided I'm going to wear something colourful instead!
Steve: And then you're off to the conference?
Jenny: Well to the hotel, yes. The conference itself starts the next day. I thought at first that it would be about a thirty-minute drive. But the roads will be busy at that time. It will probably take closer to an hour. I guess we'll arrive at the hotel by about seven thirty.

Steve: What are your plans for the first evening?

Jenny: We're seeing a play at the local theatre. After that we'll both be at the conference. Anna's going to spend some time sightseeing afterwards. The problem is, I don't think she realises the buses and trains are on strike all this week. I've decided to drive her around in my car. She won't have enough time to see everything, but hopefully she'll have seen most of the sights before she leaves. Her flight leaves on Thursday at twelve so I'll have time to drive her to the airport.

Unit 10

Language awareness: verb forms (2)
Activity 4

Laura: Petros, can you remember leaving the college last night?

Petros: No! I remember nothing!

Laura: You must do! As you were leaving you stopped me to ask me the time.

Petros: Really?

Laura: Yes. You've stopped wearing your watch since the strap broke.

Petros: No! I remember nothing at all!

Laura: I don't suppose you remembered to bring that money you owe me either?

Petros: Money? What money?

Unit 11

Part 1 Small but scary

Well, this first one tends to be very unpopular. You'll find these lovely little creatures all over the world and although they have such a bad reputation they're relatively harmless. You certainly don't have to worry about getting stung or bitten by one. They eat virtually anything they come across, even the rubbish we humans leave around so they are not all bad! They can carry disease, however, and tend to smell rather unpleasant. These flat, oval insects can often grow to more than 10 cm long.

Ahh, now these hairy spiders are found in the Americas, Asia and Africa. These creatures can grow to be more than 25 cm, big enough to eat not only insects but small animals like frogs and birds. The spiders carry venom which they inject into their prey when they bite them. However, although it's painful, their bite has not been known to kill humans and so these spiders are generally quite safe to handle. People often mistakenly believe that these creatures are insects. However, insects have six legs and as you can see, this has eight very long hairy legs.

This creature is quite widespread and is found in the Americas, Africa, Australasia, Asia and Southern Europe. Although its two front claws look very scary, the danger is in its long curved tail where the sting is found. It is with this sting that it injects venom into its victim, which can be any small creatures like spiders, frogs, mice or other insects. Although it looks very dangerous, the venom of the majority of these insects is harmless to humans even though the sting can be quite painful.

These mammals have earned a very bad reputation over the years, a reputation which hasn't been helped much by the Dracula stories! This particular species is found in South America and when open those leathery wings will spread to about 17 cm. They live off blood and will bite their sharp teeth into warm-blooded creatures like cattle and horses, and occasionally humans. The main danger as far as these animals is concerned is that they can spread disease, notably rabies.

Now, here we have another spider, this one much smaller than the previous one. These can be found in the Americas, Australasia, Asia, Southern Europe and North Africa. The female grows to about 1.5 cm, larger than the male which it often eats after mating. Apart from her unfortunate partner, this creature will eat insects. The female injects venom into its victim when it bites them. This venom can prove fatal to humans although this is more likely to be the case with young children rather than adults.

Unit 11

Part 2 Animal rights

Let me start by stating quite honestly that many thousands, if not millions, of people would have died or suffered unnecessarily had it not been for research carried out on animals. Research on animals has been in existence for centuries and a number of major discoveries, such as antibiotics in the fight against infectious diseases and insulin as a means of dealing with diabetes, came about after research had been carried out on animals. Over a thousand doctors and scientists have over the years defended vivisection as having made important contributions to advances in medicine and surgery.

We've got to address the question of whether people are more important than animals. If you accept that a human life is worth more, then you have to accept that we must use animals, when justified, for the treatment and cure of human ills. There are also safety factors to take into consideration. Most countries have laws that demand that all drugs and agricultural chemicals are tested before they're put on sale. If humans are to benefit from these advances then I'm afraid we will need to continue to make use of animals in experiments.

I think I need to make a few things clear. One criticism that is often made of scientists involved in animal experimentation is that the animals are treated cruelly. This is totally unjustified. Animals used in research are treated as well as possible. A researcher cannot expect to gain useful or accurate results if the animal is frightened or distressed.

Secondly, in contrast to statistics often quoted by animal rights groups, around six out of ten animal experiments are totally painless. They might be used in research looking at breeding patterns, or in the study of diet ... they might simply be used for taking blood samples.

Thirdly, there are some strict laws covering the use of animals in experiments. In Britain, all experiments involving animals have to be licensed and these licences are only issued if no other way of doing the experiment is possible. There must always be a named person in charge of the experiment and a vet must be available to check on the health and the welfare of the animals.

Finally, the number of experiments carried out each year on animals has been falling year by year in Britain since 1976, a point often ignored by animal rights people. And hopefully as computers become more sophisticated, numbers will drop still further. But I'm afraid that animal experimentation will be with us for the foreseeable future if science and medicine are to continue to work for the benefit of the human race. We all want to be able to stop the suffering that, for example, AIDS and cancer victims have to go through. For this reason I have no doubt whatsoever that animal experimentation is justified.

Unit 11

Language awareness: time conjunctions
Activity 1

It was the big day in the jungle: the insects were playing the elephants in the biggest football game of the year: the Cup Final. Thousands of insects and elephants had turned up to watch the match and as the two teams walked onto the pitch the supporters roared for their teams.

When both teams had warmed up the referee started the game. The elephants were good! They ran through the insects' defence like a knife through butter ... and scored! Five minutes later the same again ... past the defenders like they didn't exist ... Goal! When the referee blew the whistle to end the first half the elephants were winning 15–0.

During the half-time break the insects sat in the changing room feeling very sorry for themselves. While they were eating their oranges and criticising each other the manager went over to the butterfly who had played particularly badly and told him that he wouldn't be playing in the second half, the centipede was going to take his place. Once the manager had finished talking to the rest of the players, they went back out for the second half.

The referee started the second half and immediately the centipede got the ball. He went round one elephant, round another and another ... and scored! A few minutes later the centipede got the ball again, this time running around six elephants ... and scored! He was fantastic. When the referee blew his whistle to finish the game the insects had won 16–15 and the centipede had scored every goal!

While the insects were celebrating with the Cup, the captain of the elephants went over to the captain of the insects and said, 'That centipede was good.' 'I know,' said the insect. 'He's our best player.' 'But I've never seen anything like it in my life,' said the elephant. 'He scored 16 goals all on his own ... it's incredible.' 'I know,' said the insect. 'I told you, he's our best player.' 'But,' said the elephant, 'if he's that good, why didn't he play in the first half?' 'Well,' said the insect, 'it takes him two hours to put his boots on!'

Unit 11

Language awareness: expressing quantity
Activity 6

a Both spiders are poisonous.
b Every creature is deadly.
c All of them are insects.
d Neither of the spiders are found in Asia.

e Each creature spreads disease.
f None of the creatures are bigger than 40 cm.
g There were no creatures mentioned that are found in Europe.
h You can be stung by either of the insects.
i Both of the insects have eight legs.

Unit 12

Part 1 The kiss that can save a life

P = Presenter
T = Tim
S = Stephen

P: And now to this week's health check. Would you know what to do if you came across somebody unconscious, not breathing or with no heartbeat? Tim Ledger and Stephen Clarke certainly did and thanks to their quick thinking and first-aid skills both managed to help save the life of a loved one. It was one Saturday afternoon a few weeks before Jamie Ledger's fourth birthday. Jamie was splashing around in the bath while his parents, Tim and Judy, were sitting downstairs in the living room. Judy called up to make sure Jamie was all right and, when she got no answer, she told Tim to go upstairs to check. Listen to Tim describing what happened ...

T: I didn't think there was anything to worry about at first and complained a little bit about having to go upstairs. I looked in the bathroom but couldn't see Jamie so I thought he must be in the bedroom. I was just about to open the bedroom door when a kind of sixth sense drew me back to the bathroom. When I looked in again I saw Jamie lying face down in the water. I grabbed him quickly but he wasn't breathing, his body was very limp and his lips were blue. I thought he was dead.

P: Tim shouted downstairs to Judy. When she saw Jamie she was sure he was dead and ran screaming to neighbours to call an ambulance. Here's Tim again ...

T: I was panicking, trying to think of the procedure I had learnt in a first-aid course at work two years before. I remembered – you have to get air into the lungs. I didn't stop to try to find a pulse because in my panic I thought he would have one. I tipped his head back into the right position to blow air through his mouth. I kept telling myself I had to get it right. It was quite staggering to see his chest go up and down as I blew the air in. After about four or five minutes his body took over and he started breathing.

P: Jamie made a full recovery and Tim is eternally grateful to his employers for the first-aid course they run at work.

T: It gave me the confidence to have a go at pulling him round. Without the course I might have been tempted to try pumping the water out of his chest rather than getting oxygen in.

P: And Tim's not the only one to be thankful for having some basic first-aid skills. Kenneth Clarke has his 15-year-old son Stephen to thank ... 54-year-old Ken had been working in the garden when he came into the kitchen and suddenly fell over and hit the floor. Stephen explains what happened ...

S: There were four or five adults around the house as well as me. I was working on my bike at the time. I knew Dad had had a heart attack 'cos he wasn't breathing and I couldn't feel a pulse. No one else knew what to do, but I didn't panic. I blew air into his lungs and kept pressing his heart. I just kept going – it wasn't difficult really and after about four minutes his heart got going and he started breathing. But then he was sick and stopped again so I kept going until the ambulance arrived.

P: Ken was rushed to hospital and recovered in an intensive care unit. Ken's own father had died at the same age from a similar attack and he is proud of his son for having the self-confidence and courage to step in and take over. Stephen had completed a compulsory first-aid course at his school in Stoke-on-Trent and recently received a top life-saving award.

S: I think all schools should have these courses. I was scared, but so glad I knew what to do.

Unit 12

Part 3 Taking exams

Speaker 1
It was so so. I arrived for the exam early and was waiting a long time. This made me nervous before the interview. The examiner was kind and I could relax a little when the interview started. But I didn't speak very much. The other student who ... he was with me ... he spoke too much, I think. In the last part when we discuss something ... he talked too much. But the time it passed very quickly. I was happy when it was finished.

Speaker 2
My teacher tell me many time that it is important for to read the answers carefully. This is true I think. And also she said me finish all questions. In the writing exam I had this problem. The first question was difficult for me ... and I take too much time. When I did the second question I have to write very quickly. This isn't good because I couldn't have the time to correct my mistakes in the end.

Speaker 3
It is a good idea to read all questions in the listening exam first. This help you understand the people speaking ... you, er, understand the subject. Also answer as many questions as possible the first time of listening. When I listen the second listen I answered the questions I didn't know and check the questions I did before. I also determined to write answers on the answer sheet carefully. This is very important.

Speaker 4
In the beginning reading was very difficult for me. The reading is very long and it takes much time to finish. In the exam I try to answer the question by using the questions as a guide. I mean some questions you must read quickly to find special information and some questions you must to read more slowly. I think the reading examination was OK. I had enough time to finish all the questions.

Speaker 5
I am not very good at grammar so I was nervous of the Use of English. But I think the exam was good for me. I studied vocabulary before the exam and remembered different type of same word like 'photograph' 'photography'... 'strong' 'strength' and I did lots of examination practice before, too. I think for other students it was difficult or easy, I don't know ... some went out of the room before the end.

The authors would like to thank the following: the students at Henley College, Coventry who helped with recordings and trialling, Robert Wheeler, the designer. Thanks are also due to our editor, Andrew Juraschcek, for his patience, support and useful suggestions. Fiona Joseph also acknowledges the support given by the University of Wolverhampton Research and Development Committee.

Dedicated to Anna-Emily

The authors and publishers would like to thank the following for permission to reproduce copyright material:

Addison Wesley Longman Ltd for *English as a Foreign Language* by Felicity O'Dell; *Bella* for 'Is your boss spying on you?'; *The Big Issue* for 'Pizza peril'; Cassell for *Great Lateral Thinkers* by P. Sloane and D. Machale; *The Daily Express* for 'Focus on financial realitiies', 'Nickname that bears fruit', 'Our perfect soulmate' and 'Shore way to lend an ear'; *The Daily Mail* /Solo for 'Midnight creepers' and 'So, could you cope with a huge win?'; Dateline for 'You too can find love'; *The Guardian* for 'Can you cope in a crisis?', 'Latin grammar', 'Rum do for skateboader who was nicked for drink driving', 'The naked strewth', 'There's no place like home', 'Well it seemed like a great idea at the time' and 'What's the problem?', © The Guardian; Guinness Publishing for *The Guinness Book of Records 1996 Edition*, © Guinness Publishing Ltd; HarperCollins Australia for *The Secret World of Cults* by Jean Ritchie; HMSO for 'Summertime smog', reproduced with the permission of the Controller of HMSO; *The Independent* for 'Fighting back' by Mike Rowbottom; IPC Magazines for 'In search of true happiness' from *Ideal Home Magazine*; Kenji Kawakami for *101 Unuseless Japanese Inventions*; Lee Gone Publications for *Mrs Joyce Hoover's How to be British* by Martin Alexander Ford & Peter Christopher Legon; Mediamark Publishing and Carol Price for 'Home-made in Britain' by Carol Price; *The Observer* for 'Huge, hairy, harrowing and harmless' and 'Winner's workmates dream of lottery windfall', © The Guardian; Penguin Books for *Mother Tongue* by Bill Bryson, © Bill Bryson, reproduced by permission of Penguin Books; SHE *Magazine* for 'Animals – vivisection' by Ann Furedi; Times Mirror Higher Education for *Motivation at Work* by J. Miskell & V. Miskell; *Top Santé* for 'The weather: how does it affect you?' by Andrew Wilson; Warner Books UK for *Gridlock* by Ben Elton.

While every effort has been made to trace the owners of copyright material in this book, there have been cases where the publishers have been unable to locate the sources. We would be grateful to hear from anyone who recognises their copyright material and is unacknowledged.

The publishers are grateful to the following for permission to reproduce photographs and other material:

Action-Plus: p.106(TL, B); Allsport: p.106(TM, TR), 107; Collections: pp.19, 82(MR), 91(TL); Eye Ubiquitous: p.60, 105(TL); Frank Spooner Pictures: pp.68, 70, 151; House of English: pp.6, 8(BL),13; John Walmsley: pp.7, 19(ML, BL, MR, BR), 53(B), 143; Alexei Juraschcek: p.90 (TR); Fionnuala Ni Chiosain: p.90(BL); Oxford Scientific Films: p.76(T, M, B), 79, 125 ©London Scientific Films, 127(BR)©Harold Taylor; Pictor International: p.81, 104(TR), 116, 148(MR); Popperfoto: p.108; Redferns: p. 91(B), 95(TM); Reflections: p.30(R), 94–5, 105(ML), 138(TL, TR), 148(BL) Jennie Woodcock; Retna Pictures: p.95(TL, BM, BR), 96; Rex Features: p.58, 71, 95(TR); Robert Harding Picture Library: p.82(TR), 127(BL); Sally & Richard Greenhill: p.66; Science Photo Library: p.59; South American Pictures: p.91(TR); St John Ambulance p.137; Karl Stocker: p.90(TL); Tony Stone Images pp.8(TL, ML), 20, 24(TR, ML, MR, BR), 30(L, M), 45, 46–7, 48(ML, BL, BR) 82(TL, ML), 148(ML, BR); Zefa p.48(MR), 104(BR), 118–9

The publishers would like to thank the following for their valuable assistance in piloting and reporting on the material:

The Bell Language School, Cambridge; Centro Cultural Hispano-Britanico, Salamanca; Centro de Estudios Anglo-Norte, Salamanca; The English Institute, Vigo; Exeter Academy, Exeter; Hambakis Schools, Athens; Anna Krasopoulou-Miele, Evropaiko, Drama; University of Luton, Luton; Joanna Malliou, Omiros Schools, Athens

First published in 1997 by
Prentice Hall Phoenix ELT
A division of Prentice Hall International (UK) Ltd
Campus 400, Maylands Avenue
Hemel Hempstead
Hertfordshire, HP2 7EZ

© International Book Distributors Ltd 1997

Designed by Robert Wheeler
Illustrations by Kathy Baxendale, Roy Choules, Mark Duffin, Gillian Martin, Ed Mclachlan, Pavely Arts and Harry Venning
Studio photography by Sue Baker
Cassettes produced by Anne Rosenfeld at The Audio Workshop
Printed and bound in Malta

Library of Congress Cataloging-in-Publication Data

Joseph, Fiona.
    Candidate for FCE: Student's Book / Fiona Joseph and Peter Travis.
        p. cm.
    ISBN 0-13-531120-9
    1. English language—Textbooks for foreign speakers.
    2. English language—Examinations—Study guides.
I. Travis, Peter.
II. Title.
PE1128.J673   1996
428'.0076—dc21   96–48318
                                                         CIP

British Library Cataloguing-in-Publication Data

A catalogue record for this book is available from the British Library

ISBN 0-13-531120-9

    2   3   4   5
01   00   99   98